# Language Education in CHIN

C000062401

Hong Kong University Press thanks Xu Bing for writing the Press's name in his Square Word Calligraphy for the covers of its books. For further information, see p. iv.

### Education in *China*
#### Reform and Diversity

This series explores the dramatic changes in China's education system. By using fresh perspectives and innovative methods, each volume delves into the issues and debates that continue to challenge education in China, including cultural and linguistic diversity, regional disparity, financial decentralization, intellectual autonomy, and increased internationalization.

# Language Education in CHINA
## Policy and Experience from 1949

**Agnes S. L. Lam**

香港大學出版社

HONG KONG UNIVERSITY PRESS

**Hong Kong University Press**
14/F Hing Wai Centre
7 Tin Wan Praya Road
Aberdeen
Hong Kong

© Hong Kong University Press 2005

ISBN 962 209 750 2 (Hardback)
ISBN 962 209 751 0 (Paperback)

Secure On-line Ordering
http://www.hkupress.org

British Library Cataloguing-in-Publication Data
A catalogue record for this book is available from the British Library.

Printed and bound by Liang Yu Printing Factory Co. Ltd., in Hong Kong, China

 Hong Kong University Press is honoured that Xu Bing, whose art explores the complex themes of language across cultures, has written the Press's name in his Square Word Calligraphy. This signals our commitment to cross-cultural thinking and the distinctive nature of our English-language books published in China.

"At first glance, Square Word Calligraphy appears to be nothing more unusual than Chinese characters, but in fact it is a new way of rendering English words in the format of a square so they resemble Chinese characters. Chinese viewers expect to be able to read Square word Calligraphy but cannot. Western viewers, however are surprised to find they can read it. Delight erupts when meaning is unexpectedly revealed."

— Britta Erickson, *The Art of Xu Bing*

# Contents

## Chapter 4    Developing Minority Languages and Bilingualism

## Chapter 5    Conclusion

## Appendices

# Illustrations

# Tables

# Preface

During my exchange visits to China from about 1994, I became increasingly aware of how little I knew about language education in China and how useful it would be to learn more about it. Unfortunately, there was no general introduction to the topic. So I decided to do some research towards arriving at such a picture.

My research was fully supported by a generous grant of HK$800,000 from the Research Grants Council of the Hong Kong Special Administrative Region, China (Project No. HKU7175/98H); without it, it would not have been possible for me to do the fieldwork and employ a research assistant for the project, Kathy Chow, for three years and two months. Kathy was completely dedicated, extremely careful with her statistical analysis and interview transcription and gave me every kind of help from her heart.

I am also immensely grateful to the many institutions and individuals in China who gave me so much support and co-operation in all kindness, both in the actual surveys and interviews and in our living and transport arrangements on field trips. To protect the privacy of the participants in my study, I shall not name the institutions or the individuals. May this book, inadequate as it is, be a small memento of their trust and my lasting gratitude.

I would also like to thank colleagues at the University of Hong Kong, in particular, various colleagues in Research Services, China Affairs, the English Centre, the Department of English, the Department of Law, the Department of Linguistics and the Faculty of Education, for their friendly support for my work. Often taken for granted but so essential for research is the excellence of our university library and that at the Universities Service Center for China Studies at the Chinese University of Hong Kong.

To Hong Kong University Press, I owe my appreciation for their belief in the book and their professional support at every stage of the work. To the anonymous reviewers of my manuscript, I owe my sincere thanks for their painstaking work and valuable suggestions for improvement.

To complete this project, I have had to withdraw from the company of my family and friends on countless occasions for the last few years. Without their understanding and prayer support, I could not have worked with such perseverance. My husband, in particular, has been a constant source of encouragement.

For all these blessings and for the privilege to conduct the research and complete the writing, I give all my thanks to God.


Agnes Lam
January 2005
Hong Kong

# 1

# Introduction

## Introduction

It has been just over half a century since the People's Republic of China was established in 1949. Its political and economic developments have been well charted by China watchers (Fairbank, 1987; Goodman & Segal, 1991; Howell, 1993; J. Y. S. Cheng, 1998b; Lynch, 1998; S-W. Cheng, 2001; Garnaut & Huang, 2001; Mengin & Rocca, 2002; Laurenceson & Chai, 2003). Its educational achievements have also attracted much research attention (Agelasto & Adamson, 1998; Gu, 2001; Peterson, Hayhoe & Lu, 2001; Turner & Acker, 2002; Yang, 2002; X-F. Wang, 2003).

By comparison, although there are comprehensive accounts of specific aspects of language policy in China such as the standardization of Chinese (Wang, Z-T. Chen, Cao & N-H. Chen, 1995; P. Chen, 1999), the propagation of English in education (Sichuan Foreign Language Institute, 1993; Adamson, 2004) and the development of minority languages (Dai, Teng, Guan & Dong, 1997; M-L. Zhou, 2003), overall accounts of all aspects of language policy in China taken altogether are less readily available, particularly in English. Secondly, while there has been research on aspects such as language attitudes as related to language policy in China (for example, Bai, 1994; Zhou, 2001), there is less research relating policy implementation directly to learners' multilingual experience of policies over a period of time. This is unfortunate in the light of the current trend towards multilingual interpretations of linguistic development, both from the societal perspective as well as the individual learner's point of view (Spolsky, 1986; Edwards, 1994; Paulston, 1994; Cenoz & Genesee, 1998; Belcher & Connor, 2001; Singh, 2001; Herdina & Jessner, 2002; Pavlenko & Blackledge, 2004). While much is to be learnt from focusing on the development of a particular language or learners' experience of a specific language in China, an overall consideration of all the language policies in China together with the multilingual experience of individual learners can give insights which cannot be arrived at if the language policies or the experiences of learning particular languages are considered separately. A government has to take account of all the languages used in the community it serves when making language policy because the promotion of one language has effects on the functions of other languages in a community. From the learners' point of view, the learning of one language also affects their learning of other languages. Hence, a multilingual orientation in studying language policy and learner experience is quite necessary. Relating learner experience to policy implementation can also give an appraisal of how effective or feasible a specific policy has been and can point the way to follow-up action. In terms of theory building, such research can provide a bridge between traditional language planning research and the more recent work in the negotiation of learner identity in multilingual settings with reference to learner narratives.

In addition to theoretical concerns related to a multilingual approach to an understanding of the language education circumstances in China among linguists or applied linguists, there is also a practical need among educators in general for a general introduction to language policy and learners' experience in China in view of the vast opportunities for academic exchange between China and the rest of the world. Many of these educators interested in academic interaction with China do not read Chinese and may not have a background in linguistics and so could benefit more from an overall introduction rather than in-depth discussions of specific language policies.

The purpose of this book is therefore threefold: first of all, to provide a multilingual portrayal of language policy in China and, secondly, to study the experience of learners in China as a window to the implementation of such policy, both of which are relevant for theoretical considerations of multilingualism. A third objective is to make such information readily accessible in the form of a general introduction to educators around the world for practical purposes. This composite picture is presented at two levels: at the societal level is an analysis of the policies on the part of the state; at the individual learners' level are accounts of the actual experiences of learners educated from 1949 onwards to give reality to such policies.

In this chapter, the positioning of China in recent history is first reviewed. The educational system in China is then outlined. This is followed by a description of the linguistic scene in China — the languages involved as well as the major policies implemented from 1949. In the last part of the chapter, with reference to studies of multilingualism, the method of data collection and data presentation towards interpretation of the policies is described and the learning biographies of four learners from different age groups and locations in China (and hence different linguistic backgrounds) are presented as an indication of the issues to be explored in greater depth in later chapters.

## China in Recent History

The People's Republic of China (PRC) was established on 1 October 1949 after more than two decades of civil strife between the Communist Party and the

Guomingdang (Nationalist Party). During part of that time, China was also attacked by Japan. The immediate tasks faced by the new government in 1949 were tremendous. In addition to rebuilding the country, its economy and infrastructure, China was also faced with having to find its place in the international arena (Gray, 1991a, p. 253).

## Soviet influence in the early years

Not surprisingly, because of its political inclinations, China was initially hopeful about finding an ally in the Soviet Union and based its development in several areas including its economy and educational system on the Soviet model. A Treaty of Friendship, Alliance and Mutual Assistance was signed on 14 February 1950 with the Soviet Union (Gray, 1991a, p. 254) allowing the Soviet Union access to some ports and railways in the northeastern region of China in return for aid. But when it became apparent that the Soviet Union was less interested in providing aid to China and more interested in gaining control of parts of China, relations with the Soviet Union took a turn which made it necessary for China to look west as early as the late 1950s.

## The Cultural Revolution

By the early 1960s, China was quite ready to further its ties with the West. Unfortunately, events within China in the next few years developed into the most regrettable period of modern China — the Cultural Revolution. It is not uncommon to think that the Cultural Revolution was sparked off by political differences between Mao Zedong and other leaders, with Mao taking the stance of the proletariat while depicting his opponents as revisionist capitalist (MacFarquhar, 1991a, p. 270). Mao was anxious that the revolution in China should continue and not degenerate into another form of capitalism in which the state (instead of landlords in previous times) would exploit the peasants. To prevent this, Mao argued for training 'a new generation of totally dedicated revolutionary successors, whose [world-view] would be genuinely Marxist-Leninist (and by implication, Maoist) — hence the need for a *cultural* revolution' (MacFarquhar & Shambaugh, 1991, p. 270). He found the willing minds and bodies for these new revolutionaries in students. They became Mao's new 'army' — the Red Guards — who could bring down their teachers and other people in power through their denouncement or criticism exercises.

Although ideological issues were at stake, the Cultural Revolution could take off because of dissatisfaction with living conditions. Such dissatisfaction arose because the reforms in the early 1950s took land from the peasants towards collective production, which was not sufficiently well organized so that coercion was often used to meet production targets. When farmers were encouraged to improve their own living conditions by using their surplus energies to set up small industries in the Great Leap Forward in the late 1950s, the idealistic movement also degenerated into enforced labour, failing both in economic and ideological terms (Gray, 1991b, p. 266). Inclement weather conditions in 1960 also did not help (Dillon, 1998, p. 122). By the early 1960s, therefore, there was already much unrest within China. So when the Cultural Revolution broke out in the mid-1960s, it was not difficult to persuade the population that certain leaders should be denounced, particularly when critics were already invited to come forward to debate on political issues during the Hundred Flowers Movement initiated in 1956. Once unleashed, however, the forces of the new revolution could not be easily held back and the Cultural Revolution was not officially declared over until Mao's death in September 1976.

### Mao, Nixon, Zhou Enlai and Henry Kissinger

Even in the midst of the Cultural Revolution though, two senior statesmen were working hard on the foreign policy front to draw China and America together. They were Zhou Enlai, China's premier from 1949 to 1976, and Henry Kissinger, assistant to the president of the United States of America for national security affairs from 1969 to 1975 and also secretary of state from 1973 to 1977. In Kissinger's own words, 'That China and the United States should seek rapprochement in the early 1970s was … imposed on each other by their necessities' (1999, p. 139). Richard Nixon, president of the United States at that time, wanted to extricate America from Vietnam and needed to find 'a counterweight to Soviet expansionism' (Kissinger, 1999, p. 139). Mao shared his anxiety about the Soviet threat, particularly after the Brezhnev Doctrine of 1968, which 'proclaimed that Moscow had the right to bring any backsliding Communist state to heel by military force' (Kissinger, 1999, p.139). In a conversation between Mao and Kissinger in November 1973, subsequent to Nixon's February 1972 visit to China during which Mao already pledged that Chinese troops would not leave Chinese soil, they discussed extensively how the Soviet Union could be contained if Western Europe, China and the United States pursued a co-ordinated course (Kissinger, 1999, p. 149). This policy of active containment of the Soviet Union by both China and the United States was pursued until the early 1980s.

### Re-establishing ties with the Russians

By 1982, the Russians were less of a threat as America was determined to pursue military superiority over them and the Soviet Union had to deal with

Afghanistan and other problems abroad while its economy was declining at home. Trade between China and the Soviet Union began to increase. Relations improved further with Mikhail Gorbachev announcing his new view of the Asia-Pacific in 1986 and Sino-Soviet relations were normalized in a summit meeting in May 1989 (Yahuda, 1991, pp. 269–270). (For further details on Gorbachev's reforms and their impact on Sino-Soviet relations, see Lynch, 1998, pp. 129–130.)

## Deng Xiaoping's Open Door Policy

As China regained its importance in the balance of power between America and the Soviet Union, on the domestic front, China was also regaining its momentum for educational and economic developments after the Cultural Revolution. University enrolment resumed in 1978. In the same year, Deng Xiaoping's Policy of Four Modernizations was announced. The need for all-round modernization was first pointed out by Mao in 1963 and the four sectors — agriculture, industry, national defence as well as science and technology — were originally identified by Zhou Enlai in 1964 (MacFarquhar, 1991b, p. 279). This modernization movement soon evolved into the Reform and Opening Policy (Dillon 1998, p. 109). The 1980s saw rapid developments in many areas. In 1982, the communes — farming collectives merged with local governments — were abolished; their political functions were returned to local governments, in principle though not always in practice (Gray, 1991c, p. 267). Foreign experts were invited to visit China. Students and scholars were sent abroad. Fairbank (1987, p. 177), a renowned American China-watcher, observed, 'our increased contact of the 1980s tends as usual to build up the old American feelings about China — the curious appeals of tourism, the hope of big business deals, the respect for the character of Chinese friends and for the intelligence of individual Chinese'. He summed up the period as one of 'disillusioned optimism: China suffers from many evils, but it is a country we can get along with' (Fairbank, 1987, p. 177). For the Chinese too, it was a time of cautious optimism. The Cultural Revolution was still being remembered, and would be until around the mid-1990s, but the very horrors of that age made it unthinkable that it would ever happen again.

## China in an international era

China's development would have gone on smoothly if not for the Tiananmen Incident. In June 1989, students demanding reforms demonstrated in Tiananmen Square in Beijing and were overcome by army tanks. The international goodwill gained by China during its gradual opening up in the

1980s suffered a severe setback in the immediate aftermath of the incident. Yet, the disintegration of the Soviet Union in 1991 provided the vacuum for China to re-enter the international arena. China's desire for a rightful place in the world was articulated in her endeavour to join the World Trade Organization (WTO) and Beijing's bid to host the Olympic Games. Both dreams were realized in 2001. China joined the WTO on 11 December 2001 and will host the Olympics in 2008. The smooth transition of leadership in the central government in 2003 is yet another sign for optimism in China in the new millennium.

From this brief review of the last half century of China's history, three main themes have emerged. China's first priority is to have internal stability and improvement in the living conditions for her people. Where foreign relations are concerned, China is, by and large, consistently non-aggressive and tries hard to maintain peaceable relations with other countries (J. Y. S. Cheng, 1998a, p. 217). Its desire for international recognition has little to do with wanting to control other countries and more to do with not being bullied or humiliated as it was in the century before the present government. In fact, the three tenets of internal progress, peaceful foreign relations and national dignity have, on the whole, been features of Han Chinese rule for thousands of years. In this sense, though the system of government might have changed, the essence has not.

## Education in China

Educational developments from 1949 have often been discussed in three periods: before, during and after the Cultural Revolution (1966–1976). In the first period, the Soviet model of socialist reconstruction was adopted. While the primary and secondary education system prior to 1949 (six years of primary school, three of junior secondary and three of upper secondary) was maintained, university education was extended from four years to five years. The socialist planning system produced specialist graduates for the major sectors and the overall educational level of the population was raised during this time. During the second period, the educational system was streamlined with primary education reduced to five years, secondary education to four years and higher education to three years. The greatest disruption during the Cultural Revolution was in higher education as regular universities were closed down and academic research was discredited. The last period has seen modernization and reform and educational expansion at all levels. The system of education changed back to six years of primary school, three of junior secondary, three of senior secondary and four of higher education. Education for the first nine years was also made compulsory (Hayhoe, 1991, pp. 117–119).

Nowadays, the overall picture is promising. Compared to the figures in 1949, statistics from the Ministry of Education, People's Republic of China [MOE] (n.d.) for the year 2002 are impressive (Table 1.1).

**Table 1.1  Education in China**

| Year | Level | No. of institutions | No. of students |
|------|-------|--------------------|-----------------|
| 1949* | Primary education | 280,930 | 24,400,000 |
|  | Secondary education | 5,216 | 1,300,000 |
|  | Higher education | 205 | 116,504 |
| 2002 | Primary education | 456,900 | 121,567,100 |
|  | Junior secondary education | 65,600 | 66,874,300 |
|  | Senior secondary education | 32,800 | 29,081,400 |
|  | Subtotal | 98,400 | 95,955,700 |
|  | Regular higher education | 1,396 | 9,033,600 |
|  | Adult higher education | 607 | 5,591,600 |
|  | Subtotal | 2,003 | 14,625,200 |

* 1949 statistics are based on Gardner & Hayhoe (1991, p. 116). Other statistics are based on the Ministry of Education, People's Republic of China (n.d.).

As a whole, since 1949, there has been greater participation in education across all levels. The greatest gains have been made in secondary and higher education. There are now nineteen times as many secondary schools and ten times as many higher education institutions; correspondingly, the number of secondary school students and that of students in higher education have increased 74 times and 126 times respectively. As China modernizes, higher education is more than ever seen to be the key to improvement in the standard of living. Nowadays, university education at the initial level appears to be more available but graduate level education is still very competitive. To estimate from 2002 statistics (MOE, n.d.), of 22,818,200 students enrolling into junior secondary school, only 11,807,400 (52%) are likely to enrol into senior secondary education later. Of those enrolling into senior secondary, only 5,428,200 (46%) are likely to enrol into higher education at the initial level later — 3,205,000 (27%) into regular higher education and 2,223,200 (19%) into adult higher education. Of all those enrolling into some form of higher education at the initial level, only 202,600 (4%) may find a place at graduate level. The cumulative effect of these enrolment statistics is that about 1 in 7 (14%) Junior Secondary 1 students can hope to enter a regular higher education institution and 1 in 100 (1%) of this same cohort can become a graduate student. In addition to these enrolment trends, another phenomenon that should be highlighted is the discrepancy in educational conditions between rural and urban areas. This is not just a matter of equal opportunity but is a possible cause of social unrest if the gap in educational conditions, and hence economic prosperity, is not minimized. With the gradual decline in the birth rate, and hence the streamlining of primary education, perhaps better conditions can be envisaged for future generations.

## Language Policies in China

China is a multilingual and multidialectal country. For the majority language group, the Han Chinese, there are two main groups of dialects: the northern dialects and the southern dialects. The northern dialects can be subdivided into seven sub-groups and the southern dialects into six sub-groups (Huang, 1987, pp. 33–45). In addition, among the fifty-five ethnic minorities, over 80 to 120 languages are used (State Language Commission, 1995, p. 159; Zhou, 2003, p. 23). The official language in China is Chinese. The standard dialect, Putonghua, maps well onto the written form of modern Standard Chinese. Various foreign languages have been taught in China at different times. Of primary importance was Russian in the 1950s. Thereafter, English has been taught as the most important foreign language. Other foreign languages of secondary importance in China include Japanese, German, French and other languages for diplomatic purposes. At Beijing Foreign Studies University, for example, over thirty foreign languages are taught.

Since its establishment, the People's Republic has implemented and maintained three main language policies:
1. The standardization of Chinese
2. The propagation of English
3. The development of minority languages

### The standardization of Chinese

The standardization of Chinese took a two-pronged approach: in the script and in the pronunciation. In 1954, discussion on the simplification of the script was initiated. This was motivated by the hope that simplified characters would help to improve literacy rates. In 1956, the First Character Simplification Scheme was announced. It was confirmed in 1964 and reaffirmed in 1986. The Scheme contained 2,235 simplified characters and fourteen radicals (a radical is part of a Chinese character). The year 1956 also saw the directive that all schools for Han Chinese should teach in Putonghua. Workshops to train teachers were organized. To facilitate the learning of a standard pronunciation based on Putonghua, a phonetic alphabet, *hanyu pinyin*, was publicized in 1958. (For details of these changes, see State Language Commission, 1996.) Although Chinese dialects share one writing script, they can be quite different in pronunciation, word order for some phrases, particles and vocabulary. The northern dialect groups share more similarity in pronunciation though differences in tone and vocabulary still exist while the southern dialect groups are more dissimilar from each other. Since the standard dialect, Putonghua, is a northern dialect, native speakers of the southern dialects have the greater learning task when developing their competence in Putonghua. (See Chapter 2 for details.)

## The propagation of English

When the People's Republic was established, Russian was the most important foreign language for a short period. Many people have the impression that the learning of English was promoted only after the Cultural Revolution. In reality, English was accorded importance in China soon after relations with the Soviet Union became tense in the mid-1950s. As early as 1957, a draft syllabus for teaching English in junior secondary school was distributed. In 1961, the syllabus for English majors at university and college level was defined. There were also some foreign language schools established in China from 1960 to 1965. Even during the dark years of the Cultural Revolution, Zhou Enlai managed to deploy a remnant of foreign language majors to posts requiring foreign language expertise. In 1971, China replaced Taiwan in the United Nations and, as mentioned earlier, in 1972, Richard Nixon's visit to China cleared the way for exchange between China and America. After the Cultural Revolution was over and university admission resumed in 1978, more attention was paid to English for non-English majors and English in schools. With Deng Xiaoping's Policy of Four Modernizations announced in the same year, the prominence of English escalated and has not abated since (Lam, 2002a). (See Chapter 3 for details.)

## The development of minority languages

The total minority population of 106,430,000 constitutes only about 8.4% of the total population in China (National Bureau of Statistics of the People's Republic of China, 2001), but they live in a widespread area of about 64% of the total area of China (Dai et. al., 1997, p. 10). Literacy plans for the minorities, previously referred to as nationalities, are therefore not easy to implement. Before 1949, twenty of the fifty-five minorities already had a written form for their languages. From the 1950s to the 1980s, about half of them had new orthographies added or had their existing scripts revised; in addition, new scripts were created for another nine ethnic groups. The adoption of the Roman alphabet for several new orthographies was in line with the use of *hanyu pinyin* to propagate Putonghua (State Language Commission, 1996, p. 16). Although the minorities, apart from the cadres and teachers, have not been required to learn Putonghua, they have been encouraged to become bilingual in their own language as well as Putonghua, particularly in recent years (State Language Commission, 1996, p. 37). For minority groups small in numbers, educational or economic advancement may be possible only if they become proficient in Chinese. (See Chapter 4 for changes in policy during different periods.)

Except during the Cultural Revolution when many scholarly activities and cultural practices were repudiated, by and large, the three policies have been consistently implemented throughout the last half century. In spite of the prevailing policy directions, learners educated in different time periods and in different locations would have had different experiences. (This section was adapted from Lam [2002b]. See Gu [1997] and Gu and Hu [2002] for other sources on language policy in China.)

## The Language Education in China Project

China being so vast and parts of the terrain being not easily accessible, it is difficult to implement language policy to the same degree across the country. Other obstacles are the enormous size of the population, insufficient financial resources and the fact that many dialects are spoken among the majority population, the Han Chinese, and a multitude of languages are spoken among the minorities. To investigate into how language policies had been experienced by learners educated in different time periods, the Language Education in China (LEDChina) project was conducted. This section outlines the project logistics and objectives, the research instruments, the data collection procedures, the type of participants and the limitations in the study.

### Project logistics and objectives

The LEDChina project was supported by a grant of HK$800,000 from the Research Grants Council of the Hong Kong Special Administrative Region. The grant was mainly used to support a research assistant who was employed specifically for the project for three years and two months from January 1999 to February 2002. As I was teaching full-time at the University of Hong Kong throughout the project, all the field trips were conducted during my leave. The main research objective was to relate language policy changes to the experience of learners in China. It was necessary therefore to identify learners at different ages to participate in the study. In addition to age as the main variable for estimating policy changes as experienced by learners in different time periods, other factors considered in different parts of the project were the learners' first dialect or language (particularly for the learning of

Putonghua) and whether their birthplace was in a coastal region or the interior (particularly for the learning of English or the first foreign language).

## Research instruments

The approach taken was both quantitative and qualitative. Questionnaires were designed to arrive at an overall picture of learner experience; there was one version for Han Chinese learners (Appendix I) and another adapted version for learners from minority language groups. The learner survey questionnaire included sections on: biographical background, learning Putonghua, learning other Chinese dialects, learning minority languages, learning the first foreign language and learning other foreign languages. In addition, case interviews were conducted for selected respondents on their learning experience; again, there was one version of interview questions for Han Chinese learners (Appendix II) and another for minority language learners. The interview questions were designed to encourage the interviewee to talk freely as the objective of the interviews was to arrive at a biographical understanding of the interviewee's language experience. Such use of learning narratives is in line with the current interest in learning biographies as a research tool (for example, Chamberlayne, Bornat & Wengraf, 2000; Belcher & Connor, 2001, pp. 3–4). While the focus of the study was on the experience of learners, some discussions were also held with heads of language programmes (or their representatives) to find out how language teaching was organized in China more recently at primary, secondary and university level; six versions of these interview questions were used, one for each level (primary, secondary and university) and for each language (Chinese and English and, at university level, other foreign languages as well); (see Appendix V for a sample). To gather background information for these interviews, a questionnaire was also designed; again, six versions were prepared (see Appendix III and Appendix IV for samples). Putonghua was used in the collection of oral data and Chinese was used in the collection of written data. The samples included as appendices in this book were translated from Chinese.

## Data collection procedures

The points of entry for data collection were the universities. Most of the universities surveyed or visited were key universities or the only universities in the respective cities. The schools visited were the primary and secondary schools on their campuses. If a university chosen as a fieldwork location did not have its own secondary school or primary school, the contact person at the university hosting the research team would identify a substitute school fairly near to the university campus, where members of university staff were likely

**Photo 1**   The garden before the Guesthouse for Foreign Experts at Lanzhou University.

**Photo 2**   The bedroom of the research team on a field trip, also the location where some interviews were conducted.

to send their children to. Such procedures of choosing fieldwork locations ensured that the institutions participating in the study were among the best ones in the respective cities, which made it a little more possible to have some comparison of learners from different regions. To protect the privacy of the informants, the exact locations are not specified in the discussion of the data. This is because in some locations, there was only one key university or just one university and hence only one department head of Chinese and one/two department heads of foreign languages. A narrative on a learner recruited through the university also gives very specific information about the interviewee's age and career path. So it would have been quite easy to deduce who the informants were if the locations had been identified.

The initial survey data collection was conducted by post and interviews of learners as well as discussions with heads of language programmes were conducted during field trips to a northern coastal city, a southern coastal city, a northern interior city and a southern interior city, with some supplementary interviews of learners conducted in another northern interior city. Cities in provinces adjacent to the sea were classified as coastal cities. For example, Xiamen, located in Fujian, a province adjacent to the sea, was classified as a coastal city and Lanzhou, located in Gansu, was classified as an interior city. 'Northern' and 'southern' refer to north or south of the line posited between northern Chinese dialect regions and southern Chinese dialect regions (Map 1).

**Map 1**     Northern and Southern Chinese dialects
Based on Ramsey (1987, Figure 5) & Huang (1987, p. 33–45).

## Participants in the study

As the types of respondents required for the study were rather specific, it took several attempts in about two-and-a-half years to achieve a good data pool on:
1. the learning experience of Han Chinese
2. the experience of learners from ethnic minorities
3. the perspectives of language programme providers

**Han Chinese learners**: For the main part of the study involving Han Chinese learners, through contact persons based in twenty-four universities and another twenty-three individuals, 739 questionnaires were sent out and 460 questionnaires were returned. Of those returned, 415 were usable. These 415 respondents were classified into five age groups: 46 to 50, 41 to 45, 36 to 40, 29 to 35 and 24 to 28, according to their age in the year 2000. The years these groups of learners entered primary school correspond roughly to the phases of historical change in China. Learners were also categorized according to the location of their birthplace into 'northern coastal', 'southern coastal', 'northern interior' and 'southern interior'. Their age, dialect and location information are summarized in Table 1.2.

**Table 1.2  Age, dialect and location of Han Chinese respondents**

| Location | Number of respondents (Percentage) | | | | | |
|---|---|---|---|---|---|---|
| | *24 to 28* | *29 to 35* | *36 to 40* | *41 to 45* | *46 to 50* | *Total* |
| Northern coastal | 29 (7.0%) | 21 (5.1%) | 12 (2.9%) | 19 (4.6%) | 20 (4.8%) | 101 (24.3%) |
| Southern coastal | 21 (5.1%) | 22 (5.3%) | 11 (2.7%) | 16 (3.9%) | 10 (2.4%) | 80 (19.3%) |
| Northern interior | 53 (12.8%) | 53 (12.8%) | 33 (8.0%) | 20 (4.8%) | 19 (4.6%) | 178 (42.9%) |
| Southern interior | 14 (3.4%) | 9 (2.2%) | 14 (3.4%) | 13 (3.1%) | 6 (1.4%) | 56 (13.5%) |
| Total | 117 (28.2%) | 105 (25.3%) | 70 (16.9%) | 68 (16.4%) | 55 (13.3%) | 415 (100.0%) |

Note: 'Northern' and 'Southern' refer to north and south of the dialect line and 'Coastal' and 'Interior' refer to whether the birthplace of the respondent was in a province adjacent to the coast.

Of the 415 respondents, 196 (47.2%) were male and 218 (52.5%) were female with 1 (0.2%) respondent not indicating his/her sex; 153 (36.9%) were born in a rural area and 235 (56.6%) in an urban area with 27 (6.5%) not indicating whether their birthplace was rural or urban; 97 (23.4%) were from the Chinese language profession; 193 (46.5%) were from the foreign language profession; 76 (18.3%) were teaching other subjects and 49 (11.8%) had another occupation. To minimize any skewing of the data, respondents from the Chinese language profession were excluded from the data pool in the analysis of the average university graduate's experience of learning Chinese in Chapter 2; likewise, respondents from the foreign language profession were excluded from the data pool in the analysis of the average university graduate's experience of learning foreign languages in Chapter 3. In addition to questionnaire data, interviews were conducted with thirty-five Han Chinese learners. This number of interviewees is comparable to the study of thirty-two ethnic students in Lee (2001).

**Learners from the ethnic minorities**: A small parallel study on learners from the minorities was also conducted. Through contact persons in four institutions and another five individuals, 133 questionnaires were sent out and 95 were returned. Of those returned, sixty were valid. Their age information is summarized in Table 1.3.

Table 1.3 **Age of learners from minority language groups**

| Age | Number of respondents (Percentage) |
| --- | --- |
| 24 to 28 | 12 (20.0%) |
| 29 to 35 | 17 (28.3%) |
| 36 to 40 | 14 (23.3%) |
| 41 to 45 | 10 (16.7%) |
| 46 to 50 | 7 (11.7%) |
| Total | 60 (100.0%) |

Of the sixty respondents, forty (66.7%) were male and twenty (33.3%) were female; forty-two (70.0%) were born in a rural area and eleven (18.3%) in an urban area with seven (11.7%) not indicating whether their birthplace was rural or urban. As respondents differed greatly in their first languages and the number of respondents was small, the information thus collected was mainly used as background information to cross-check with interview data. Interviews conducted with seventeen learners from various minority groups proved more fruitful.

**Heads of language programmes**: Requests for language programme information were also sent to 105 heads of language programmes. Of the seventy-one who responded, sixty-nine provided usable information (Table 1.4).

**Table 1.4  Heads of language programmes**

| Type of institution | Number of respondents (Percentage) | | |
|---|---|---|---|
| | Chinese language programme | Foreign language programme | Total |
| Primary school | 10 (14.5%) | 9 (13.0%) | 19 (27.5%) |
| Secondary school | 9 (13.0%) | 9 (13.0%) | 18 (26.1%) |
| University | 12 (17.4%) | 20 (29.0%) | 32 (46.4%) |
| Total | 31 (44.9%) | 38 (55.1%) | 69 (100.0%) |

Each respondent was reporting on how the teaching of Chinese or English/ foreign languages was organized at his/her institution at a specific level of education — primary, secondary or university. The information from these respondents was used as background information to prepare for interviews of heads of programmes at each level and for each language during field trips. Eventually, on-site discussions were held with twenty-nine programme respondents.

## Limitations in the study

These various means of data collection provided first-hand information for the understanding of the three language policies in China. The main limitation in this study is that all the learners surveyed or interviewed were university graduates. This was necessary as the purpose of the study was to track the learning experience of the same learners through all levels of education in China. Another limitation is that most of the respondents in the learner survey were teachers. These two limitations need to be kept in mind in the interpretation of the data as the picture that has emerged is probably more representative of academically successful learners. In a report on minority students at a university in China (Lee, 2001), the argument is made that the study of those who make it to university may empower the next generation of learners more than documenting the experience of learners who fail to do so. There is some truth in that argument although most of the learners in the present study seem to have successes as well as failures at different stages of their lives and for learning different languages or dialects, all of which may be useful for teachers and learners to know. Another advantage of studying the sample in the present study is that the participants understood more easily the nature of research and co-operated more readily. In any case, during the time the participants in the present study were within the educational system, the historical policy changes they experienced as learners, the focus of this study, would have been similar to those experienced by learners not included in the study, granted, of course, that there would have been individual and regional variation which would surface in the interviews.

## A Multilingual Approach to Language Education

Before the presentation of some project data for discussion, it is useful to first identify the central issue and methodological concerns in the multilingual approach adopted in this study.

With around 5,000 languages in the world used in about 200 countries (Crystal, 1987, p. 360), multilingualism is in reality very widespread. Not surprisingly, therefore, multilingual orientations to understanding language education circumstances in various countries have gathered momentum in the last two decades. One of the earliest international academic gatherings devoted to the study of multilingualism was the first Symposium organized in 1984 by the AILA (International Association of Applied Linguistics) Scientific Commission on Language and Education in Multilingual Settings (Spolsky, 1986, p. 1). Other works which have appeared in the last several years include Edwards (1994), Paulston (1994), Cenoz and Genesee (1998), Belcher and Connor (2001), Singh (2001), Herdina and Jessner (2002) and Pavlenko and Blackledge (2004).

A central issue in multilingual settings is the availability of education in and through the mother tongues of learners with different home languages (Spolsky, 1986, p. 1; Nunan & Lam, 1998, p. 121) and how taking advantage of such provision may or may not empower learners to have total personal fulfilment within the national milieu. This is a concern both for the state as well as individual learners from social strata or ethnic groups with little access to power or status in a multilingual or multidialectal society. It is a dilemma because learning the language or dialect of the dominant group may result in less competence in one's own language or dialect, variously discussed as language shift (Paulston, 1994, p. 38; Nunan & Lam, 1998, p. 121), language loss, language deterioration and/or attrition (Herdina & Jessner, 2002, pp. 93–98), but not learning the dominant language may result in social marginalization. Among more recent work, a more optimistic note is struck in the emphasis on the dynamic learning biographies of individual learners who have achieved some measure of multilingual abilities (Belcher & Connor, 2001) or the model of continuous negotiation of identities in multilingual contexts (Pavlenko & Blackledge, 2004). Such research seems to point to more possibilities for achieving individual multilingualism or recreating multilingual selves. However promising these newer conceptions about individual multilingualism may be, the issue remains that governments and learners in multilingual settings have to make choices concerning linguistic development which are guided by societal considerations and which will have social implications.

A land of many languages and dialects, China is also faced with making linguistic choices; so are learners in China. Focusing on one language or dialect means less learning resources for others. Interestingly enough, language policy making in China tends to be compartmentalized with different administrative units taking charge of Chinese language matters, foreign language education and language minorities affairs; hence competition for national support for these areas of work is apparently less direct. At the individual level, the language experience of learners in China is certainly not linguistically discrete; each learner tends to be exposed to more than one language and more than one dialect. Hence, a multilingual approach is quite essential for an appreciation of the realities of language education in China.

A multilingual orientation in data collection and presentation can offer insights which are less readily available than when the learning experience of each language is considered discretely. While it may be less feasible to review all the language policies in China synchronically in the same breath, it is entirely possible and appropriate to present individual learning experiences of any particular language against the multilingual background of each learner. In this book, therefore, the tracking of policy measures and the analysis of survey data will focus on one language at a time while the interview data on learners will be presented compositely, that is, with the experiences of all the languages in a learner's repertoire mentioned, however briefly. For example, in Chapter 2 on the learning of Standard Chinese, the policy review will focus on the standardization of Chinese and the survey data will focus on the overall learning experience of Chinese by learners; but in the learning biographies focused on learning Standard Chinese, each learner's experience of other Chinese dialects or foreign languages will also be mentioned briefly so that the reader can reflect on the learner's success or failure of learning Standard Chinese with reference to the interviewee's multilingual or multidialectal experience.

Another feature of the presentation of the learning biographies in this book is that instead of grouping fragments of different learners' experience under central themes, each learner's experience is first integrally presented as individual learning biographies before they are discussed as a whole. (To minimize overlap between stories, the biographies presented were carefully selected from the pool of data and very much abridged.) This presentation mode is adopted so that the reader can have a more vivid and realistic picture of learners from different backgrounds as individuals trying to define their own learning selves in a multilingual and/or multidialectal context. Other recent examples of a similar method of presenting learning biographies are found in Belcher and Connor's (2001) *Reflections on Multiliterate Lives*, Turner and Acker's (2002) *Education in the New China: Shaping Ideas at Work* and some articles in Benson and Nunan's (2002) *The Experience of Language Learning*.

# Four Learners' Experiences

As mentioned earlier, the policy shifts at different times as well as the linguistic variation in China have resulted in a range of language learning circumstances. As an indication of the differences in learning experiences, here are excerpts from interviews of four learners from different backgrounds. The age specified was that of the interviewee in 2000. Pseudonyms are used (and will be in all references to interview data later). The four learners, from the oldest to the youngest, are:

1. Lian: Southern Chinese from the coastal region, female, aged 50, a library administrator
2. Wei: Northern Chinese from the interior region, male, aged 38, a mathematics/philosophy teacher
3. Bao: Zhuang minority, male, aged 32, a news agency editor
4. Shan: Northern Chinese from the interior region, female, aged 26, a Chinese language teacher

## Lian (Southern Coastal Chinese Interviewee 34, female, aged 50, a library administrator)

**Background**: I was born in the city in the Wuyi county in Zhejiang in 1950. In 1958, when I was seven or eight, I entered primary school. In 1964, I entered junior secondary school, also in the same county. After that, I enrolled in a technical college but when the Cultural Revolution began, classes were cancelled. So in 1968, I started working in a textile factory. Then from 1973, I worked in a company producing salted eggs and century eggs. In 1984, I came to Guangxi. I first worked in the Nationalities Research Institute as an information officer. In 1985, I studied political education at this university [in the southern interior of China] and graduated in 1988. I now work in the library of the university.

    **The Wuyi dialect**: There are eleven dialects in Zhejiang. Every county has a different dialect. Most people can understand five or six of them. My first dialect is the Wuyi dialect. The dialects in that county are very special. That county was like a 'dialect island'. People who could speak that dialect were all in that county. There were very few speakers. Outside that county, people could not understand that dialect. My husband can also speak my dialect because he grew up in Zhejiang. My child, born in Wuyi, also learnt this dialect. Now my child is working in Wuhan. When we talk on the telephone or go out together, we speak this dialect and we can keep our conversations secret because people around us cannot understand it. When I visit my maiden home, I also speak the Wuyi dialect.

**Learning Putonghua**: I learnt Putonghua when I was growing up in the county because everyone spoke Putonghua in the city then. I did not have to learn Putonghua purposely. The teachers at the school also used Putonghua because they were from different parts of China. It was like that in primary school and also in secondary school. In the technical college that I attended, Putonghua was also used as the medium of instruction because the college was for the whole province. Students came from all over the province, so they could only communicate in Putonghua. I never felt any difficulty in learning Putonghua because I used it from Primary 1.

**Switching between Putonghua and other dialects**: Among colleagues at my present workplace, Putonghua is spoken. Sometimes they speak Baihua [the dialect spoken in her present location in Guangxi] with each other, but when there are visitors from another place coming here to discuss something, they will use Putonghua. I can understand Baihua because when the locals chat with each other, they speak Baihua. I cannot speak Baihua well and do not enjoy speaking it. My husband's family is in Wuhan. When we visit them, I speak Putonghua. They can understand me. When they speak the Wuhan dialect, I can understand them too though I cannot speak it well. I also understand the Sichuan dialect and the Guiliu dialect a little because I often go to villages to do research. In the villages, if you do not understand their dialects, it is very hard to collect information.

**Learning English**: I learnt English from junior secondary school. After that, I learnt on my own through the correspondence course supported by television broadcasts. I studied at a television university for two years from 1989 to 1990. I also used the cassette recorder to listen to tapes and bought books to read. It was a very dead way to learn. I could understand a little, remember some words. My English was good for examinations. In those days, the teacher's standard was rather low. Her own English was not too good so she could not teach well. Few people learnt English well. To learn well, you have to rely on yourself. We are assessed very often, for example, for promotion at our workplace. If you do not study, it will not do. I was already assessed twice for promotion, five years between each assessment. If you want to be promoted again, then you need to be assessed again. If you do not want promotion, then you will not be assessed. On the mainland, a lot of us study for the purpose of assessment.

**Importance of interaction**: The environment affects learning particularly. If you are living in a certain language environment, even if you do not specially work hard at learning a language, you will still be influenced and learn some of it. If you pay attention in addition and try to learn it intentionally, you will learn fast. If you do not have that environment, even if you try very hard to learn, you will still have a huge obstacle. It is like my learning of English. I can listen to tapes, read books, memorize words but without the opportunity to interact, it is very difficult for me to improve. When I have learnt the language to a certain level and I have mastered a certain amount of vocabulary, I know what it means and I can understand what I read but I cannot speak it. The best way to learn a language is to have a combination of someone teaching you and someone to practise communication with you. I do not have the opportunity to practise or interact. So my oral language cannot improve. It is rather difficult to find someone to interact with me in English. There are many foreign language teachers in our university but they are all busy with their own work. You will not feel good about taking up their time.

**English in Hong Kong**: I was in Hong Kong once. I was on an exchange programme at the Chinese University in April 2000. When I met students, they all spoke Cantonese or English. Since I could not speak Cantonese well, when I had to ask them questions about certain matters, I could only use English. My English was rather rusty but under those circumstances, I was forced to use it. After a period of time, I was better and felt there was much improvement. When I meet a foreigner, we must speak English. So even if I cannot speak English well, I must still speak it. So environment affects learning very much.

**English in France**: In September 2000, I was also in France to do research on the Yao and Miao ethnic groups [ethnic minorities from China] living in France. The first generation of these groups there could still speak some Chinese but their second generation could only speak French and some of them could speak a little English. Since I could not speak French, we could only communicate in English. I could also buy things and ask for directions in English. The environment forced me to improve. I was very happy about it. Language could help me solve problems. If you are travelling and do not speak English at all, you will not dare to go and buy things. You are like a dumb person. Some of the people who went with me were older and could not speak English. They did not even dare to buy anything. So I could only be brave and went to shop for them. They were very grateful to me.

## Wei (Northern Interior Chinese Interviewee 31, male, aged 38, a mathematics and philosophy teacher)

**Background**: I was born in Tongwei in Gansu in 1962. I grew up in a rural area and completed my primary and secondary education there. In 1979, I enrolled in a teacher training university in the provincial capital and graduated in 1983. Upon graduation, I taught mathematics in a teachers' training college in Dingxi, a small city, for five years. In 1988, I came to this university [in the northwestern region] to do my master's degree. Since I graduated in 1991, I have been teaching mathematics and philosophy at this university.

**The Tongwei dialect**: The dialect I know best is of course the Tongwei dialect because I grew up in my home village. I learnt this dialect from my parents. This should be considered my mother tongue because I could speak it from a young age. Dingxi was near my home so I could speak the Dingxi dialect too, which was similar to the Tongwei dialect. I can learn my dialect well because it was spoken all around me.

**Putonghua**: I did not learn Putonghua very well. I also learnt it from my parents but all along, I could not speak it well. The teachers in my primary and secondary schools did not use Putonghua to teach, not even in Chinese lessons. My classmates and I did not use Putonghua for interaction. Only when I went to university at the provincial capital in 1988 did I learn Putonghua. That was because the students came from all over the country and they could not understand my dialect. Actually in class, we were required to use Putonghua but I did not make much effort in learning it well at school. So at university, I had to learn it on my own from listening to broadcasts and listening to other people speaking in Putonghua. Because I teach mathematics and philosophy here, the teaching involves the disciplinary knowledge more. So even if my Putonghua is not so good, the effect is not so great. It is quite difficult to learn Putonghua when a person has grown up.

**English**: I learnt a little English. I learnt some words. A few days ago, some visitors from overseas came to visit our department and basically we could communicate about academic matters, not very well, but we could interact. My father at first did not know any English. He was a farmer. But my grandfather was a *ju³ren²* [a person who passed the local qualifying examination in the civil service examinations in imperial China] in the Qing dynasty. So my father studied a lot under my grandfather. Later, my father studied English by himself. He could read English books but could not pronounce the words. So from a young age, I liked English because I was influenced by my father. At university, I liked English particularly. Perhaps that was why I spent more time on it. I relied on self-study because, in those days, the standard of English teaching was rather low. At university, we were using a series of books produced by Nankai University but those were more suitable for developing professional English. At that time, I wanted to learn English more widely. So I studied the set of books by Xu Guozhang by myself. In my third year at university, I became interested in English literature and read a series on English literature. I also read a poetry anthology including the poetry of Byron. That was the first book I read in English by myself. Now I have basically no problem in reading English but writing is very difficult, very difficult. I am still continuing to learn. I hope I can write academic papers in English and publish internationally. That would be best.

**Russian**: I also studied Russian when I was at university but I have forgotten almost all of it now. If I use a dictionary, I can still read some Russian books.

**Learning languages**: I think not having an environment to use the language is the greatest obstacle. Learning a language takes a lot of time. It is definitely not enough just to depend on the teacher. It demands a lot of work by ourselves and is a matter of self-study. It does not matter which method you use to learn as long as you practise more, read more, listen more, write more, speak more and interact more.

**Policy recommendations**: Universities should be stricter. If you cannot pass the Band 4 examination [the national examination for university students in China; more details in Chapter 3], you cannot get your degree. But that is not strict enough. The environment for using English creatively is also inadequate. For example, the television broadcast time in English is not long enough. Putonghua learning should also be a long-term policy. It is best to force people to learn it when they are young. A person who cannot speak Putonghua well should not be a teacher. The policy should be more strictly implemented in primary school and then secondary school. At university, we could be more relaxed about this because many students already know Putonghua by the time they get to university. In the cities, they have television and radio broadcasts and children generally can speak Putonghua. Those who cannot speak Putonghua well are from the rural areas. The state should send better university graduates to the rural areas or pay teachers there better and should develop the vast rural areas. If the economy and the living conditions in the rural areas are better and we can attract better teachers there, then children from rural areas will learn better. Even nowadays, educational conditions in rural areas are still very bad.

## Bao (Minority Interviewee 15, male, aged 32, a news agency editor)

**Background**: I was born in 1968 in a small city in the Debao *xian*[4] [county] in Guangxi. In 1975, I entered primary school and in 1980, I entered secondary school also in Debao. In 1986, I left for Guangzhou to study at the university specializing in economics and international trade. Upon graduation in 1990, I came to [a city in the southern interior] to work at the Guangxi branch of the China Commodities Inspection Bureau (CCIB) until 1995. Thereafter, I worked at two commercial companies before I joined the news agency in 1999 to work as an editor on international current affairs.

**The Zhuang language**: I learnt the Zhuang language from speaking it at home from birth. It was very natural for me. In primary school, the teachers would usually speak Putonghua in class. If we did not understand any Chinese words in class, the teacher would also provide explanations in the Zhuang language and would also converse with us in the Zhuang language outside class. My friends and I would speak in the Zhuang language because most of the people living in that area spoke that language.

**Putonghua**: In secondary school, not all the teachers came from the local area. Some were not from the Zhuang minority group. They all taught in Putonghua. All of us could basically understand Putonghua and there was no need to teach us in the Zhuang language any more. We would speak Putonghua with the teachers even outside the classroom but continued to speak the Zhuang language with our classmates. Apart from classes, there was little opportunity to learn Putonghua. There was no television in those days. But Putonghua movies influenced me a lot. I remember being carried by adults to go to Putonghua movies. I could not understand most of it but I remember the screen shots and bits of the stories. When I was in Primary 4, around 1978 or 1979, because of the war in Vietnam, many Chinese soldiers would come to our district. We would meet these soldiers and they would ask us for directions and we would have to reply in Putonghua. So there was a chance to speak it. I also began to listen to Putonghua radio broadcasts from Senior Secondary 1. That improved my Putonghua a lot. But because we lived in the Zhuang district, my Putonghua was not quite complete. Even in senior secondary school, when I met vocabulary I did not understand, there was no one to ask because the people sitting near me were also Zhuang people and were in the same situation. Several of the phrases came from the north but we had not lived in the north before. So we could not understand them.

**Chinese literature at university**: Only when I went to university did my Putonghua become perfect. At university, there were classmates from many different provinces. When I heard them using different phrases, slowly I understood their meanings. In my first year at university, we also had Chinese lessons twice a week for a year. We studied classical Chinese literature. Unfortunately, our teacher was an old lady whose Putonghua was very poor. She tried to teach in Putonghua but used a lot of Cantonese in between. I could still understand most of it because the Chinese dialect used in Guangxi, Baihua, is still quite similar to Cantonese but my classmates from Sichuan and some other places could not follow her lessons. We were assessed but if we could not pass our Chinese assessment, we could still graduate.

**English in secondary schooldays**: I started learning English from Junior Secondary 1. But the learning during those early years was very inefficient. The teachers' standard of English was not very good. Teachers taught English in Putonghua, both in junior secondary and senior secondary school. The tools for learning were also not very advanced. We did not have tape recorders. In senior secondary school, I listened to BBC [British Broadcasting Corporation] and VOA [Voice of America] a little but my listening was not systematic. There was no guidance and no book. There was also no opportunity to use it.

**English at university**: Only when I went to university did the teacher teach English in English. Because our university specialized in international trade, we had English lessons throughout our four-year programme, except for the last semester. A foreign teacher interviewed each of us to stream us into either the fast class or the slow one. He would ask questions like: 'What is your name?

Which province did you come from? What is your province famous for?' I could understand all his questions but, according to the Chinese way of expression, I felt I should be humble and said there was nothing special in my province and I was put in the slow class. The foreign teacher came from a special American organization, which had a contract with the Ministry of Education to send teachers here and to allow teachers to go to America for training. He taught the fast class. The slow class was taught by foreigners employed directly by the university. Sometimes, it was this person. Sometimes, it was another person. Sometimes, the teacher just taught for half a year and ran away. So it was not so good. Even though there was an English Corner for us to try to speak to each other, there was no atmosphere for us to say much. In the slow class, everyone's standard was not high. So when the teacher asked us to do discussion, the result was that I felt we were wasting a lot of time. At university, there were tapes we could listen to but the supply of electricity in Guangzhou in those days, from 1986 to 1990, was not adequate. So only when it was dark would electricity be supplied to the dormitories. So though some of us had tape recorders, we could not use them because if we had to use batteries, they would run out soon and they cost a lot of money. There was also a language laboratory; we could go there to listen to tapes but there were only forty to fifty seats but there were over a thousand students.

**English at work**: When I was working at the CCIB, I had to use English very often. With foreigners, I used English. There were also a lot of visitors from Hong Kong. With these Hong Kong visitors, we would speak in Chinese, often Cantonese, but fax and Telnet communication was all in English. Between 1995 to 1997, when I was working in a commercial company, I was also posted to Hong Kong for a few months periodically and would use Cantonese and English.

**Learning English nowadays**: I am still learning English now. I listen to VOA and CCTV9 [a national channel]. I also browse the Internet in English. For example, if I want to know about cars, I can find the information there. I think if there can be more English newspapers, use of Chinese and English on the streets, like in street names, and the government can invite more foreigners to come and interact with us, that will enhance our English.

**Languages as wealth**: I consider languages my wealth; the more I know, the better. My best language now is Putonghua. My second best language is the Zhuang language. After that come Cantonese, Baihua, English and Japanese (which I studied for one-and-a-half years at university) in that order. My wife is Chinese. She cannot speak the Zhuang language. My child is just one year old now. I plan to teach my child the Zhuang language, Putonghua and English. These three should be enough for him.

## Shan (Northern Interior Chinese Interviewee 11, female, aged 26, a Chinese language teacher)

**Background**: From the time I was born in 1974 till I entered university, I was living in Huhehaote [or Hohhot], the capital of Inner Mongolia. The population was about 1 million. In 1980, I entered primary school. In 1986, I went to junior secondary school and in 1989, senior secondary school. In 1992, when I was 18, I came to Beijing for my university education. I did a double degree in biomedical engineering and scientific editing for five years. From 1997, I have been studying for my master's programme in economics part-time. I teach Chinese part-time at this university [in Beijing]. I teach the reading of newspapers and magazines in Chinese and Chinese characters for beginners.

**The Shanxi dialect**: Although I was born in Inner Mongolia, my parents were originally from Shanxi. So they speak the Shanxi dialect at home. Usually, they speak the Shanxi dialect and I speak Putonghua at home. But if we have a visitor from Shanxi, then I will try to speak the Shanxi dialect because the visitor will then feel that we are very close. But normally I do not speak the Shanxi dialect at home.

**Putonghua**: My best language is Putonghua. In primary and secondary school, my Chinese teachers used Putonghua to teach and some teachers of other subjects also used Putonghua to teach. I have a strong wish to learn dialects. I am very surprised I have this interest. I just feel China is so vast and the southern dialects are so different from the northern dialects. I am very curious about other people's dialects.

**Tianjinhua**: I can also speak the Tianjin dialect a little. This might be because the factory where my parents worked moved from Tianjin to Inner Mongolia. So several older workers were from Tianjin, about 30 percent of them. In China, workers in one factory often lived together in dormitories. We went to their homes to play and their children also came to our homes to play. So from the time when I was small, I listened to this type of sounds and they became familiar. I cannot speak much but I can speak it.

**Dongbeihua**: I can speak very good Dongbeihua [northeastern dialects] though I have never been there. I have two good friends from that region. Because Dongbeihua has a rather strong accent, I thought it rather interesting when I listened to it. So I frequently felt I wanted to learn it. Now I can communicate with my two friends in Dongbeihua and other people cannot tell which region I came from and think I am like them.

**Other dialects**: I have little difficulty in picking up northern dialects. At the moment, I am learning a little Shaanxihua and Shandonghua. I feel it is very simple. It is only adjusting some sounds. The phrasing and sentence structure are not very different. But for the dialects in the south across the Jiang [Chang Jiang or the Yangtze River], for example, in Shanghai, Jiangsu, Zhejiang, I cannot learn anything; it is very difficult. I can guess where people are from but I am unable to learn their dialects.

**Large English classes**: I started learning English in Junior Secondary 1. There were sixty students in one class. Most of the time, we read aloud together after the teacher. It was like many people singing together, like a chorus. Only when we were reading did we feel it was more orderly. If you had questions, you could not stop to ask them. After the lesson, because there were sixty people, soon you would lose the interest to ask questions. There were too many people. Everyone was walking in and out and only you would be asking questions; it seemed a little stupid. In China, this is a very big problem. After we have been studying for some time, there will not be the concept of asking questions any more. No one was willing to ask questions. Even if there were really questions, I tried to control myself and did not want to ask them. When I was in senior secondary school, it was a little better. There were forty-eight people in one class. It was rather difficult to learn a second language in a big class. If we spoke, the teacher could not hear us properly.

**English for examination**: My reading and writing in English are good. This might also be related to the fact that in the university entrance examination in 1992 only reading and writing were assessed. For people like us coming from a small and faraway place, the only route to leave that place and have any advancement is to enter university. It seemed as if we only had one thought in our brains — to learn the answers to all the questions that might appear in the examination. If we were given a question paper, we all did it and the teacher would then check the answers with us and ask, 'For this question, what to choose? Choose "a". That's correct. Why is it correct?' I have actually been learning English for many years, thirteen years since 1986. But I only learnt and paid attention to listening and speaking English from my university days for the purpose of interacting with other people. Before that, it was only to study it as an examination subject. In many 'small places' [that is, not big cities] in the northern part of China, it is like this, probably all like this.

**English outside class**: At university, once the English lesson was over, I switched quickly back to Putonghua. I felt if I continued to speak English, people would judge me and would laugh at me or say that my English was not good. In the dormitory, four of us shared the front room and we had an agreement — we would speak English every night. But we only maintained this for three days because it was very painful. There were many things we could not communicate in English because we did not know the words and when other people saw us not being able to communicate, they would laugh at us and asked what we were doing. I do not know whether the English I speak is different from that spoken by other people. We only had a foreign teacher once in my third year. So when I speak with people from other countries now, sometimes I wonder if they can understand me and if what I speak is English. This is my big obstacle and is hard to overcome.

**TOEFL and GRE**: Most of my classmates were sitting for the TOEFL [Test of English as a Foreign Language] examination and the GRE [Graduate

Record Examination]. So I took those examinations too. If not, people would think I was very strange. There was also a school to help students prepare for these examinations. It was called a school but it was really a tutorial company. The classes were quite frightening. Eight hundred people would have the lesson together in a big hall or a warehouse. The atmosphere was stressful. Lessons were very expensive. But the company seemed to be able to get the question papers. Last year's papers — they would be able to have them this year. The TOEFL course is about five hundred *yuans* [or Renminbi, the Chinese currency] and the GRE course is about eight hundred. The course is about ten weeks long. Every week, there are about three to four lessons, two-and-a-half hours for each lesson. Every time after a lesson, I would get a headache because there were too many people and it was too crowded. So in the end, I studied by myself instead.

**Japanese**: I also learnt Japanese at university for about a month but there was a time clash with something else I had to do. So I gave it up. It was also because there were too many people in the class — about forty-odd students. So it was rather tiring. We learnt from zero level but it was very repetitive. I already knew something and we had to say it over and over again. The course was free of charge. You had to pay a deposit but, if you passed the examination, it would be refunded to you. I lost my refund. It was not a requirement and you could choose to learn Japanese, French, German or even Russian. Very few people chose Russian.

**Songs and television drama**: I liked learning the songs in television drama too. I found these songs particularly useful for learning languages. The most popular songs in those days were those from Hong Kong and Japan. I would use my own method to write down the words even if I did not know the language. For example, if the song is in Cantonese and it is slow and the words are not fast and colloquial, if I like the song, I will try to write it down. When I was at university, I loved listening to old English songs, very nice to listen to, very famous songs. I do not like the noisy songs. The words are clearly pronounced in the old songs and the words are very meaningful. I also liked learning dialects from short plays on television.

## Relating Learner Experience to Policy Implementation

The four learning biographies presented above give some indication of the variation in experience depending on the historical period the learner was educated in, the native dialect or language of the learner, whether the learner grew up in a rural or an urban area and other idiosyncratic personal or family circumstances. By and large, the younger the learner, the more mature the policy implementation, the better the learning conditions are. But there are regional and individual circumstances that give rise to differences in the experience of policy implementation even within the same time zone.

The following observations made with reference to the four learning stories are not intended to be generalizations but will focus on: the learning of Putonghua, the role of other Chinese dialects, the learning of English, the experience of minority learners and other observations on language learning in multilingual China.

## Learning Putonghua

Although Putonghua has been propagated from around 1955, its spread in certain areas is incomplete; learners coming from rural or minority language areas in recent years may still face difficulty or feel a sense of inferiority about their ability to acquire an accurate or respected accent. In contrast, those growing up in coastal cities are usually in a more advantageous position by virtue of the fact that cities attract speakers from other dialect areas and Putonghua has to be the common dialect used among these speakers. Lian, the oldest of the four learners, entered Primary 1 in 1958, during the early years when Putonghua was first propagated as the national dialect from 1955. As she grew up in a city in the coastal region, it was not surprising that she was educated in Putonghua from Primary 1. Students going there from all over the province and teachers from other places could only communicate in Putonghua. In contrast, Wei, though younger, grew up in a rural area in the northern interior region; his teachers at school did not use Putonghua even in Chinese lessons; so he felt he did not learn Putonghua well until he went to university in 1988. Likewise, Bao, from the Zhuang minority, was taught in a mixture of the Zhuang language and Putonghua. Both of them cited the need to learn on their own from listening to broadcasts in Putonghua. Shan, the youngest of the four, reported that all her teachers used Putonghua to teach all subjects at all levels. Interestingly, both Bao and Shan, the younger two, reported Putonghua as their best language nowadays.

## Other Chinese dialects

In spite of the spread of Putonghua, other Chinese dialects and minority languages still have a role to play, particularly in enhancing intimacy or rapport between speakers. Lian reported the use of the Wuyi dialect with her husband and her child so as to keep their conversations 'secret' or unknown to people around them. She also reported the use of several other dialects with her husband's relatives and with villagers during her research. Wei stated that his best dialect was the Tongwei dialect and indicated that his Putonghua was not so perfect. Bao considered languages as wealth and planned to teach his child the Zhuang language along with Putonghua (and English). Shan also expressed her intrinsic interest to learn several other northern Chinese dialects, similar to her own, but felt that southern Chinese dialects were very difficult for her, perhaps because they were so different from her own.

## Learning English

In the face of less than ideal circumstances for learning English such as large classes, learners tend to have to do a lot of learning on their own. Lian was convinced that she had to rely on herself to learn well because the teacher's standard was rather low; she spent a lot of time on tapes and books, though it was 'a very dead way to learn'. She was motivated by the assessment for promotion every five years. She was also pleased that she could use English in Hong Kong and in France. Likewise, Wei relied on self-study and the first book he read by himself was a poetry anthology. He felt he could handle reading but found writing very difficult. Bao also tried to learn on his own but electricity was supplied to dormitories only when it was dark; so he could not use tape recorders often. Shan's story showed that some learners took the initiative to learn from each other by agreeing to speak English among themselves every night in the dormitory. Her story also highlighted the culture of taking examinations such as the TOEFL and the GRE and the commercial courses targeted at passing these examinations. But the class size of those courses was so huge — eight hundred students in one class — that she preferred to study by herself instead. While conditions for learning English have improved in terms of technical support such as television and tape recorders, it is evident that learning English in China nowadays still suffers from insufficient opportunity to use the language for interaction.

## Minority learners

Bao came from the largest minority group in China, the Zhuang people. Even so, his story still gives an idea of the additional difficulties that minority language learners may face in China. In the learning of Putonghua, he had the further difficulty of having to learn it partly through other Chinese dialects which were not his home language. Although he was taught partly in the Zhuang language and partly in Putonghua in primary school, in secondary school, he would come across vocabulary from the north and at university, his Chinese teacher used a lot of Cantonese. In spite of this, however, Bao was positive about learning Putonghua and considered learning languages to be the acquisition of wealth. His repertoire included Putonghua, the Zhuang language, Cantonese, Baihua, English and Japanese. Though he was multilingual, the very fact that Putonghua became his best language underscores the problem faced by minority learners (Lee, 2001, p. 30): competence in Putonghua facilitates their academic and economic advancement, but that will inevitably mean lesser use of their own languages even if they may not lose them altogether. (This issue will be further explored in Chapter 4.)

## Becoming multilingual in China

Much as these are accounts of what happened in the past while the learners were going through the education system, they also point to some of the circumstances in recent years because these learners seem not to have stopped their language development at the end of their education. Their stories illustrate various circumstances that can enhance learning such as parental influence (for example, Wei's interest in learning English because his father was interested), the need for interaction (for example, Bao's improvement in Putonghua at university and Lian's use of English while shopping in France), assessment for educational and career advancement (as for all four learners in learning English) and the usefulness of informal learning opportunities such as radio, movies, television and songs (as for Bao in learning Putonghua and Shan in learning different languages). Because these learners have done so much learning on their own, it comes as no surprise that they should recommend increasing radio and television broadcasts to enrich the opportunities for independent learning. What stands out most in all these stories is the self-awareness that these learners have about their learning experience and about their motivation for learning and using their various languages and dialects.

## Summary

In this chapter, I have reviewed briefly the overall context of developments in China, its domestic goals and foreign policy, the character of its education system and the language policies it has maintained consistently in the last half century. I have also provided a glimpse of how these policies have been experienced by learners from different time periods and with different linguistic backgrounds. Putonghua is still being propagated and English is of paramount importance as China moves comfortably into an age when international discourse is vital for its well-being. The main issues seem to be how to facilitate the learning of these two languages nationally and, at the same time, to maintain cultural coherence for the various dialect and minority language groups in the multilingual and multidialectal setting of China.

In the chapters to follow, details will be provided on the three major policies: the standardization of Chinese (Chapter 2), the ascendancy of English (Chapter 3) and language developments among minority ethnic groups

(Chapter 4). In each of these chapters, the policy steps will first be traced and the actual experiences of learners will then be presented. In the concluding chapter (Chapter 5), I shall summarize the experience of language learning in China as well as identify some trends in language education in China as a prediction of what lies ahead in the years to come.

# 2

# Propagating Standard Chinese

## Introduction

In the last chapter, the three major language policies in China were introduced. Of the three policies, the one which has been most widely implemented for the longest period is the propagation of standard Chinese among the majority ethnic group, the Han Chinese. This chapter is focused on this policy. The chapter begins with an outline of the major policy measures in the standardization of Chinese from 1949. Against this background, an overall picture of how the policy has been experienced is provided through a summary of survey data from 318 Han Chinese learners from different age cohorts, dialectal backgrounds and locations in China. To complement the survey data, four case histories of Han Chinese learners focused on their learning of Chinese against their multilingual background are also presented and discussed. The final part of the chapter presents perspectives from some heads of Chinese programmes on the teaching of Chinese in China from primary school to university level in recent times.

## The Standardization of Chinese

When the People's Republic of China was established in 1949, one of the first targets in education was to promote literacy among the majority ethnic group, the Han Chinese (and also among the language minorities, which will be discussed in Chapter 4). To this end, the Chinese script was simplified and standardized. At the same time, to propagate Putonghua (Common Speech) as the standard dialect, a romanized script, *hanyu pinyin*, based on the Roman alphabet, was adopted in parallel. This second measure has been especially important because of the great dialectal variation in the pronunciation of Chinese characters by people in different regions. While both policies — the simplification of the script and the propagation of a standard dialect — were initiated in the mid-1950s, they have been periodically reaffirmed by the state; in recent years, more measures have also been announced.

## Simplification of the Chinese script

Before measures from 1949 are presented, it is necessary to provide some background to the Chinese script, which has had a long history. The script probably began developing with the establishment of the Xia dynasty in the twenty-first century BC and became established by the Shang dynasty beginning in the sixteenth century BC. This gives it an age of about 3,500 years old (Norman, 1988, p. 4; State Language Commission, 1995, p. 35). Although it has been classified as an ideographic or logographic script in that it is meaning-based (Taylor & Olson, 1995, p. 2), there is actually a phonetic component in many characters (about 80% of characters in general use by one count) (State Language Commission, 1995, p. 39). The methods of character formation have been referred to as the *liu⁴shu¹* (六书) or six methods of writing in the dictionary *Shuowen Jiezi* compiled by Xu Shen (Norman, 1988, p. 67) in 121 AD during the Han dynasty (Malmqvist, 1994, pp. 7–8). They are illustrated in Table 2.1.

**Table 2.1  Six methods of writing**

| Method | Character | Pinyin | Meaning |
|---|---|---|---|
| 1. Pictograph *xiang⁴xing²* (象形 ) | 日 | *ri⁴* | 'sun' |
| 2. Ideograph *zhi¹shi⁴* (指事) | 三 | *san¹* | 'three' |
| 3. Compound ideograph *hui⁴yi⁴* (会意) | 明 | *ming²* | 'bright' ('sun' and 'moon' combined) |
| 4. Phonetic compound *xing²sheng¹* (形声) | 河 | *he²* | 'river' |
| 5. Loan character *jia³jie⁴* (假借 ) | 花 | *hua¹* | character for 'flower' borrowed to mean 'spend' |
| 6. Derivative graph *zhuan³zhu⁴* ( 转注 ) | 考 老 | *kao³* from *lao³* | 'test' derived from 'old' |

Based on Malmqvist (1994, p. 23) and State Language Commission (1995, pp. 37–39).

With such a long history, the Chinese script has undergone several changes, the most well-known being its codification during the Qin dynasty (221 to 207 BC). Throughout its development, the tendency has been towards simplification with some loss of its pictographic quality and the conversion of earlier rounded strokes to more linear and angular representations (Norman, 1988, p. 62). This has been explained with reference to the wider use of the writing system in society.

The total number of Chinese characters has been estimated to be under 55,000 (Norman, 1988, p. 71; Su, 1994, p. 10). This is the number of characters in comprehensive dictionaries. Most users have a vocabulary of about 4,000 to 6,000 characters depending on their needs. In a list of characters in general use published by the Guojia Yuyan Wenzi Gongzuo Weiyuanhui (State Language Commission), often abbreviated as Guojia Yuwei, in 1988, the number is about 7,000 (State Language Commission, 1996, p. 229). The great number of characters existing and the much smaller number of characters in general use means that there are many characters which are not in frequent use or no longer used. The characters no longer in use are called $si^3zi^4$ (死字), dead characters. Cheng X-H. (1991, p. 28) lists altogether ninety-one characters relating to horses, many of which are no longer in use. Some examples are: $gua^1$ (騧), 'brown horse with a black mouth', $biao^1$ (驫), 'several horses galloping together' and $lai^2$ (騋), 'horse over seven feet tall'. At the same time, by the 1950s, because of the different degrees of literacy in the population, some characters had developed variant forms or $yi^4ti^3zi^1$ (异体字). For example, $chuang^1$ (窗) meaning 'window', had five variant forms ( 窻 窓 窻 牎 牕 ) (Cheng X-H., 1991, p. 26). The great number of dead characters and the proliferation of variant forms in the society made it difficult for learners. It was to combat such circumstances that the Chinese government decided to standardize the Chinese script from the 1950s (Table 2.2).

**Table 2.2 Standardization of the Chinese script**

| Year | Event |
|------|-------|
| 1954 | Government directive to initiate discussion on the simplification of the script. |
| 1955 | Publication of *List of Standard Forms for Variant Characters*. There are 795 character groups in the revised publication of this list (with changes in 1986 and 1988 incorporated later). Through this list, 1,025 variant characters were discarded. |
| 1956 | Announcement of the implementation of the *First Character Simplification Scheme* with 515 simplified characters and 54 radicals. A radical is the part in a character common to several characters. For example, 艹 signifies 'grass' and is found in these characters $hua^3$ (花), $qin^2$ (芹), $cha^2$ (茶) meaning 'flower', 'celery' and 'tea' respectively. Sometimes, it can also be a character in itself. |
| 1964 | Confirmation of *First Character Simplification Scheme*. Except for four radicals ( 纟 讠 钅 饣 ), all simplified radicals when used as single characters should also be used in the simplified form. |
| 1977 | Publication of *Second Character Simplification Scheme*, which did not meet with acceptance by the population. |
| 1983 | Publication of *List of Standardized Radicals (Draft)* for dictionary design. |
| 1986 | Confirmation of disuse of the 1977 *Second Character Simplification Scheme*. |
| 1986 | 1964 *Character Simplification List* published again with 2,235 simplified characters and 14 radicals. |
| 1988 | Publication of the *List of Frequently Used Characters* (3,500 characters). |
| 1988 | Publication of the *List of Characters in General Use* (7,000 characters). |
| 1992 | Publication of regulations for the use of Chinese characters in publications. |

Based on information from State Language Commission (1996).

To effect all these changes, there was selection of forms already in use in the community as well as further simplification following such patterns of use. For the choice of a standard form over other variant forms in the *List of Standard Forms for Variant Characters*, the determining criteria were not entirely clear. There seemed to be a few principles: simpler forms were preferred over more complex forms; forms in common use were preferred over less commonly used forms; forms already used in the established literature were preferred over newly derived non-standard forms. These principles could be conflicting in certain instances and some consensus within the team working on the lists of characters would have to be reached. As for the design of new simplified characters, two methods of character design from the *liu⁴shu¹* mentioned above were frequently used: phonetic compound (Method 4) and loan character (Method 5). Both methods allow the creation of new simplified characters based on existing characters with similar sounds. Other methods used were to borrow from the older simpler form (云 to replace 雲 meaning 'cloud') or to adopt the cursive form ( 书 to replace 書 meaning 'book') of a character. In some cases, the same character has ended up with more than one meaning. The character, *mian⁴* (面) is now used for both 'face' and 'noodle' and *hou⁴* (后) now means both 'empress' and 'behind'.

However it was achieved, the result was that a single form of a character was thereafter propagated by the state to replace the several forms previously in use. While the action by the state precipitated the changes, it was not the initial motivation for the changes. The initial motivation was the proliferation of dead characters and variant characters in common use and the need in the society for the character set to be simple enough for it to be learnable by the general population. When the state tried to implement the *Second Simplification Scheme*, which was less based on forms in popular use, it did not succeed to have it accepted by the public. (See Lam, 1998, and Chen, 1999, pp. 148–163, for more details on script reform.)

### Propagation of Putonghua and hanyu pinyin

While the reforms on Chinese characters were taking place, a phonetic alphabet was also developed in parallel to enhance the learning of the standard dialect, Putonghua, which was generally based on the northern dialects, using the Beijing dialect as the standard pronunciation and *baihuawen*, a modern literary variety popularized from the early twentieth century in China, as the standard for its grammatical phrasing (State Council, 1956; State Language Commission, 1996, p. 12). This standard variety is also referred to as Mandarin in some parts of the world such as Taiwan and Singapore. The popularization of Putonghua began in the mid-1950s and was reaffirmed in the 1980s.

In 1954, the Zhongguo Wenzi Gaige Weiyuanhui (Commission on

**Photo 3**   Plaque on the wall of a secondary school in Xiamen: 'Language is a mark of a country's nationhood.'

Language Planning of China) was established (Wang et al., 1995, p. 63). After a national conference on language and script in October 1955, a directive from the State Council dated February 1956 initiated the propagation of Putonghua (State Council, 1956; reprinted in Wang et al., 1995, pp. 765–768, and State Language Commission, 1996, pp. 11–15). What follows is a paraphrase of this document.

1. **Schools**: From the autumn of 1956, except for the ethnic minority regions, all primary and secondary schools should begin to include the teaching of Putonghua in Chinese classes. From 1960, students from grades above Primary 3, secondary school students and those in teacher training colleges should basically be able to speak Putonghua; Putonghua should be used as a medium of instruction in primary schools and teacher training colleges for all subjects; teachers in secondary schools should also basically teach in Putonghua. The teaching on Putonghua should also be increased in the Chinese curriculum in higher education. Younger teachers and teaching assistants in higher education should enrol for short Putonghua courses if they could not speak Putonghua.

2. **The army**: The Chinese subject in the education of the People's Liberation Army and its affiliated schools should be taught in Putonghua. New recruits to the army and new entrants to military schools should be able to speak Putonghua within a year.

3. **Youth groups and factories**: As far as possible and progressively, Putonghua should be propagated among youth groups and workers' organizations and should be adopted in cultural tuition programmes in factories.

4. **Broadcasting and entertainment**: Broadcasting stations all over the country should co-operate with the regional Tuiguang Putonghua Gongzuo Weiyuanhui (Committees to Promote Putonghua) to offer Putonghua seminars. Broadcasting stations in various dialect areas should broadcast some programmes in Putonghua so that listeners could learn Putonghua

by and by. All broadcasting personnel, actors in the movie industry, professional actors in drama and singers should receive Putonghua training. Even those in Peking opera or other types of performances should support the propagation of Putonghua by and by.

5. **The press**: Personnel for all newspapers, news agencies, magazines and publishers should learn Putonghua grammar and phrasing. The Ministry of Culture should monitor this development so that the confusion in the use of phrasing and sentence structure could be minimized in two to five years' time.

6. **Service personnel**: All personnel in the transport and communication services should learn Putonghua. In large cities, those in public health services, the police, the justice and cultural departments should do likewise. Organizations supporting such services should provide a training programme so that staff having to deal with the public frequently should be able to learn Putonghua within a specified period of time.

7. **Interpreters**: Interpreters dealing with the outside world should use Putonghua as far as possible.

8. **Hanyu pinyin**: The Commission on Language Planning of China should complete the *hanyu pinyin* scheme within the first half of 1956 to facilitate the teaching of Putonghua and the romanization of Chinese characters.

9. **Dictionaries and dialectal differences**: The Language Research Institute in the Chinese Academy of Sciences should complete a dictionary to illustrate the correct pronunciation of Putonghua within 1956 and a Modern Chinese dictionary by 1958; in collaboration with the Ministry of Education and the Ministry of Higher Education and organizing the manpower in teacher training colleges and the Chinese departments in universities, it should also complete within 1956 and 1957 a preliminary survey of dialects in each county. Within 1956, the education offices in each province should provide booklets on the characteristic differences between Putonghua and the respective local Chinese dialect(s). The Ministry of Education and the Ministry of Broadcasting should develop large quantities of tapes to enhance the teaching and learning of Putonghua. The Ministry of Culture should do film productions for the propagation and teaching of Putonghua.

10. **Training**: To develop cadres for the propagation of Putonghua and to train teachers of Chinese and administrative cadres in secondary schools and teacher training colleges, the Ministry of Education should offer Putonghua classes frequently. All organizations and groups should send suitable cadres to be trained. Similarly, the education offices in all provinces, cities and counties should organize short training courses for teachers of Chinese in primary schools and teacher training colleges and local organizations and groups should send suitable personnel for training.

11. **Committees**: The State Council established the Committee to Promote

Putonghua to unify and lead the national propagation of Putonghua, with its work on an everyday basis carried out by the Commission on Language Planning of China (responsible for planning and monitoring the project), the Ministry of Education and the Ministry of Higher Education (responsible for the teaching of Putonghua, teacher training and developing teaching materials), the Ministry of Culture (responsible for publicity, publications and the production of tapes and films) and the Language Research Institute in the Chinese Academy of Sciences (responsible for the research on standardizing Putonghua phonology, vocabulary and grammar). Every province and municipality should establish a similar committee to oversee the work at the regional level.

12. **Minority groups**: In the ethnic minority regions, Putonghua should be propagated among the Han Chinese living in those regions. The teaching of Chinese in minority schools should use Putonghua as a standard. Chinese programmes in minority areas should be broadcast in Putonghua as much as possible. Each autonomous region could set up a Committee to Promote Putonghua as necessary to organize and lead the work of propagating Putonghua.

From the 1956 directive, it is clear that the propagation of Putonghua was planned as an all-encompassing policy involving the schools, the media and other public services with specific implementation targets and follow-up action at both national and regional levels. The manpower resources mobilized for policy implementation were immense and the roles of respective units were clearly specified.

By 1958, the *Hanyu Pinyin Scheme* to describe the pronunciation of this standard dialect was completed as planned and approved by the National People's Congress. Prior to the adoption of this scheme, there was a pronunciation scheme using symbols written with strokes like in Chinese characters. But in the 1958 scheme, the symbols became letters from the Roman alphabet. For example, ㄅ became [b], ㄆ became [p], ㄇ became [m] and ㄈ became [f]. In the adoption of the *Hanyu Pinyin Scheme*, there was the borrowing of a Roman alphabet (used in English) with Chinese sounds. What is particularly interesting is that since the propagation of *hanyu pinyin*, it became more than an aid to pronunciation. In Chinese publications, Chinese characters are of course printed in preference to *hanyu pinyin*. In non-Chinese publications however, *hanyu pinyin* is now accepted as a mode of representing Chinese graphically. This became more so as *hanyu pinyin* gained more acceptance outside China, especially since its adoption by the United Nations Secretariat in 1979 (Wang et al., 1995, p. 549). (See Hsia, 1956; Barnes, 1974; Seybolt and Chiang, 1979; Cheng C-C., 1986; Jernudd, 1986; Rohsenow, 1986; and Zhou, 1986, for further discussion on language reform in China and State Language Commission, 1996, for the relevant documents.)

Since all schools for Han Chinese students were to teach in Putonghua from the autumn of 1956, workshops to train teachers were organized from 1956 to 1960 by the Ministry of Education and the Language Research Institute (Wang et al., 1995, p. 292). In 1961, the National Committee to Promote Putonghua was integrated with the Commission on Language Planning of China (Wang et al., 1995, p. 287). The initial fervour for this work, however, was soon overtaken by economic measures in terms of the national impetus. After that came the Cultural Revolution during which schooling was extremely irregular and the work of propagating Putonghua suffered a severe setback. The local offices for promoting Putonghua were largely disbanded (Wang et al., 1995, p. 287). Not surprisingly, therefore, it has been noted that, with exceptions in certain locations, 'very little attention was paid to the promotional work in the 1960s and 1970s' (Chen, 1999, p. 26). See, however, Wang et al. (1995, pp. 541–549) for a list of the promotion activities from 1960 to 1980, which serves as an indication that the policy was not abandoned even during those unfavourable years.

After the Cultural Revolution, with the educational system revived, interest in propagating Putonghua also resumed. In August 1978, a directive from the Ministry of Education reaffirmed the need to train teachers in Putonghua (Wang et al, 1995, p. 289) and training workshops were offered again from 1979 (Wang et al., 1995, pp. 292–293). In 1982, the revised *Constitution of China* (Chapter 1, Article 19) reaffirmed that Putonghua should be promoted all over the country (National People's Congress, 1999, p. 11). A notice from the State Council dated 16 December 1985 renamed the Zhongguo Wenzi Gaige Weiyuanhui (Commission on Language Planning of China) as the Guojia Yuyan Wenzi Gongzuo Weiyuanhui (State Language Commission); it still remained directly under the State Council (State Language Commission, 1996, p. 28). The 1986 national conference reasserted various aspects of the initial 1956 policy (Chen, 1999, pp. 26–27). Throughout the 1980s and early 1990s, several documents were issued to standardize the use of *hanyu pinyin* in domains such as: place names in China such as mountains and rivers (1984), using word boundaries to combine the *hanyu pinyin* form of characters (1988) and names of ethnic groups or nationalities in China (1991). The promotion of Putonghua was also reaffirmed with directives on its use in: characters with more than one pronunciation (1985), cities open for tourism (1986), teacher training colleges and universities (1987), primary schools (1990), public transport (1991) and secondary schools (1993) (Wang et al., 1995, pp. 728–825).

Of all the measures initiated in the 1980s, one deserves special mention. It was the move towards standardization in assessing proficiency in Putonghua proposed at the 1986 national conference. In 1988, the State Language Commission began a three-year project to investigate this issue, testing teachers, students and personnel in certain occupations in a number of cities.

The proficiency standards that were arrived at were published by the State Language Commission and distributed to all provinces, autonomous regions and municipalities in 1992 for piloting. In 1994, the standards were revised and redistributed for implementation (State Language Commission, 1996, p. 354). After further endorsement by the Commission, the standards were formally distributed again in December 1997 (State Language Commission, 1997). There are six grades in the grading scheme for the Putonghua Shuiping Ceshi (PSC or Putonghua Proficiency Test) testing both reading and conversation (Table 2.3).

### Table 2.3 Putonghua Proficiency Test Grading Scheme

| Grade | Criteria |
|---|---|
| 1A | Accuracy in pronunciation, vocabulary and grammar. Natural intonation. Fluent expression. Loss of marks within 3%. |
| 1B | Accuracy in pronunciation, vocabulary and grammar. Natural intonation. Fluent expression. Occasional errors in pronouncing sounds and tones. Loss of marks within 8%. |
| 2A | Basically correct pronunciation. Natural intonation. Fluent expression. Occasional errors in pronouncing a few difficult sounds. Very few errors in vocabulary and grammar. Loss of marks within 13%. |
| 2B | Inaccurate articulation of some tones and sounds. More errors in pronouncing difficult sounds. Intonation without obvious influence from another dialect. Occasional use of phrasing and grammar from another dialect. Loss of marks within 20%. |
| 3A | More errors in pronunciation. More errors in difficult sounds than frequently encountered. Mostly inaccurate tones. More obvious dialectal intonation. Errors in vocabulary and grammar. Loss of marks within 30%. |
| 3B | Many errors in pronouncing sounds and tones. Prominent influence from another dialect. Obvious dialectal intonation. More errors in vocabulary and grammar. Occasionally incomprehensible to people from other regions. Loss of marks within 40%. |

Paraphrased from State Language Commission (1997).

While the Putonghua Proficiency Test was intended for native speakers of Chinese, with particularly high requirements for broadcasting personnel and teachers, the teaching of Chinese to non-native speakers was not forgotten. In 1987, the Guojia Duiwai Hanyu Jiaoxue Lingdao Xiaozu (State Leading Group for Teaching Chinese as a Foreign Language) was set up to co-ordinate the teaching of Chinese to non-native speakers in China and outside China (Consulate General of the People's Republic of China in San Francisco, n. d.). In 1988, another national standardized test, the Hanyu Shuiping Kaoshi (HSK or Chinese Proficiency Test of China), was established (*China Daily*, 26 February 2002, cited in China Internet Information Center, 2001) to measure the Chinese proficiency of foreigners, overseas Chinese and other non-native learners of Chinese from the ethnic minorities in China (Ni, Zhao & Peng, 1998, p. 3). HSK, now well-known internationally as the standard test for Chinese as a Foreign Language (China Education and Research Network, n.d.), can be taken at three levels: basic, elementary-intermediate and advanced. The advanced test assesses listening, reading, writing and interviewing abilities (HSK Center, n.d.).

In summary, while the early emphasis in the 1950s was on propagation, the later impetus from the 1980s has gone beyond mere propagation. Not only should one be able to speak Putonghua; one should also be able to do so competently and obtain certification for it.

## Some recent measures

Though the twin policies of script reform and the propagation of Putonghua were initiated half a century ago and much work was completed by the 1990s, the standardization of Chinese is still pursued with vigour even in the last few years. In a directive from the Ministry of Education and the State Language Commission dated 29 February 2000, the target for the use of Putonghua to spread all over the country by 2010 has been set; in the light of the information age, Putonghua proficiency and the use of the simplified script to enhance language use are considered all the more necessary for mastering scientific and cultural knowledge. In terms of the Putonghua Proficiency Test, all teachers should attain Grade 2B; teachers of Chinese should attain Grade 2A and those teaching pronunciation should attain Grade 1B. Even administrative personnel in the Ministry of Education and schools should attain Grade 3A. Teachers of Chinese in minority schools should also attain at least Grade 3A (see Chapter 4 on the ambivalence concerning the learning of Putonghua by minority learners). In the codification of the script, there is also ongoing work. As recently as 19 December 2001, for example, a list of vocabulary with variant forms was published for use by 31 March 2002 (Ministry of Education, 2002, pp. 382–383). A good amount of attention has also been paid to computing standards for keyboard entry for characters. During my field trips to China, I also saw plaques on the walls of schools and dormitories still exhorting teachers and students to 'speak Putonghua' and to 'write standardized characters' while reminding them that 'language is the mark of a country's nationhood'. Of all the recent measures, the clearest indication of policy intent is the *Zhonghua Renmin Gongheguo Guojia Tongyong Yuyan Wenzi Fa* (The Law on Language Use of the People's Republic of China), which was announced on 31 October 2000; it reaffirms that Putonghua and standardized characters are the speech and the script to be used throughout the nation (Article 2), though minority groups still have the freedom to use and develop their own languages and scripts (Article 8) (Editorial Committee, China Education Yearbook, 2001, p. 813). (See Chapter 5 for more details on the latest trends.)

**Photo 4**   Slogan on the wall of the International Exchange Center at Guangxi Nationalities College: 'Speak Putonghua. Write standardized characters.'

That recent measures have been implemented does not mean that the standardization of Chinese has not been successful. On the contrary, as the following sections will show, the policy as a whole has been largely successful though individuals may vary in their experiences. The continual work has been necessary because China is too vast a land and China's population of 1.2 billion is too large for state initiated language planning to pervade completely within half a century.

## The Overall Experience of Han Chinese Learners

The policy to promote a standard dialect to unify the country and a simplified script to enhance literacy has not been experienced in the same way by Han Chinese learners at different time periods, with different first dialects and from different locations. To illustrate such differences, I shall now present survey results from 318 Han Chinese learners (Lam, 2002). Respondents were approached through the universities (and secondary schools affiliated to or contacted by the universities) in major cities throughout China. The data set of 318 learners used in this analysis of the experience of learning Chinese was derived from the master data pool of 415 Han Chinese learners (see Chapter 1, 'The Language Education in China Project', pp. 10–17) by excluding those from the Chinese language profession to prevent skewing of data. All of them had completed university education. They were grouped into five age groups according to their age in 2000: 46 to 50, 41 to 45, 36 to 40, 29 to 35 and 24 to 28. The age intervals were roughly five years apart, except for an adjustment made for the early and later periods of the Cultural Revolution (1966–1976). Respondents were asked questions on: when they began learning Putonghua, whether they were taught in Putonghua, the independent learning activities they engaged in and their use of Putonghua upon leaving secondary school. The responses were analysed for age, dialect (northern versus southern) and location (coastal versus interior) effects. The Loglinear Analysis involving the Chi-square statistic ($\alpha = 0.05$), a robust test suitable for categorical data and unequal cell sizes, was used for analysing most of the data. The Analysis of Variance was also used for analysing some data ($\alpha = 0.05$). Small differences in sample sizes for various aspects were due to missing data. In the following sections, the most salient effects of age, dialectal background and location are presented.

## Effects of age

The age of the respondents did not seem to make a difference on when they started learning Putonghua but did affect when they started learning how to write Chinese ($\chi^2 = 32.35$, df = 12, p = 0.0012) (Table 2.4). For learners in the younger cohorts (aged 29 to 35 and 24 to 28), more of them began learning how to write Chinese at home. This was especially so for the youngest group, 65.1% of whom had started learning how to write Chinese before primary school. This probably reflects the higher literacy rates among their parents as a result of educational expansion in China under the present regime.

Younger learners also seemed to have more access to technical support in learning Putonghua outside the classroom, perhaps because such resources became more affordable from the mid-1980s. They practised more with tapes and materials outside the classroom ($\chi^2 = 22.21$, df = 12, p = 0.0352), watched more television ($\chi^2 = 24.88$, df = 12, p = 0.0154), saw more movies or watched more video tapes ($\chi^2 = 24.26$, df = 12, p = 0.0188) and listened to or sang songs more often ($\chi^2 = 23.04$, df = 12, p = 0.0274) (Table 2.5).

Apart from taking advantage of technical support more, younger respondents also wrote more letters in Chinese ($\chi^2 = 35.44$, df = 12, p = 0.0004). Among the oldest group, only 63.1% wrote letters as an activity to learn Chinese better but in the youngest group, 90.7% did so, perhaps because more could afford to pay for the postage necessary to send letters. It is also important to remember that even the youngest group in the present study was between twenty-four to twenty-eight years old. Teenagers nowadays, particularly those in urban areas, if surveyed, may report a lesser use of letters since more may be using the telephone or e-mail. Those in rural areas, however, may still be

**Table 2.4 Time at which respondents started learning how to write Chinese**

| Age group | Number of respondents (Percentage) | | | | |
|---|---|---|---|---|---|
| | *From birth* | *From kindergarten* | *From primary school* | *From secondary school or later* | *Total* |
| 46 to 50 | 1 (2.6%) | 17 (44.7%) | 19 (50.0%) | 1 (2.6%) | 38 (100.0%) |
| 41 to 45 | 6 (11.3%) | 13 (24.5%) | 33 (62.3%) | 1 (1.9%) | 53 (100.0%) |
| 36 to 40 | 9 (16.1%) | 10 (17.9%) | 37 (66.1%) | 0 (0.0%) | 56 (100.0%) |
| 29 to 35 | 17 (20.7%) | 18 (22.0%) | 46 (56.1%) | 1 (1.2%) | 82 (100.0%) |
| 24 to 28 | 24 (27.9%) | 32 (37.2%) | 29 (33.7%) | 1 (1.2%) | 86 (100.0%) |
| Total | 57 (18.1%) | 90 (28.6%) | 164 (52.1%) | 4 (1.3%) | 315 (100.0%) |

**Table 2.5 Respondents using technical support outside class to learn Chinese**

| Age group | Number of respondents (Percentage) | | | | |
|---|---|---|---|---|---|
| | *Using tapes and materials* | *Watching television* | *Seeing movies or watching video tapes* | *Listening to or singing songs* | *Total in that age group* |
| 46 to 50 | 11 (29.0%) | 25 (65.8%) | 21 (55.3%) | 20 (52.6%) | 38 (100.0%) |
| 41 to 45 | 17 (31.5%) | 33 (61.1%) | 29 (53.7%) | 29 (53.7%) | 54 (100.0%) |
| 36 to 40 | 15 (26.3%) | 43 (75.5%) | 35 (61.5%) | 36 (63.1%) | 57 (100.0%) |
| 29 to 35 | 35 (50.0%) | 68 (81.9%) | 58 (69.9%) | 56 (67.4%) | 83 (100.0%) |
| 24 to 28 | 43 (50.0%) | 73 (84.9%) | 57 (66.3%) | 59 (68.6%) | 86 (100.0%) |

using letters more often as a mode of communication. No significant change over time was found for the use of other learning activities outside the classroom such as conversing with others in Putonghua, listening to the radio, checking the dictionary and reading newspapers, magazines or books.

Over the last half century, the use of *hanyu pinyin* (a romanized script to aid the pronunciation of Putonghua) has gained increasing acceptance. Younger learners were likely to think it easier to learn ($\chi^2 = 18.57$, df = 8, p = 0.0173); just over 70% in the two younger groups of respondents thought so (Table 2.6). The only exception to this trend was the group aged 36 to 40, who was most affected by irregular schooling during the Cultural Revolution.

The learning of simplified characters was rated easy by all age cohorts, both in learning to read them (96.4%) and to write them (93.7%). With the general acceptance of the simplified script, the perception and use of complex characters also changed ($\chi^2 = 24.27$, df = 12, p = 0.0187) (Table 2.7). About half (49.2%) of all age cohorts found the writing of complex characters difficult, indicating again that simplified characters were accepted from the early days of the campaign. In addition, while there was some fluctuation in

**Table 2.6  How respondents rated the difficulty in learning *hanyu pinyin***

| Age group | Number of respondents (Percentage) | | | | |
|---|---|---|---|---|---|
| | *Easy* | *Neutral* | *Difficult* | *Did not use hanyu pinyin* | *Total* |
| 46 to 50 | 20 (62.5%) | 10 (31.3%) | 2 (6.3%) | 0 (0.0%) | 32 (100.0%) |
| 41 to 45 | 34 (66.7%) | 14 (27.5%) | 3 (5.9%) | 0 (0.0%) | 51 (100.0%) |
| 36 to 40 | 22 (42.3%) | 22 (42.3%) | 4 (7.7%) | 4 (7.7%) | 52 (100.0%) |
| 29 to 35 | 60 (73.2%) | 13 (15.9%) | 9 (11.0%) | 0 (0.0%) | 82 (100.0%) |
| 24 to 28 | 59 (70.2%) | 19 (22.6%) | 5 (6.0%) | 1 (1.2%) | 84 (100.0%) |
| Total | 195 (64.8%) | 78 (25.9%) | 23 (7.6%) | 5 (1.7%) | 301 (100.0%) |

Note: 'Difficult' and 'Did not use' were pooled together in the Loglinear Analysis because the number of respondents for some cells was too small.

**Table 2.7  How respondents rated the difficulty in writing complex characters**

| Age group | Number of respondents (Percentage) | | | | |
|---|---|---|---|---|---|
| | *Easy* | *Neutral* | *Difficult* | *Did not write complex characters* | *Total* |
| 46 to 50 | 4 (11.4%) | 9 (25.7%) | 15 (42.9%) | 7 (20.0%) | 35 (100.0%) |
| 41 to 45 | 5 (9.8%) | 16 (31.4%) | 25 (49.0%) | 5 (9.8%) | 51 (100.0%) |
| 36 to 40 | 2 (3.7%) | 12 (22.2%) | 28 (51.9%) | 12 (22.2%) | 54 (100.0%) |
| 29 to 35 | 7 (8.6%) | 23 (28.4%) | 42 (51.9%) | 9 (11.1%) | 81 (100.0%) |
| 24 to 28 | 4 (4.8%) | 11 (13.1%) | 40 (47.6%) | 29 (34.5%) | 84 (100.0%) |
| Total | 22 (7.2%) | 71 (23.3%) | 150 (49.2%) | 62 (20.3%) | 305 (100.0%) |

the non-use of such characters by earlier cohorts of learners, perhaps because of the lesser attention paid to the promotional campaign in the 1970s, among the youngest cohort, 34.5% did not use any complex characters at all in their writing and only 4.8% of them found writing complex characters easy.

The age effects as a whole point to the gradual acceptance of Putonghua and *hanyu pinyin* over the past decades and the better learning conditions experienced by younger learners. The simplified script was also basically accepted by the population from the early days of its propagation.

## Effects of the first dialect

While age did not affect the time respondents were introduced to Putonghua, their native dialect background did ($\chi^2 = 14.99$, df = 4, p = 0.0047) (Table 2.8). Respondents with a southern dialect as their first dialect began learning

**Table 2.8 How first dialect affected the time respondents began learning Putonghua**

| First dialect | Number of respondents (Percentage) | | | | | |
|---|---|---|---|---|---|---|
| | At home from birth | From kinder-garten | From primary school | From secondary school | At university or at work | Total |
| Northern dialect | 77 (36.3%) | 33 (15.6%) | 59 (27.8%) | 8 (3.8%) | 35 (16.5%) | 212 (100.0%) |
| Southern dialect | 14 (13.6%) | 21 (20.4%) | 51 (49.5%) | 3 (2.9%) | 14 (13.6%) | 103 (100.0%) |
| Total | 91 (28.9%) | 54 (17.1%) | 110 (34.9%) | 11 (3.5%) | 49 (15.6%) | 315 (100.0%) |

Putonghua later. There was also an interactive effect between first dialect and location ($\chi^2 = 11.89$, df = 4, p = 0.0182). Southern dialect speakers in the interior region began learning Putonghua latest; 47.4% of them learnt it from primary school, 5.3% from secondary school and 31.6% only when they entered university or started working.

In secondary school, northern dialect respondents also had significantly more class time devoted to learning Putonghua (F = 3.945, $df_1$ = 1, $df_2$ = 301, p = 0.048). They had on the average 7.805 lessons per week (sd = 3.207) in secondary school while southern dialect speakers had 7.085 lessons (sd = 2.410). This difference is interesting because the general impression was that curricula in China tended to be rather uniform over different parts of the country. The results indicate that there was some variation after all. (See also the section 'Teaching Chinese in China Today' in this chapter, pp. 59–70.) There was no significant difference in primary school on class time devoted to learning Chinese but a related issue was whether teachers of Chinese used Putonghua as a medium of instruction. On this point, there was an interactive effect between dialect and location with the southern interior dialect regions having the least use of Putonghua in Chinese lessons in primary schools ($\chi^2$ = 9.64, df = 2, p = 0.0081); up to 31.6% of the teachers of respondents from that area did not use Putonghua to teach Chinese (Table 2.9).

The differences in the classroom arising from dialect backgrounds extended to the use of Putonghua to converse with classmates in primary school ($\chi^2$ = 31.46, df = 2, p < 0.0001) and secondary school ($\chi^2$ = 23.78, df = 2, p < 0.0001) but not at university ($\chi^2$ = 3.74, df = 2, p = 0.1541) (Table 2.10). In the schools, more northern dialect speakers used Putonghua more often. At the university level, Putonghua was used frequently by most respondents (around 85%) from both dialect backgrounds.

At home, while learning Putonghua, northern dialect speakers also enjoyed more conversational support ($\chi^2$ = 35.74, df = 3, p < 0.0001) (Table 2.11). In most cases, it was not because there was no one at home who could speak

**Table 2.9  The use of Putonghua by Chinese teachers in primary school**

| First dialect | Location | Number of respondents (Percentage) | | | |
|---|---|---|---|---|---|
| | | Putonghua used by all teachers to teach Chinese | Putonghua used by some teachers to teach Chinese | Putonghua not used to teach Chinese | Total |
| Northern dialect | Coastal | 55 (62.5%) | 22 (25.0%) | 11 (12.5%) | 88 (100.0%) |
| | Interior | 56 (45.5%) | 42 (34.1%) | 25 (20.3%) | 123 (100.0%) |
| Southern dialect | Coastal | 43 (66.2%) | 21 (32.3%) | 1 (1.5%) | 65 (100.0%) |
| | Interior | 13 (34.2%) | 13 (34.2%) | 12 (31.6%) | 38 (100.0%) |
| Total | | 167 (53.2%) | 98 (31.2%) | 49 (15.6%) | 314 (100.0%) |

**Table 2.10 The use of Putonghua when conversing with classmates outside class**

| Level of education | First dialect | Number of respondents (Percentage) | | | |
|---|---|---|---|---|---|
| | | Putonghua usually used | Putonghua used sometimes | Putonghua not used | Total |
| Primary | Northern | 99 (46.7%) | 37 (17.5%) | 76 (35.8%) | 212 (100.0%) |
| | Southern | 22 (21.2%) | 42 (40.4%) | 40 (38.5%) | 104 (100.0%) |
| Secondary | Northern | 102 (48.1%) | 55 (25.9%) | 55 (25.9%) | 212 (100.0%) |
| | Southern | 24 (23.1%) | 50 (48.1%) | 30 (28.8%) | 104 (100.0%) |
| University | Northern | 181 (85.8%) | 26 (12.3%) | 4 (1.9%) | 211 (100.0%) |
| | Southern | 86 (84.8%) | 18 (17.3%) | 0 (0.0%) | 104 (100.0%) |

**Table 2.11  The use of Putonghua at home when learning Putonghua**

| First dialect | Number of respondents (Percentage) | | | | |
|---|---|---|---|---|---|
| | Putonghua used by everyone at home | At least one other family member spoke Putonghua | Family preferred to speak a dialect at home | No one else knew Putonghua at home | Total |
| Northern | 69 (33.2%) | 49 (23.6%) | 65 (31.3%) | 25 (12.0%) | 208 (100.0%) |
| Southern | 8 (7.8%) | 27 (26.2%) | 58 (56.3%) | 10 (9.7%) | 103 (100.0%) |
| Total | 77 (24.8%) | 76 (24.4%) | 123 (39.5%) | 35 (11.3%) | 311 (100.0%) |

Putonghua but because the families with a southern dialect background preferred to speak in that dialect (56.3%).

Not surprisingly, therefore, the patterns of current use of Putonghua also show that northern dialect speakers use Putonghua more often at home ($\chi^2 = 15.02$, df = 2, p = 0.0005), with friends ($\chi^2 = 7.1$, df = 2, p = 0.0287) and when

**Table 2.12 The current use of Putonghua by respondents**

| Domain of use | First dialect | Number of respondents (Percentage) | | | |
|---|---|---|---|---|---|
| | | Putonghua used very often | Putonghua used sometimes | Putonghua not used | Total |
| At home | Northern | 148 (71.8%) | 27 (13.1%) | 31 (15.0%) | 206 (100.0%) |
| | Southern | 54 (52.9%) | 32 (31.4%) | 16 (15.7%) | 102 (100.0%) |
| Shopping/ in restaurants | Northern | 171 (83.8%) | 28 (13.7%) | 5 (2.5%) | 204 (100.0%) |
| | Southern | 60 (57.7%) | 39 (37.5%) | 5 (4.8%) | 104 (100.0%) |
| With friends | Northern | 171 (83.8%) | 30 (14.7%) | 3 (1.5%) | 204 (100.0%) |
| | Southern | 76 (73.1%) | 26 (25.0%) | 2 (1.9%) | 104 (100.0%) |
| At government offices | Northern | 185 (90.2%) | 17 (8.3%) | 3 (1.5%) | 205 (100.0%) |
| | Southern | 88 (84.6%) | 16 (15.4%) | 0 (0.0%) | 104 (100.0%) |
| At work | Northern | 199 (95.7%) | 9 (4.3%) | 0 (0.0%) | 208 (100.0%) |
| | Southern | 92 (88.5%) | 12 (11.5%) | 0 (0.0%) | 104 (100.0%) |

shopping or in the restaurants ($\chi^2 = 24.53$, df = 2, p < 0.0001); there is, however, no significant difference at work ($\chi^2 = 5.61$, df = 2, p = 0.0605) or at government offices ($\chi^2 = 3.95$, df = 2, p = 0.1388) (Table 2.12). In terms of how widely Putonghua is used, the domains rank from the least use to the greatest use as follows: at home, in shops or restaurants, with friends, at government offices and at work. Putonghua is used very often in official, formal or work-related communication by both northern and southern dialect speakers at least 85% of the time, but dialects still have a role to play in informal interaction at home, particularly for southern dialect speakers; only 52.9% of those respondents reported using Putonghua at home very often. In the south, dialects are also still used to some extent in shops and restaurants; only 57.7% of the southern dialect speakers reported using Putonghua very often in such settings.

To summarize on dialect effects, northern dialect speakers have enjoyed more favourable conditions for learning Putonghua than southern dialect speakers. These conditions still prevail in informal situations though Putonghua is now generally used at the university level and at work, whatever the dialect background.

## Effects of birthplace location

Apart from dialect effects, there were also effects arising from the birthplace location (coastal versus interior) of the respondents. In general, respondents who grew up in coastal areas enjoyed better learning conditions than those born in the interior.

**Table 2.13 How location affected the time respondents began learning Putonghua**

| Location | Number of respondents (Percentage) | | | | | |
|---|---|---|---|---|---|---|
| | At home from birth | From kinder-garten | From primary school | From secondary school | At university or at work | Total |
| Coastal | 57 (37.3%) | 28 (18.3%) | 52 (34.0%) | 3 (2.0%) | 13 (8.5%) | 153 (100.0%) |
| Interior | 34 (21.0%) | 26 (16.0%) | 58 (35.8%) | 8 (4.9%) | 36 (22.2%) | 162 (100.0%) |
| Total | 91 (28.9%) | 54 (17.1%) | 110 (34.9%) | 11 (3.5%) | 49 (15.6%) | 315 (100.0%) |

More of the respondents from coastal regions started learning Putonghua at home from birth (37.3%) while a good number of those growing up in the interior only learnt Putonghua after secondary school (22.2%) ($\chi^2 = 16.82$, df = 4, p = 0.0021) (Table 2.13).

Another interesting location effect was in the degree to which teachers at different educational levels used Putonghua even when teaching other subjects (Table 2.14). At every level, more teachers of respondents born in the coastal regions used Putonghua when teaching other subjects such as mathematics, science and so on. The differences were statistically significant at the primary ($\chi^2 = 26.77$, df = 2, p < 0.0001), secondary ($\chi^2 = 32.48$, df = 2, p < 0.0001) and university ($\chi^2 = 14.05$, df = 2, p = 0.0009) levels.

**Table 2.14 The use of Putonghua by teachers of other subjects (e.g., mathematics)**

| Level of education | Location | Number of respondents (Percentage) | | | |
|---|---|---|---|---|---|
| | | Putonghua used by all teachers | Putonghua used by some teachers | Putonghua not used | Total |
| Primary | Coastal | 82 (53.6%) | 52 (34.0%) | 19 (12.4%) | 153 (100.0%) |
| | Interior | 46 (28.6%) | 57 (35.4%) | 58 (36.0%) | 161 (100.0%) |
| Secondary | Coastal | 79 (51.6%) | 62 (40.5%) | 12 (7.8%) | 153 (100.0%) |
| | Interior | 38 (23.6%) | 83 (51.6%) | 40 (24.8%) | 161 (100.0%) |
| University | Coastal | 106 (69.7%) | 45 (29.6%) | 1 (0.7%) | 152 (100.0%) |
| | Interior | 77 (49.4%) | 73 (46.8%) | 6 (3.8%) | 156 (100.0%) |

Other location effects were also obtained in terms of how frequently respondents used Putonghua with their classmates or the degree to which they engaged in learning activities outside the classroom. As a whole, learners in coastal regions have enjoyed more favourable conditions.

## *Summary*

To summarize, the survey found effects relating to all three variables: age, first dialect and birthplace location.

**Changes over time**: Results according to the age variable indicate that the simplified script was accepted from the early years of the promotion campaign, and Putonghua and *hanyu pinyin* have gradually been accepted. Whether a change of language attitude led to greater use of Putonghua or vice versa is a complex issue (Zhou, 2001, p. 245) but the finding that younger people are more willing to speak Putonghua is quite certain. It has even been observed that by the late 1990s, it was 'almost impossible to elicit responses in the local variety' in Shanghai and Guangzhou if a conversation was initiated in Putonghua (Zhou, 2001, p. 246). The findings also indicate that younger learners enjoy better learning conditions such as technical resources.

**First dialect**: More northern dialect speakers began learning Putonghua from birth while most southern dialect speakers did so within the formal education system. Northern dialect speakers used Putonghua more often when interacting with classmates outside class in primary and secondary school and had more interaction in Putonghua at home. At university and at work, whether in the south or the north, Putonghua has been widely used.

**Coastal versus interior**: Learners in coastal regions have also enjoyed better learning circumstances. Teachers in coastal regions use Putonghua more at all levels of education, perhaps because the more affluent coastal regions have attracted populations which are more mixed in terms of dialectal background; hence, the use of Putonghua is more necessary to facilitate interdialectal communication. The region with the least favourable conditions for learning Putonghua appears to be the southern interior.

# Four Case Histories

To consider how far the general picture of learning Chinese based on the survey data was true of individual experience, case interviews of thirty-five Han Chinese learners were conducted (see Chapter 1, 'The Language Education in China Project', pp. 10–17). Interviewees were selected according to the three variables investigated in the survey: age, first dialect and birthplace location (coastal versus interior). This section presents excerpts from four learning histories: two from each dialect group/location, one older and one younger (adapted from Lam, 2002). The learners were interviewed in Putonghua. Each interview took about an hour. In the excerpts to follow, the interviewee's age was that in 2000. All names are pseudonyms. The interviewer's comments are put in square brackets.

The main issue in reviewing these learning biographies is whether individual experiences were consistent with the policy trends and survey findings: that younger learners, northern dialect speakers and those growing up in coastal regions experienced more favourable conditions for learning Putonghua. If not, what circumstances would result in a learner's deviation from the prevailing trends? Secondly, although the focus of this chapter is the propagation of standard Chinese, it is useful to consider the learning of Putonghua in the light of the total multilingual experience of learners (see Chapter 1, 'A Multilingual Approach to Language Education', pp. 17–18). To this end, some information about the interviewees' experience of other languages is also included in the excerpts to follow. We could consider, for example, how their learning of Putonghua was affected by their learning of other dialects or language, how important learning Putonghua was relative to their learning of other languages, whether the learning of other dialects or languages took away learning time and energy from their learning of Putonghua or whether Putonghua learning had been so dominant or circumstantially natural that it led to lesser motivation in learning other dialects or languages.

The four learners to be considered are:

1. Yan: Northern Chinese from the interior region, male, aged 44, political scientist
2. Xin: Northern Chinese from the coastal region, female, aged 27, English teacher
3. Tian: Southern Chinese from the interior region, male, aged 38, Chinese teacher
4. Danny: Southern Chinese from the coastal region, male, aged 28, hotel employee

## Yan (Northern Interior Chinese Interviewee 12, male, aged 44, a political scientist)

**Background**: I was born in 1956 near Changan [now Xian]. I started going to school in 1962. In those days, because of the Cultural Revolution, school was irregular. In 1970, I went to a senior secondary school away from home. I was the only one from my class that entered a senior secondary school. In 1973, I returned to my village as a *zhi¹ qing¹* [intellectual youth]. I worked as a farmer. From 1975 to 1977, I studied at a Teachers' College in Xian. After that, I taught politics for half a year in a secondary school. In 1978, the universities resumed admission and I came to this university [in the northern interior]. Upon graduation in 1982, I started teaching political science here.

**The Xian dialect**: I spoke the Xian dialect from birth because it was spoken around me. I was educated in the Xian dialect even during my junior secondary schooldays. Even in senior secondary school, not every teacher taught us in Putonghua. My Chinese teacher even pronounced my name wrongly in Putonghua. He was a good teacher though.

**Putonghua at Teachers' College**: It was only during my Teachers' College days that I had a teacher who emphasized the standardization of the Chinese language. He was a member of the Commission on Language Planning of China. He prepared materials on the differences between Putonghua and the Xian dialect and requested that we should use Putonghua in class and when conversing. There was also another teacher who left a deep impression on me. She was from the south of Shaanxi. There were some characters she could not pronounce in the standard way. She was always asking the other teacher how to pronounce some characters correctly. These two teachers made a big impact on me. I became willing to speak and to learn Putonghua.

**Other Chinese dialects**: Time and again, I visited other cities like Liaoning, Beijing, Wuhan and Chengdu to attend short courses or conferences. I can understand several Chinese dialects because of my contact with speakers of different dialects, especially during my visits to other cities. During my visits, it was natural to speak Putonghua. In Liaoning, for example, for half a year as Visiting Scholar, I only spoke Putonghua.

**Russian**: In senior secondary school, the foreign language I studied was Russian. I still remember sayings like 'Wish Chairman Mao ten thousand birthdays'. I have forgotten everything else.

**The handicap of poor English**: I started learning English at university. I did so for two years. Even after graduation, I still tried to learn it on and off but I did not succeed. This is my regret because my failure to learn English well is a big handicap to my research and my career. If we wish to get promoted, we must pass a foreign language examination.

## Xin (Northern Coastal Chinese Interviewee 26, female, aged 27, an English teacher)

**Background**: I was born in 1973 in a village in Shandong [in the northern coastal region]. I went to the primary school in my village. For secondary school, I attended a more proper county school but teachers there still taught in our *jia¹ xiang¹ hua⁴* [home village speech]. In 1992, I came to this university [in the northern interior]. Now I teach English here.

**The Shandong dialect**: I learnt the Shandong dialect definitely from imitating my family while young. My teachers and classmates also spoke this dialect, even in secondary school. When reading passages aloud in class, we used Putonghua. When we conversed, we used our *jia¹ xiang¹ hua⁴*. Even our Chinese teacher used our *jia¹ xiang¹ hua⁴* to teach us.

**Putonghua at university**: When I left home to go to university, to communicate with my classmates, because they could not understand the Shandong dialect (though it was very similar to the standard dialect), I imitated other people and spoke Putonghua. So I actually learnt how to speak Putonghua only from 1992. Before that, I was exposed to Putonghua through the radio and television. When I first started speaking Putonghua at university, I had to overcome many difficulties, such as in tone and vocabulary. The main difficulty was tone.

**Dialect switching**: I spoke Putonghua at university but when I went home to Shandong, I spoke my *jia¹ xiang¹ hua⁴*. The first summer I went home, I found my behaviour very funny. Everyone was speaking my *jia¹ xiang¹ hua⁴*. I knew I should too but when I forgot how to say something in my *jia¹ xiang¹ hua⁴*, I used Putonghua. They were very surprised and I did not even realize it. Later, I was aware of that. After one or two years, I began to switch between my home dialect and Putonghua easily. Now I can speak my *jia¹ xiang¹ hua⁴* the moment I get off the train; the moment I get on the train, I can switch to Putonghua.

**Inferiority**: Because I grew up in a village, when I came to university in this big city, I felt inferior. I did not dare to speak with other people in my dialect. Some classmates came from Beijing and other big cities. They could speak Putonghua very fluently and communicate their thoughts very well. So I wanted to imitate their Putonghua pronunciation or some of their sentences that were more fun.

**Interest in learning English**: I studied English from junior secondary school. My first English teacher spoke standard English fluently. Because of her, I became interested in learning English. In junior secondary school, we began with the alphabet and learnt a lot of grammar and vocabulary. Only in my last year in senior secondary school did I begin to converse in English because there was an oral English test I had to pass.

**Dormitory life**: Once I entered university, there were many more lessons in oral English and more practice even outside the classroom. Seven of us shared one room in our dormitory. We were from different provinces and spoke different dialects. Since we were all English majors, we decided to speak English the moment we entered the dormitory. I also listened to tapes and saw foreign movies. Sometimes, I listened to the news programmes on CCTV [a national channel]. We also tried to talk with our *wai⁴ jiao¹* [foreign teachers] more so that our spoken English could be more standard.

**German**: It was compulsory to learn a second foreign language. When I first started learning German, my interest was greater. But in the graduate courses, the emphasis was on grammar and I paid less attention.

# Tian (Southern Interior Chinese Interviewee 24, male, aged 38, a Chinese teacher)

**Background**: I was born in 1962 in Jiangxi [in the southern interior]. My first dialect is Kejiahua [the Hakka dialect]. I spoke Kejiahua till I was eighteen when I came to this university [in the northern interior] in 1980. I graduated in 1984. Since then, I have been teaching Chinese here.

**No market for Putonghua**: At school, we were taught in Kejiahua. What the teachers spoke was closer to written Chinese but it was not Putonghua. In pronunciation, it still seemed like a dialect. After classes, my classmates and I conversed in Kejiahua. In junior secondary school, we had a very young music teacher from the local region. Her husband was from another region. So she spent some time with him elsewhere. She could speak very standard Putonghua. In her first lesson, she tried to teach in Putonghua; the whole class laughed because we were not used to being spoken to in such standard Putonghua. When the class was over, the students imitated her way of speaking and said she was singing. After that, she did not dare to teach again in Putonghua. Later in secondary school, there were two teachers who came from other provinces and spoke fairly standard Putonghua. Since they were from elsewhere, they did not mind speaking to us in Putonghua. In our region at that time, there was no market for Putonghua. Unless you were from another province, if you spoke Putonghua, people would think you were trying to $da^3$ $guan^1$ $qiang^1$ [speak like an official] and would laugh at you or talk about you. Kejia people have a saying 'Rather sell the land of the ancestors than change the speech from the ancestors.'

**Putonghua at university**: I was exposed to interaction in Putonghua only when I came to this university. Because this is a big city with many people from other provinces, Putonghua is commonly spoken, especially on campus. Throughout my four university years, I spoke only Putonghua, except when I was with friends from my home village. My Putonghua became more and more standard year by year. Now I am equally fluent in Kejiahua and Putonghua though some people say my Putonghua has a southern accent. I do not know. When I was in the south, my Putonghua pronunciation was considered standard. But to northerners, my Putonghua is non-standard and has a southern accent. My vocabulary may also have elements from my dialect.

**English for university admission**: For people my age, the learning of English only began at a very old age. We started learning it only when our senior secondary education was about to end. At that time, university admission had just resumed. It was for the purpose of gaining entry into university that we all learnt English. We had very little time to prepare for it. So we all gave up. Because my English was so poor, I was assigned to learn Japanese.

**Japanese**: I studied Japanese for four years but did not learn it well. I have lost most of it.

**English for work**: After graduation, because of occupational needs, I started learning English. My university organized a course for young teachers. But I did not keep up with the course. In 1998, the university sent me to another university for half a year to study English. It was at that time that I learnt English more systematically. The course was to prepare people to take an examination so that they could be sent overseas by the State for visits or attachments.

**The painful way**: I also tried learning English on my own using tapes and books such as *New Concept English*. It was a very stupid and painful way to learn. Recently, I learnt a lot from browsing web sites in English. I can now manage simple everyday conversations and read articles in my discipline. But my writing and listening are not too good.

### Danny (Southern Coastal Chinese Interviewee 18, male, aged 28, a hotel employee)

**Background**: I was born in Gulangyu [an island off Xiamen in the southern coastal region] in 1972 and went to school and university in [a southern coastal city]. I studied management as an undergraduate. In 1993, I began working at the reception counter of a hotel. In October 1998, I came to this university [the same southern coastal city] to study English.

**Minnanhua, Putonghua and respecting others**: I speak Minnanhua [a Fujian dialect] and Putonghua equally well. I learnt Minnanhua from my grandmother who took care of me. Putonghua was not used at home. When I was four, I went to kindergarten and was taught in Putonghua. Outside the classroom, my classmates and I still conversed in Minnanhua but we spoke Putonghua with the teachers. In [the same southern coastal city], we have a lot of visitors from other provinces. In a group of three or four people, if one does not speak Minnanhua, we immediately switch to Putonghua. This is a kind of respect for that person.

**Cantonese**: I also learnt Guangdonghua [Cantonese] from television dramas and video tapes from Hong Kong. In the hotel where I worked, we had some visitors from Hong Kong and Macau. Some overseas customers also spoke Cantonese. Around 1994 and 1995, I met a Cantonese friend from Hong Kong who could not understand any Putonghua. Since I was interested in languages, I bought two or three Cantonese tapes and spent two or three weeks listening to the tapes 'with all my life' [with total dedication]. I wanted to communicate with him. Besides, in my industry, knowing one more language is very advantageous. In 1997, when I went to a world tourism exhibition in Hong Kong, I could shop in Cantonese.

**English**: I started learning English from Primary 5. I could handle writing and the examinations but my listening and speaking were very poor. A friend with a relative overseas bought some tapes and hotel management books for me. There was a book on conversations at a five-star hotel. But it was difficult for me to learn by myself. Anyway, the hotel I was working in was only a three-star hotel so the requirements were not very high. In 1996, I tried applying for a job in the Marco Polo Hotel. At the interview, they asked me to speak English with them. I could understand but could not speak fluently. In 1998, I worked at a private club for half a year. There were some foreigners going to that club. I thought if my English was better, I could do better. So I quit my job and came here [a university in the same southern coastal city] to really learn English, not for a qualification.

## Discussion

These four case summaries serve to illustrate the effects of several variables on the experience of policy by learners: age, dialect and location. Their learning of Putonghua can also be considered in the context of their total linguistic experience.

**Change in attitude**: The two younger learners, Xin and Danny, were evidently more open to learning Putonghua than the two older learners, Yan and Tian, during their younger days. Yan was at first not particularly interested in learning Putonghua, perhaps because not all his teachers taught in Putonghua when he was at school. Only when he saw his teachers at Teachers' College so keen to pronounce the characters correctly did he become willing to speak and learn Putonghua. Likewise, when Tian was at school, his classmates used to laugh at a teacher who tried to speak accurate Putonghua with them. He pointed out that in those days, relinquishing one's dialect was considered more negatively than selling the ancestral land. In contrast, though Xin was taught very much in the Shandong dialect and only learnt to speak Putonghua at university, she was very keen to do so and in fact felt inferior that she did not have an urban accent. Unlike the other three who were not taught consistently in Putonghua until after secondary school, Danny was taught in Putonghua from kindergarten and felt that as long as there was one person in a group who could not understand his dialect, then a group of people should speak Putonghua as a kind of respect for that person. What is interesting about the difference between Xin and Danny is that while Danny experienced better conditions for learning and Xin did not, they were both positive about learning and using Putonghua. This argues strongly for the acceptance of Putonghua among younger learners in China.

**First dialect**: As northern dialect speakers, Yan and Xin should have expected an easier time in learning Putonghua. But Yan's schooling years overlapped with the Cultural Revolution during which the promotion of Putonghua was not pursued with as much enthusiasm. Xin also reported great difficulty in acquiring the correct tones and vocabulary in Putonghua at university though she was exposed to Putonghua through the radio and television earlier. This could be because she started speaking Putonghua only as an adult. Tian, whose first dialect was a southern dialect, reported that though his pronunciation was considered rather standard in the south it was still considered non-standard by northeners. At least, he thought they would think so. In contrast, Danny, also a southern dialect speaker, did not report any difficulty with learning Putonghua, perhaps because he started learning it from kindergarten. Danny's story shows that as long as learners start learning Putonghua early and have the opportunity to use it, even if it is not used at home, they can learn it well.

**Location**: The survey results indicate that learners in coastal regions experienced better learning conditions. That is probably true in general but Xin's case shows that this cannot always be assumed. Xin came from a coastal province but spent most of her early years in a village. She felt inferior because she could not speak Putonghua as fluently as her university classmates from the big cities. This underscores the fact that the use of Putonghua has been more widespread in urban areas than in rural areas and that such a circumstance empowers urban dwellers and places rural dwellers at a disadvantage. In terms of academic and economic opportunities, the divide between urban and rural regions is probably greater than that between coastal and interior regions.

**Dialects versus Putonghua**: Despite the success in propagating Putonghua in education, especially at university, and in urban life, native dialects still seem to have a social role to play, particularly in the learners' home towns and villages. All four learners retained competence in their own dialects and switched comfortably between their dialects and Putonghua as appropriate. Yan and Danny also reported learning other dialects in relation to their work. Bidialectal or multidialectal competence in China is perceived positively; the acquisition of such competence does not seem to affect adversely learners' attitude to their own dialects, to themselves or to Putonghua. In other words, bidialectalism or multidialectalism in China is additive (Cummins, 1984, pp. 57–58; Lam, 2001, p. 95). This should not be surprising if one remembers that flexible choice of varieties within a wide repertoire to meet communicative needs is the hallmark of a competent speaker.

**English versus Putonghua**: All four learners reported the need to have competence in English to add to their professional competitiveness. Yan needed to pass a foreign language examination to get promoted. Xin was an English teacher. If Tian's English was good, he could be sent abroad for attachments. Danny needed English for his hotel work. English or the failure to learn English as successfully as they wished apparently occupied their learning selves at one time or another. Xin's pact with her dormitory mates to use English with each other was also premised on the fact that they were all from different provinces and spoke different dialects. Like Putonghua, English can be used as an interdialectal language; outside China, in Singapore, for example, it is not uncommon to see Chinese from different dialect groups conversing with each other in English; on the China mainland though, Putonghua is a more ready option. As younger learners acquire more competence in English and Putonghua becomes the first dialect of a certain sector of the population, code-switching between English and Putonghua in interdialectal discourse might happen even on the China mainland. Meanwhile, it is not inaccurate to note that, relatively speaking, English seems to feature a little more prominently in learners' stories than their learning of Chinese, perhaps because competence in Chinese is often taken for granted. So much attention given to English is considered detrimental to learners' improvement in Chinese by some teachers of Chinese, as will be discussed in the next section.

## Teaching Chinese in China Today

The survey results and the learning biographies have provided a general understanding of how Chinese has been learnt. To find out how Chinese is now taught in China, discussions with heads of Chinese programmes at each educational level were held in four cities (not to be named to protect the privacy of the informants) from different regions:
1. Northern coastal region
2. Southern coastal region
3. Northern interior region
4. Southern interior region

The findings are now presented according to the three levels of education: primary, secondary and higher. It must be emphasized that the programmes described below are only examples, probably of the best scenarios, and so should not be taken as typical of circumstances all over China, particularly not of rural areas which tend to enjoy less advantageous conditions.

### Chinese in primary education

All the four primary schools visited offer two semesters in a year with twenty to twenty-two weeks in each semester, often inclusive of assessment. Lessons are forty minutes long. About one-third of the class time in primary school is devoted to learning Chinese. On the basis of eighteen teaching weeks per semester, the total number of class hours spent on studying Chinese in primary school ranges from 1,685 to 1,944 lessons or 1,123 to 1,296 hours. Table 2.15 provides an overview of the circumstances.

**Table 2.15 Teaching of Chinese in four primary schools**

| Location of school | Coastal region | | Interior region | |
|---|---|---|---|---|
| | Northern city | Southern city | Northern city | Southern city |
| No. of Chinese teachers | 35 | About 29* | 18 | 8 |
| Adequacy of Chinese teachers[+] | Slight shortage but manageable | No shortage | Slight shortage but manageable | Too many teachers |
| Equipment | Fully equipped[#] | Fully equipped | No compact disk player, video projector, computers, language learning software or internet access | No language learning software or internet access |
| No. of students | 1,500 | 1,308 | 814 | 300 |
| No. of students per class | 44 | 52 | 48 | 35 |
| No. of lessons per week | 30 | 27 | 32 | 31 |
| No. of Chinese lessons per week | 8.5@ | 9 | 9 | 7.8 |
| Textbooks used are published by | Education Commission of the City | District Education Commission | Ministry of Education | Ministry of Education |
| Assessment before entry | Oral interview | Oral interview for class placement | No entry test | No entry test |
| Assessment at the end of Primary 6 | District examination | School examination | District examination | City examination |
| Students' skills upon graduation[+]: | | | | |
| Pronunciation | Excellent | Good | Good | Good |
| Conversation | Very good | Good | Good | Good |
| *Hanyu pinyin* | Very good | Very good | Good | Very good |
| Simplified characters | Excellent | Very good | Good | Passable |
| Writing letters | Very good | Very good | Good | Good |
| Listening to news broadcasts | Passable | Good | Passable | Good |
| Reading newspapers | Passable | Good | Good | Good |
| Data source code | 11-021-001 | 21-171-009 | 12-251-003 | 22-881-010 |

* Number estimated from the total number of 70 teachers in the school.
[#] 'Fully equipped' means 'With: library, cassette recorder and tapes, video recorder and tapes, overhead projector, compact disk player and compact disks, computer and language learning software, video projector and internet access.'
@ The greatest range is in the northern coastal city with 12 lessons in Primary 1 and 7 lessons in Primary 6.
[+] According to the head of the programme.

**Photo 5**    The dormitory in the Primary School at Guangxi Nationalities College. Teachers take turn to stay overnight here to take care of the students sleeping in the same room.

**Photo 6**    Children writing on the blackboards in the playground of the Primary School at Lanzhou University.

In general, the two schools in the coastal cities are better equipped than those in the interior. The coastal schools also use textbooks published by district education bodies rather than depend on those published by the state. The proficiency in Chinese achieved by Primary 6 graduates reported by the heads of Chinese teaching is best in the northern coastal city, then in the southern coastal city, while the levels achieved in schools in the interior are still good on the whole.

In conversations with the heads of Chinese programmes at these primary schools, several interesting views emerged. A major current concern is that teachers would need to pass the Putonghua Shuiping Ceshi (PSC or Putonghua Proficiency Test) every five years. Chinese teachers have to achieve at least 87 marks out of 100 (Grade 2A) on this test while other teachers have to achieve 80 marks (Grade 2B) (Table 2.3). This Putonghua assessment is also linked to their promotion prospects. Other current teacher development initiatives are short in-service courses and increasing the number of graduates with university degrees teaching in primary school. As for learning activities, small group interaction, drama performance, storytelling, Putonghua public speaking competitions and reading have all been cited as useful activities young learners in China enjoy. In the northern interior, in the 1970s, there was still some resistance to speaking Putonghua in the villages but now, according to one informant, Putonghua is taught and spoken in the villages as well. What the interior needs are two types of support: more teacher training and better employment conditions as well as books and equipment such as language laboratories and computers. For example, in the northern interior city visited, it was reported that only five or six schools had language laboratories.

## Chinese in secondary education

The four secondary schools visited offer two semesters in a year with eighteen to twenty-two weeks in each semester, often inclusive of assessment. Lessons are forty-five minutes long. On the basis of eighteen teaching weeks, the total number of class hours for studying Chinese in secondary school ranges from 1,015 to 2,376 lessons or 761 to 1,782 hours. Table 2.16 provides an overview.

Class time for Chinese in secondary schools ranges from 11 lessons per week in the school in the northern interior to 4.7 lessons per week in those in the two coastal cities. The provision of equipment is also uneven with some schools having almost everything and other schools rather poorly resourced. Interestingly, all four schools reported using textbooks published by the state. Higher education admission examinations being the most crucial event in a student's life, schools cannot afford to experiment with other teaching materials at this stage. In terms of student achievement, those in the northern

**Table 2.16  Teaching of Chinese in four secondary schools**

| Location of school | Coastal region | | Interior region | |
|---|---|---|---|---|
| | *Northern city* | *Southern city* | *Northern city* | *Southern city* |
| No. of Chinese teachers | 13 | 17 | 15 | 4 |
| Adequacy of Chinese teachers[+] | Slight shortage but manageable | No shortage | Slight shortage but manageable | No shortage |
| Equipment | No compact disk player, compact disks, computers, language learning software or internet access | Fully equipped[#] | No internet access | No overhead projector, compact disk player, compact disks, language learning software, video projector or internet access |
| No. of students | 1,000[*] | 1,200 | 1,800 | 300 |
| No. of students per class | 50 | 50 | 64 | 51 |
| No. of lessons per week | 32 | 33 | 30 | 35 |
| No. of Chinese lessons per week | 4.7 | 4.7 | 11 | 5.5 |
| Textbooks used are published by | Ministry of Education | Ministry of Education | Ministry of Education | Ministry of Education |
| Assessment before entry | District examination | District examination | District examination | Provincial examination |
| Assessment at the end of Senior Secondary 3 | City examination | Provincial and National examinations | National examination | Provincial and National examinations |
| Students' skills upon graduation[+]: | | | | |
| Pronunciation | Excellent | Passable | Good | Passable |
| Conversation | Excellent | Good | Good | Passable |
| *Hanyu pinyin* | Very good | Good | Good | Passable |
| Simplified characters | Excellent | Excellent | Good | Passable |
| Writing letters | Very good | Excellent | Passable | Good |
| Listening to news broadcasts | Excellent | Good | Good | Passable |
| Reading newspapers | Excellent | Excellent | Passable | Good |
| Data source code | 11-022-001 | 21-172-008 | 12-252-005 | 22-882-009 |

[*]  This school only offers 3 years of senior secondary school.

[#]  'Fully equipped' means 'With: library, cassette recorder and tapes, video recorder and tapes, overhead projector, compact disk player and compact disks, computer and language learning software, video projector and internet access.'

[+]  According to the head of the programme.

coastal city seem to fare best; in the southern coastal city, the second best, and those in the interior are mostly 'Passable' or 'Good'. Like the evaluations for primary school performance, this is only reported data and the heads of Chinese programmes in the interior cities might have been too humble to claim more for their graduates. Yet, this very humility might be linked to the sense of inferiority in terms of competence in Putonghua among some of the learners coming from the interior regions.

With reference to the discussions with the heads of Chinese programmes in secondary schools, four of their observations come to the forefront. First, proficiency in Chinese at this level is often taken for granted. For example, there is a special programme offered at four senior secondary schools, three in Beijing and one in Shanghai, for one hundred junior secondary school graduates from all over the country to enter directly into university after completing senior secondary school; these special students do not have to sit for the national higher education admission examinations. Since these students come from various provinces like Guangdong, Xinjiang, Hubei and so forth, their Putonghua might not be so good but they are selected if they come first or second in science subjects like mathematics, chemistry and biology in national competitions. In general, parents and students seem to worry more about the students' performance in science subjects and English and less about their competence in Chinese or Putonghua. For example, if students are given leave of absence for a period, upon their return, they will ask the science or English teachers to give them some make-up lessons but they will not ask the Chinese teachers for such help. Secondly, for a long time, some of the content in the Chinese textbooks first compiled in the 1970s and 1980s were quite out-of-date. Some reading passages were based on political speeches made by national leaders on the Great Leap Forward, people's communes and so on; both teachers and students found it difficult to be interested in such content from the past. In a series published in the 1990s, a few articles by Mao Zedong are still included. Thirdly, while students find it easy to define the areas for revision for science subjects or English, they find it hard to know what exactly to study for their Chinese examinations. The nature of the national Chinese test for entry into higher education with sixty marks on basic knowledge (such as pronunciation of Chinese characters and the accuracy of sentence structures), forty marks on reading and fifty marks on writing is also not quite inspiring. Despite such conditions, teachers appear to be trying their best to introduce learning activities that have a good degree of learner involvement such as producing a newspaper for the school, debates, role plays and competitions.

## Chinese in higher education

The Chinese departments in the four universities visited offer two semesters in a year with eighteen to twenty weeks in each semester, often inclusive of two weeks of assessment. Lessons are forty-five to fifty minutes long. The total period of time spent on studying Chinese as a major at undergraduate level ranges from about 1,510 to 1,845 hours. Before entry into university, all degree level students must pass the examination for Chinese in the higher education admission examinations. Chinese major students at the end of their programme are not always required to take the national Putonghua Shuiping Ceshi (Putonghua Proficiency Test) but they may choose to do so themselves if they intend to go into teaching or broadcasting.

In addition to Chinese degree programmes consisting of courses in Chinese literature and/or linguistics, there is a separate Chinese as a Foreign Language programme, mainly for foreigners or overseas Chinese. Generically termed as Duiwai Hanyu Jiaoxue (Teaching Chinese as a Foreign Language), these vary from short exchange courses of a few weeks' duration (in collaboration with universities in Hong Kong or other countries) to more comprehensive semester-long courses of about 320 hours, sometimes with three semesters in a year. These courses for visitors tend to occur in universities in the coastal or border regions. Overseas students in the Chinese as a Foreign Language programmes are usually not required to pass any national examination at the end of their studies but they may wish to assess their own standards by taking the national Hanyu Shuiping Kaoshi (Chinese Proficiency Test) designed for non-native speakers of Chinese.

In some universities, courses in Chinese literature or linguistics are also open as electives to students not majoring in Chinese. Graduate level studies in Chinese, particularly at the Doctor of Philosophy (PhD) level, are not available in all universities. Sometimes, Putonghua enhancement courses may also be offered for students who are likely to become teachers. At a university in the northern interior region (Source of data: 12-493-002), for example, all three thousand students, whether majoring in Chinese or not, are required to take a thirty-hour Putonghua course offered at two lessons per week, fifty minutes per lesson, for eighteen teaching weeks for one semester.

Table 2.17 provides an overview of some aspects of the teaching of Chinese at university level. With reference to Table 2.17, the higher enrolment for Chinese as a major in the university in the southern interior city can be attributed to the fact that it has a great number of minority learner students. Another point worth noting is that at university level, the students in the two universities in the north were evaluated more highly than those in the south by their heads of department. Again, care must be taken in interpreting such views as some of the professors might be speaking humbly about their students and their 'Good' might actually mean 'Excellent'. That granted, it should not

**Table 2.17 Teaching of Chinese in four universities**

| Location of university | Coastal region | | Interior region | |
|---|---|---|---|---|
| | *Northern city* | *Southern city* | *Northern city* | *Southern city* |
| No. of Chinese teachers | 27 | 26 | 31 | 60 |
| Adequacy of Chinese teachers[+] | Slight shortage but manageable | | | |
| Equipment | Fully equipped[#] | No video player, video tapes, compact disk player, compact disks, language learning software or video projector | No compact disk player, compact disks, language learning software, video projector, internet access | Fully equipped |
| No. of students | | | | |
| Chinese as a major | 300 | 200 | 245 | 1,040 |
| Chinese as a foreign language | 260 | 0 | 0 | 57 |
| Graduate students | 15 | 40 | 38 | 6 |
| Other students* | 1,000 | 0 | 337 | 1,330 |
| Average no. of students per class | | | | |
| Chinese as a major | 30 | 50 | 60 | 50 |
| Chinese as a foreign language | 15 | Not applicable | No information | No information |
| Materials used are published/ written by | Other universities and teachers at this university | Ministry of Education and teachers at this university | Ministry of Education | Ministry of Education and teachers at this university |
| Chinese major students' skills upon graduation[+]: | | | | |
| Pronunciation | Excellent | Passable | Good | Good |
| Conversation | Excellent | Passable | Good | Good |
| *Hanyu pinyin* | Excellent | Good | Passable | Good |
| Simplified characters | Excellent | Good | Excellent | Good |
| Writing letters | Excellent | Good | Excellent | Very good |

*(continued on p. 67)*

*(Table 2.17 continued)*

| Listening to news broadcasts | Excellent | Good | Very good | Good |
|---|---|---|---|---|
| Reading newspapers | Excellent | Good | Excellent | Very good |
| Giving a speech | Very good | Passable | Passable | Passable |
| Writing academic /technical essays | Very good | Passable | Good | Good |
| Listening to academic/ technical talks | Excellent | Good | Excellent | Good |
| Reading academic / technical materials | Excellent | Passable | Excellent | Good |
| Data source code | 11-023-001 | 21-173-011 | 12-253-003 | 22-883-012 |

\* Non-Chinese-major students, students on distance learning programmes and non-degree students

\# 'Fully equipped' means 'With: library, cassette recorder and tapes, video recorder and tapes, overhead projector, compact disk player and compact disks, computer and language learning software, video projector and internet access.'

+ According to the head of the programme.

**Photo 7**   Student hostels at Yanan University in the style of *yaodongs* or cave houses.

**Photo 8**    A student hostel at Xiamen University.

**Photo 9**    Building to house overseas students at Lanzhou University.

**Photo 10**  Center for Overseas Academic and Cultural Exchange at Tsinghua University.

be surprising that students in the north should fare better in some aspects of Chinese studies because Putonghua, the standard dialect, is a northern dialect, and maps well onto the written form of Modern Chinese. In interviews with both learners and heads of programmes, it has also been pointed out that universities, as places where speakers from all dialect backgrounds congregate, are where all students have to learn to communicate in Putonghua if they have not yet done so before.

From discussions with heads of programmes, a few developments are worth highlighting. First, Chinese as a major is becoming more attractive in double degree programmes. A student can study three years in a discipline such as computer science and then take courses for two years in the Chinese department to graduate with a double degree in computer science and editing/publishing. Secondly, the propagation of Putonghua is by no means completed. As one professor noted, people in many rural districts in the south are still not speaking Putonghua; Putonghua is basically the language of educated people; and in economically more advanced cities like Shanghai, the Shanghai dialect may actually be preferred in some social circles. This observation has to be seen in the context of China as an agricultural country. Thirdly, resources are insufficient, particularly in the interior. Because of difficult working conditions, teachers often leave the interior region. One university in the interior sent ten teachers away to be trained; only two returned. Finally, as Chinese opens up more and more to foreigners in the decades ahead, it is to be expected that the Chinese as a Foreign Language programmes will become more and more popular. (See Chapter 5 for more discussion on this point.) In fact, some foreigners have already gone beyond such Chinese proficiency courses to do a degree in Chinese studies in China. The expansion in such programmes presents a challenge to Chinese language teachers. They are increasingly called upon to incorporate an understanding of second language acquisition or applied linguistics into their teaching. Many are capable of rising to the challenge with more teacher training.

## Summary

This chapter serves as a review of a policy initiated about half a century ago. The policies of Putonghua propagation and the use of standardized characters are still maintained with renewed rigour. While the policies have in general been very successful, there are still students going through education, especially at the primary level, in their dialects among the poorer rural areas, particularly in the interior. With more access to education and population movements to big cities and perhaps more interdialectal marriages, Putonghua may emerge as the home language for more Han Chinese people, particularly in urban areas, in the years to come. As China becomes more international in its outlook, attention is being focused on the learning of English but this very openness will in turn attract foreigners to learn Chinese and enrich the pedagogical openness of Chinese language education in China. In the next chapter, the foreign language experience of Han Chinese learners will be discussed.

# 3

# Promoting English and Other Foreign Languages

## Introduction

Of the three language policies in China introduced in Chapter 1, the one the international community is most aware of in recent years is the promotion of English as the most important foreign language. This chapter is an overview of three aspects of this policy: policy changes concerning foreign language education at different times, the experience of different cohorts of learners in different locations and how the current teaching programme is organized. In terms of government policy, apart from a very brief interlude with the Russian language in the 1950s as part of an attempt to find an ally in the Soviet Union, English has been upheld as the most valuable foreign language in China, especially from 1977 after the Cultural Revolution ended. From then on, the teaching of English has spread considerably beyond the nurturing of English major students, with a great deal of attention given to enhancing the English competence of non-English major students in universities as well as English in the school sector. To illustrate the foreign language learning experience of different cohorts of learners, some statistics on a survey of 415 learners as well as four learning biographies will be presented. The chapter ends with a discussion of current curricular structures from primary school to university with reference to information provided by heads of English or foreign language programmes at different educational levels.

## Foreign Language Policy from 1949

China's interaction with the Western world and culture started about two thousand years ago as trade through the Silk Road (Fu, 1986, p. 1) but the learning of foreign languages as part of a national agenda is much more recent, beginning in the mid-1800s after China lost the Opium War in 1842. From that time onwards, the learning of foreign languages has been motivated by the desire for China to acquire Western knowledge to withstand foreign aggression and to establish itself as a modern nation with economic, scientific and military might. With the establishment of the People's Republic of China in 1949, though there might have been periodic modifications in rhetoric, the instrumental motivation in learning foreign languages has not changed in essence. The promotion of the learning of foreign languages remains intricately tied to the development of China's global perspective — its economic and scientific advancement and desire for international stature.

As pointed out in Chapter 1, in discussions of education in China, three periods have usually been identified (Hayhoe, 1991):
1. The period of socialist construction (1950–1965)
2. The period of the Cultural Revolution (1966–1977)
3. The period of four modernizations (1978–1988)

In a review of English Language Teaching in China, Scovel (1995) adopted a similar demarcation:
1. The first period (1949–1965)
2. The second period (1966–1976)
3. The third period (1977–Present)

The broad division into three periods is very much a historical recognition of the upheaval caused by the Cultural Revolution (the second period) with the first period being the time before it and the third period being the time after it. In terms of foreign language learning, in hindsight, it is possible to have finer distinctions. Although Russian was made the most important foreign language in the early years of the Republic (Xu, 1990, p. 3; Scovel, 1995, p. 3), by the late 1950s, English was 'returned to its original status as the most important foreign language' (Scovel, 1995, p. 3). Pride and Liu (1988, p. 43) have therefore subdivided the first period around 1960 to recognize this important policy change. I would also subdivide the Cultural Revolution period into two periods: an early period when all things foreign were repudiated and a later period from around 1971 when interest in foreign language learning was somewhat tentatively revived, though not fully pursued, in the light of China's joining the United Nations and better relations with America. The post-Cultural Revolution period (from 1977 to the present) could also be further subdivided because, with the onset of the 1990s, China became increasingly interested in playing a role in international affairs beyond its own modernization agenda. This divide from around 1991 was less apparent when it occurred and more identifiable in hindsight as China rose in international stature. The six policy periods relating to foreign language education (Lam, 2002) thus identified are listed in Table 3.1.

While this broad demarcation marks the major shifts in policy stance, for an understanding of the developments at different educational levels, it is useful to highlight some significant events during each of these periods. In the account which follows (Lam & Chow, 2001), many of the events occurring

Table 3.1  Six phases in foreign language education in China

| Historical period | Phase in foreign language education | Years |
|---|---|---|
| Before the Cultural Revolution | 1. The interlude with Russian<br>2. The back-to-English movement | Early 1950s<br>1957–1965 |
| During the Cultural Revolution | 3. Repudiation of foreign learning<br>4. English for renewing ties with the West | 1966–1970<br>1971–1976 |
| After the Cultural Revolution | 5. English for modernization<br>6. English for international stature | 1977–1990<br>From 1991 |

before 1989 were selected and summarized from the detailed chronology of important events in English language education compiled by the Sichuan Foreign Language Institute (1993) with reference to policy papers, committee minutes and other sources. Other accounts of policy trends can also be found in Fu (1986), Li, Zhang and Liu (1988), Dzau (1990), Troutner (1996) and Adamson (2004).

## The interlude with Russian: Early 1950s

Because China's initial concept of its place in the world was to align itself with the communist nations, the foreign language that received a lot of initial attention in the early 1950s was Russian, it being the language of the most influential communist nation then. The dream of finding an ally in the Soviet Union was soon shattered because the Soviet Union did not treat China as an equal and did not provide the aid in the manner as promised (Lynch, 1998, p. 115). So towards the end of that period, the teaching of other languages, especially English, resumed.

Some notable events during that period were:

| | |
|---|---|
| 1949 | Beijing Foreign Language Institute (teaching both English and Russian) was established as a result of amalgamation of various foreign language teaching units. |
| | Russian lessons were broadcast on the Beijing People's Broadcasting Station. |
| 1950 | National plans to teach foreign languages in junior secondary school at three lessons per week and senior secondary school at four lessons per week were announced. |
| | Russian departments were established in nineteen higher education colleges and Russian training courses were organized in several party, government and military sections. |

| | |
|---|---|
| 1951 | National plans to teach Russian and to train 10,000 cadres with knowledge of Russian by 1954 were announced. |
| | By this year, Russian departments were established in at least thirty-four universities and colleges. |
| 1953 | A press report from the State emphasized the importance of English in the secondary school curriculum because it was an international language though Russian had to be learnt so as to learn from the Soviet Union; the rationale given was 'Even in the Soviet Union, foreign languages taught include English, French and German.' |
| | Since fewer English teachers were needed for secondary schools, the training of English teachers at teacher training universities and colleges was reduced in scope. |
| | Russian was required as the main foreign language for undergraduates. |
| 1954 | Foreign language teaching in junior secondary school was discontinued by a notice from the Education Ministry. |
| 1955 | A three-year syllabus for Russian majors at university level was completed for implementation from 1955 to 1956. |
| 1956 | Zhou Enlai announced that it was necessary to expand foreign language education. The plan was to increase enrolment for English, German and French majors from 1956. |
| | Beijing Foreign Language Institute admitted graduate students in English. |
| | Draft syllabi for teaching Russian and English in the senior secondary school were distributed. |

## The back-to-English movement: 1957–1965

In the late 1950s, from about 1956 or 1957, it became increasingly apparent that the Soviet Union could not be relied upon as a friendly nation. China began to look towards the West. From about 1961, China was ready to pursue better ties, at least economically, with the West. During this period, English displaced Russian as the most important foreign language in China. A particularly interesting development in this period was the establishment of foreign language schools. Though small in number, they constitute an important tradition in foreign language learning in China. Another significant step was to extend the learning of English to science and technology university students. Had there not been a Cultural Revolution, this back-to-English movement would probably have accelerated with further momentum.

Some notable events during that period were:

| | |
|---|---|
| 1957 | The number of graduates in Russian and other Eastern European languages exceeded demand. Admission of Russian majors stopped for a year and training in Russian dwindled from this year onwards while training of majors in English and other languages increased. |
| | A draft syllabus for teaching English in junior secondary school was distributed. |
| 1958 | The number of foreign language lessons in senior secondary school increased from four to five lessons per week. |
| 1959 | The Education Ministry announced that from 1959 to 1960, the better schools should start the teaching of foreign languages in junior secondary with one-third of them teaching Russian and two-thirds teaching English and other languages. |
| | Where possible, majors in foreign languages at college or university level should study a second foreign language apart from the main one, which was usually Russian or English. |
| | At the recommendation of Zhou Enlai, Beijing Foreign Language Institute established its own secondary school on campus. In that secondary school, the languages taught were Russian, English, French, German and Spanish. |
| 1960 | Beijing Foreign Language School was established to teach English from Primary 3 as a pilot scheme. |
| | The Education Ministry decided that the People's Education Press should develop a new set of English materials for primary and secondary schools. |
| 1961 | The syllabus for English majors at university and college level was defined. The four main areas of evaluation of student performance in the syllabus were:<br>a. Love of the country and a global spirit.<br>b. Mastery of the English language and English/American literature, British and American history, politics, economics and culture and general knowledge of Chinese language and literature.<br>c. English competence and reading ability in a second foreign language.<br>d. Good health and physique. |
| 1962 | Owing to a lack of teachers, 65% of junior secondary schools had not started teaching foreign languages. |
| | The first English syllabus for non-English majors (Science and Technology) was distributed. |

| 1962 | Materials for English majors (by Xu Guozhang and others) and non-English majors (Science and Technology) were published. |
|------|-------------------------------------------------------------------------------------------------------------------------|
| 1963 | Ten foreign language schools to start teaching foreign languages from Primary 3 were proposed so as to develop a group of personnel with specially high competence in foreign languages — English, Russian, French, Spanish, German, Japanese and Arabic. |
|      | The Education Ministry announced there should be more teacher training for teaching English and more English classes for students. |
| 1964 | There were not enough experts in English and other languages and an oversupply of Russian majors. |
|      | The three-year plan to send 2,000 students abroad to increase the number of cadres with knowledge of English and other languages was announced. |
|      | Other forms of education — evening college, correspondence courses, radio and television programmes — were proposed. |
|      | English was established as the first foreign language in higher education. |
|      | Shortage in foreign language teachers was to be met by importing teachers from overseas and by retraining teachers of Russian to teach English. |
| 1965 | The slogan *you$^4$ hong$^2$ you$^4$ zhuan$^1$*, literally 'red and expert', meaning 'to love the party and the people and to be an expert in one's area of learning' was propagated. The concern was that foreign language learning would expose students to all sorts of unpatriotic ideologies. Unless learners loved the party and the people, their knowledge of foreign languages would not help the country. |
|      | By 1965, fourteen foreign language schools training learners in foreign languages from Primary 3 were in place in Beijing (two schools), Shanghai, Tianjin, Sichuan, Nanjin, Changchun, Wuhan, Hangzhou, Tongshan, Haerbin, Guangzhou, Luda and Xian. |

## Repudiation of foreign learning: 1966–1970

From 1966 to 1976, the Cultural Revolution swept throughout the country making the learning of foreign ideas (including foreign languages) condemnable. That was a time when farmers and workers were honoured and traditional scholars were distrusted. Foreign language learning suffered the same fate as scholarly studies in Chinese. Yet, even during those dark years for foreign language learning, Zhou Enlai did manage to save a remnant of the foreign language majors and deploy them to jobs requiring foreign languages.

Some notable events during that period were:

| 1966 | Classes stopped at the start of the Cultural Revolution. |
|---|---|
| 1967 | The slogan *bu⁴ xue² ABC, zhao⁴yang⁴ gan⁴ ge²ming⁴* or 'it is possible to bring about revolution even without learning ABC' (meaning 'one does not need to learn foreign languages or foreign knowledge to revolutionize the country') became popular. |
| 1968 | Zhou Enlai instructed the Foreign Affairs Ministry to send the foreign language majors to a few selected work camps so that they could later be redeployed to do work related to their foreign language training. |
| 1969 | Many foreign language teachers and students were denounced as 'only expert and not red' and suffered greatly. |
| 1970 | Some foreign language students were deployed to various jobs related to foreign languages. Peking University and Tsinghua University in Beijing started admitting worker-farmer-and-soldier students as a pilot scheme. |

## English for renewing ties with the West: 1971–1976

In the midst of the Cultural Revolution, in 1971, the United States formally recognized China as a member of the United Nations, taking Taiwan's place. Further diplomatic talks between Zhou Enlai and Henry Kissinger proved fruitful. In February 1972, Richard Nixon visited China resulting in Sino-American discourse towards commercial, cultural and educational exchange (Lynch, 1998, p. 93). In spite of these overtures, it was only after Mao's death and the end of the Cultural Revolution in 1976 that China could quicken its pace of modernization and fully realize its strategic intentions to open its door to the West and Western learning.

Some notable events during that period were:

| 1971 | Beijing Foreign Language Institute also admitted farmer-and-soldier students. |
|---|---|
| 1972 | The slogan of 'red and expert' for foreign language training was revived. |

| 1972 | Sixteen students were sent to England to learn English and twenty were sent to France. |
| 1973 | Shanghai People's Broadcasting Station collaborated with Fudan University and Shanghai Foreign Language Institute to broadcast Japanese and French learning programmes respectively. |
| | Beijing Foreign Language Institute was instructed by the State to recruit students from all over the country. |
| | Anti-culture (whether Chinese or foreign) sentiments prevailed again. |
| 1974 | The slogan of 'not learning ABC can still bring about revolution' became even more widespread. Foreign language education, especially in secondary schools, suffered a severe setback. |
| 1975 | The draft for developing Chinese-foreign language dictionaries was announced. The foreign languages involved were English, Japanese, Russian, French, German, Spanish, Arabic among others. |
| 1976 | Mao died. The Cultural Revolution ended when the Gang of Four lost their power. |

### English for modernization: 1977–1990

The 1980s were the time of Deng Xiaoping's Policy of Four Modernizations (first announced in 1978): to modernize agriculture, industry, science and technology and defence. The Four Modernizations Policy soon evolved into the Reform and Opening Policy (Dillon, 1998, p. 109). The Reform and Opening Policy made it absolutely necessary for the Chinese to learn English and other foreign languages. More and more educational, occupational and economic advantages became attached to learning English and other foreign languages. During that period, the policy directions from the State met with tremendous support in terms of syllabus design and materials development from English language professionals in China as well as some eminent ELT experts from overseas. ELT became established as a professional discipline during those years.

Some notable events during that period were:

| 1977 | The reinstatement of admission to higher education was announced. |
| 1978 | Plans to teach foreign languages from Primary 3 were announced. Three main weaknesses in foreign language education prior to 1978 were pointed out at a seminar hosted by the Education Ministry: |

| | |
|---|---|
| 1978 | a. overemphasis of Russian.<br>b. too much attention on foreign language majors and insufficient attention on non-foreign-language majors.<br>c. discontinuation of foreign language teaching in junior secondary school from 1954 to 1959.<br><br>Foreign language training should be 'like a dragon' meaning it should be a continuous process from primary school to university.<br><br>Foreign language training became linked with the Four Modernizations.<br><br>Recruitment of foreign teachers to teach in China resumed. |
| 1979 | More support for foreign language teaching in primary and secondary school was announced.<br><br>Curricula for foreign language majors and teachers were drafted and announced.<br><br>The plan to restore the fourteen foreign language schools first established in 1964 was announced.<br><br>Among the 222,273 cadres with a knowledge of foreign languages in 1979, 145,843 (65.6%) specialized in English. |
| 1980 | First conference on 'Applied linguistics and ELT' was held in Guangzhou with participation from twenty-two higher education institutions in China and three institutions from Hong Kong.<br><br>Experts from China visited the Hong Kong Examinations Authority and devised the English Proficiency Test.<br><br>Materials development teams were established for various foreign languages taught in higher education. |
| 1981 | First batch of PhD and master degree student quotas were announced. Quotas for English far exceeded those for other foreign languages. |
| 1982 | English was announced as the main foreign language in secondary school. |
| 1983 | The College English syllabus was discussed at a meeting in Shanghai.<br><br>Four centres for training teachers for English majors and six centres for training teachers for College English for non-majors were established. |
| 1984 | The College English syllabus for Science and Technology students was completed for implementation from 1985. |

| 1984 | Research projects on various aspects of learning English at university level were conducted. |
| | Draft syllabi for training teachers to teach English at secondary schools were made available. |
| | The issue of which international organization for foreign language professionals in China to join was discussed at a meeting of the Foreign Language Teaching and Research Association in China in December. |
| 1985 | It was announced that the Band 4 and Band 6 standardized exams for College English would be implemented in 1987. Bands 1 to 3 and 5 could be examined within each institution. For College English, there were altogether six bands with all students expected to pass Band 4 after two years of studying English at the university. |
| | An ELT Conference was held in Guangzhou Foreign Language Institute with participation from several countries and participants like M. A. K. Halliday, Henry Widdowson and Alan Maley. |
| 1986 | First official delegation from China attended the TESOL (Teaching English to Speakers of Other Languages) conference in Anaheim near Los Angeles. They introduced the College English syllabus in China at the conference. |
| | Student quotas for graduate studies in English for Specific Purposes became available in China. |
| | Fu Ke published *A history of foreign language teaching in China* (in Chinese). |
| 1987 | Teachers of several foreign languages met to discuss syllabi for teaching foreign languages at university level. |
| | By 1987, the number of foreign languages taught at university had expanded to include many languages. |
| | A first book on *The teaching of College English* was published by the Beijing Municipality College English Teaching and Research Association. Another was published by the Foreign Language Teaching and Research Association. |
| 1988 | Li Liangyou, Zhang Risheng and Liu Li published *A history of English language teaching in China* (in Chinese). |

**Photo 11** Plaque for Sister Brigid Keogh, who made a lasting contribution to the Department of Foreign Languages at Yanan University and was made a permanent resident of China.

**Photo 12** The front of the International Exchange Center at the Guangxi Nationalities College.

## English for international stature: From 1991

Although China gained tremendous goodwill through its Open Door policy during the 1980s, this goodwill suffered a severe setback at the turn of the decade because of the 1989 Tiananmen Incident. By the turn of the decade, China was in need of an opportunity to rise to international grace again. When the Soviet Union disintegrated in 1991, the balance of power in the global arena made it possible for China to adopt an increasingly international stance. Economic openness was enhanced through various trade arrangements. Such an international outlook called for a corresponding openness in terms of foreign language learning.

As a professional discipline, ELT in China also became more international in the 1990s. Collections of essays often covering various conferences on ELT were published in China; examples were: Li (1990), Department of English Quality Review Team (1992), College Foreign Language Teaching and Research Association (1994), Xu (1996), Chen and Yang (1997) and Liu and Wu (2000). Another interesting publication during this time was a handbook by Zhou (1995) covering all aspects of teaching English in secondary schools. Publications outside China included: Dzau (1990), Ross (1993), Cortazzi and Jin (1996), Troutner (1996) and The British Council and State Education Commission (1996). At the same time, syllabi and materials from primary school to adult education were designed or revised during this period.

Some notable events during this period were:

| | |
|---|---|
| 1990 | In May 1990, guidelines for teaching English in primary school were made public. |
| 1992 | In June 1992, the draft English syllabus for junior secondary school was published. |
| 1993 | In May 1993, the draft English syllabus for senior secondary school was published. (A revised version was published in May 1996.) |
| 1995 | The National English Test for evaluating staff for recruitment or promotion into different staff grades was initiated. In 1999, the use of a generic test was discontinued and the testing of English was integrated with four fields: humanities, science and technology, health, and economics and finance. |
| 1999 | The Public English Test System (PETS) was publicized as a test to replace the Waiyu Shuiping Kaoshi (WSK or English Proficiency Test). <br><br> A revised syllabus for English majors at university was drafted and circulated for consultation; it was submitted to the Ministry of Education in December 1999. Upon approval, it was made public in March 2000 for implementation. In the new syllabus, there are three components: |

| | |
|---|---|
| 1999 | a. English as a skill: for example, listening and writing<br>b. English as a field of study: for example, English linguistics and literature<br>c. English as related to a profession: for example, diplomacy, trade, military affairs |
| 2000 | First approved in 1999, the National Research Center for Foreign Language Education was established at Beijing Foreign Studies University in March 2000 to conduct research in foreign language education and in bilingualism.<br><br>In 2000, the International Association of Teachers of English as a Foreign Language (IATEFL) also endorsed the establishment of a China branch. |
| 2001 | China joined the World Trade Organization on 11 December 2001. The impact of this event on education was so great that a special policy plan in response to this event was published on the Ministry of Education web site.<br><br>In the same year, Beijing's successful bid to host the 2008 Olympic Games was announced. |
| 2002 | In July 2002, the TESOL (Teachers of English to Speakers of Other Languages) Candlelight project was announced in July 2002 by the Ministry of Education. This teacher training project was funded by a charitable organization based in Beijing and the teachers were recruited from Canada. The target was to provide a 130-hour course to 6,800 to 7,500 teachers within two years. Teachers from all over the country were invited to go to Beijing for training (Ministry of Education 2002).<br><br>In August 2002, the first IATEFL China conference was held in Tonghua in the Jilin province.<br><br>2002 also saw China joining AILA (International Association of Applied Linguists) in the form of CELEA (China's English Language Education Association). |

## Summary

From this review of policy trends in the light of changes in foreign relations, it is evident that, apart from a very brief interlude with the Russian language in the early years of the Republic and non-learning during some years of the Cultural Revolution, English has been promoted as the most important foreign language in China. As China enters the new millennium, it is well poised for further developments in English language education across the curriculum from primary school to graduate studies. A few of these changes will be highlighted in Chapter 5.

## The Overall Experience of Han Chinese Learners

With reference to the six policy phases just described, it is to be expected that Chinese learners of English from different times should differ in learning experience. There might also be effects according to their first dialect since northern dialect speakers could arguably have less learning to do for Putonghua and hence perhaps more spare learning capacity for learning English. Learners from the coastal region might also benefit from the greater opportunity to use English.

The three variables of age, first dialect and childhood location were investigated in a survey of 222 non-foreign-language specialists and 193 foreign language specialists, or 415 learners in total (Lam, 2002); 318 of these respondents were the same respondents as for the survey on learning Chinese reported on in Chapter 2; in fact, both surveys were administered as different parts of one questionnaire (see Chapter 1, 'The Language Education in China Project', pp. 10–17, and Appendix I). Respondents were approached through the universities and secondary schools in major cities throughout China. All the respondents were Han Chinese and had completed university education. They were grouped into five age groups according to their age in 2000: 46 to 50, 41 to 45, 36 to 40, 29 to 35 and 24 to 28. The years these groups of learners entered primary school correspond roughly to the first five phases of foreign language policy changes in China (Table 3.1). (At the time of data collection, the sixth phase was too recent for the corresponding cohort to have completed university education.)

Both batches of respondents, foreign language specialists and non-foreign-language specialists, were asked the same questions concerning when they started learning their first foreign language (meaning 'their most important foreign language'), class time for such learning, the use of the foreign language during their learning as well as their current use of the language. Some brief information was also collected on their learning of their second foreign language (meaning 'an additional foreign language'), if any.

Results from the two batches of respondents were then analysed separately for effects relating to the three variables of age, first dialect and birthplace location and then compared. The Loglinear Analysis involving the Chi-square statistic ($\alpha = 0.05$), a robust test suitable for categorical data and unequal cell sizes, was used for analysing most of the data. The Analysis of Variance was also used for analysing some data ($\alpha = 0.05$). Since eight of the 222 non-foreign-language specialists did not learn any foreign language, the data pool for analysing the actual learning experience of non-foreign-language specialists was reduced to 214. Small differences in sample sizes for various aspects arose when respondents did not answer some questions.

The foreign language learning experience of non-foreign-language specialists is more typical of most university graduates in China and is the focus of this section. The most salient effects of age, dialectal background and birthplace location in the non-foreign-language specialists' experience in learning their first foreign language, which was English for 90.7% of them, are first presented. Then, the experience of foreign language specialists learning their first foreign language, also English for 96.2% of them, will be briefly discussed. Finally, the experience of learning the second foreign language by mostly the foreign language specialists will be outlined.

## Age effects in learning the first foreign language: Non-foreign-language specialists

As a whole, younger respondents experienced better conditions for learning the foreign language in many ways: they started learning earlier; they had better support at school and there were more resources at their disposal outside the classroom for them to do more on their own to learn the foreign language. As a result, they were more open to using the language.

The main foreign language learnt by most respondents (90.7%) was English. Even the oldest group (46 to 50), entering primary school from 1956 to 1960, had 55.6% learning English as their first foreign language. For the other age groups, there was a steady increase in English learners from 91.4% (for Age Group 41 to 45) to 98.5% (for Age Group 24 to 28). This age effect is significant ($\chi^2$ =33.44, df = 8, p <0.0001) and accords with the policy shift from Russian to English around 1960.

Most older respondents learnt their foreign language only at university (54.5% for Age Group 46 to 50) while most younger learners did so from secondary school (88.2% for Age Group 24 to 28) (Table 3.2). These age differences are significantly different ($\chi^2$ =56.32, df = 8, p <0.0001). A similar pattern for learning to write a foreign language was found ($\chi^2$ =56.61, df = 8, p <0.0001).

For those who studied their foreign language in secondary school (183 respondents), there had been a steady increase in foreign language class time over the years (Table 3.3) with the two recent cohorts having 5.5 to 6.5 lessons of 45 minutes each per week. This difference is statistically significant (F = 13.963, $df_1$ =4, $df_2$ = 171, p = 0.000). Foreign language class time at university remained stable.

**Photo 13** Plaque at the entrance of the Department of Foreign Languages at Lanzhou University in three languages: Chinese, English and Russian.

**Photo 14** Plaque at the entrance of the Department of Foreign Languages at Xiamen University in three languages: Chinese, English and Russian.

**Table 3.2  Time respondents started learning to speak their foreign language**

| Age group | Number of respondents (Percentage) | | | | |
|---|---|---|---|---|---|
| | From primary school | From secondary school | At university | At work | Total |
| 46 to 50 | 1 (4.5%) | 9 (40.9%) | 10 (45.5%) | 2 (9.1%) | 22 (100.0%) |
| 41 to 45 | 1 (2.8%) | 24 (66.7%) | 10 (27.8%) | 1 (2.8%) | 36 (100.0%) |
| 36 to 40 | 0 (0.0%) | 29 (80.6%) | 6 (16.7%) | 1 (2.8%) | 36 (100.0%) |
| 29 to 35 | 8 (16.0%) | 39 (78.0%) | 2 (4.0%) | 1 (2.0%) | 50 (100.0%) |
| 24 to 28 | 8 (11.8%) | 60 (88.2%) | 0 (0.0%) | 0 (0.0%) | 68 (100.0%) |
| Total | 18 (8.5%) | 161 (75.9%) | 28 (13.2%) | 5 (2.4%) | 212 (100.0%) |

Note: No respondents learnt their foreign language before primary school. 'At university' and 'at work' were pooled together in the Loglinear Analysis because the number of respondents for some cells was too small.

**Table 3.3  Increase in class time for foreign language learning in secondary school**

| Age group | No. of lessons per week (45 minutes/lesson) | | Total no. |
|---|---|---|---|
| | Mean | Standard deviation | of respondents |
| 46 to 50 | 4.727 | 1.849 | 11 |
| 41 to 45 | 3.778 | 1.717 | 27 |
| 36 to 40 | 4.310 | 2.422 | 29 |
| 29 to 35 | 5.500 | 1.448 | 48 |
| 24 to 28 | 6.500 | 2.328 | 68 |
| Total | 5.383 | 2.260 | 183 |

Foreign language teachers at secondary school for different age groups also used the foreign language increasingly during foreign language lessons (Table 3.4). This increase accelerated to about 80% in the two most recent cohorts entering secondary school from about 1977 onwards ($\chi^2 = 51.38$, df = 8, p < 0.0001), which was when the Cultural Revolution ended and the educational system was revived.

A similar trend occurred at university (Table 3.5). For younger cohorts entering secondary school from about 1977 onwards, more teachers used the foreign language more often in foreign language lessons ($\chi^2 = 17.75$, df = 8, p = 0.0232).

**Table 3.4 Use of the foreign language in foreign language lessons in secondary school**

| Age group | Number of respondents (Percentage) | | | | |
|---|---|---|---|---|---|
| | Foreign language used by all teachers | Foreign language used by some teachers | Foreign language not used by teachers | No foreign language lessons | Total |
| 46 to 50 | 0 (0.0%) | 9 (40.9%) | 2 (9.1%) | 11 (50.0%) | 22 (100.0%) |
| 41 to 45 | 0 (0.0%) | 15 (44.1%) | 11 (32.4%) | 8 (23.5%) | 34 (100.0%) |
| 36 to 40 | 1 (2.7%) | 17 (45.9%) | 12 (32.4%) | 7 (18.9%) | 37 (100.0%) |
| 29 to 35 | 1 (2.0%) | 39 (78.0%) | 8 (16.0%) | 2 (4.0%) | 50 (100.0%) |
| 24 to 28 | 0 (0.0%) | 54 (79.4%) | 14 (20.6%) | 0 (0.0%) | 68 (100.0%) |
| Total | 2 (0.9%) | 134 (63.5%) | 47 (22.3%) | 28 (13.3%) | 211 (100.0%) |

Note: 'Used by all teachers' and 'Used by some teachers' were pooled together in the Loglinear Analysis because the number of respondents for some cells was too small.

**Table 3.5 Use of the foreign language in foreign language lessons at university**

| Age group | Number of respondents (Percentage) | | | | |
|---|---|---|---|---|---|
| | Foreign language used by all teachers | Foreign language used by some teachers | Foreign language not used by teachers | No foreign language lessons | Total |
| 46 to 50 | 1 (4.8%) | 17 (81.0%) | 1 (4.8%) | 2 (9.5%) | 21 (100.0%) |
| 41 to 45 | 4 (11.8%) | 25 (73.5%) | 4 (11.8%) | 1 (2.9%) | 34 (100.0%) |
| 36 to 40 | 3 (8.6%) | 26 (74.3%) | 4 (11.4%) | 2 (5.7%) | 35 (100.0%) |
| 29 to 35 | 9 (18.4%) | 36 (73.5%) | 3 (6.1%) | 1 (2.0%) | 49 (100.0%) |
| 24 to 28 | 21 (31.3%) | 44 (65.7%) | 1 (1.5%) | 1 (1.5%) | 67 (100.0%) |
| Total | 38 (18.4%) | 148 (71.8%) | 13 (6.3%) | 7 (3.4%) | 206 (100.0%) |

Note: 'Foreign language not used' and 'No foreign language lessons' were pooled together in the Loglinear Analysis because the number of respondents for some cells was too small.

Respondents were also asked whether they did a variety of activities to enhance their learning outside the classroom. Age effects were found for the following activities:

1. Using the foreign language to converse with classmates outside the classroom in secondary school ($\chi^2 = 13.18$, df = 4, p = 0.0104)
2. Practising on their own with tapes and materials ($\chi^2 = 16.79$, df = 8, p = 0.0324)
3. Watching television ($\chi^2 = 13.66$, df = 4, p = 0.0085)
4. Seeing movies or watching video tapes ($\chi^2 = 18.87$, df = 4, p = 0.0008)
5. Listening to songs or singing songs ($\chi^2 = 21.3$, df = 8, p = 0.0064)
6. Reading newspapers or magazines ($\chi^2 = 35.54$, df = 8, p < 0.0001)
7. Reading books ($\chi^2 = 15.52$, df = 8, p = 0.0498)

Although only one-third of the respondents used the foreign language outside the classroom with classmates in secondary school (Table 3.6), it is still encouraging to find that some learners were not afraid to practise in this way while learning. Bear in mind that the youngest two cohorts would have gone to secondary school from 1977 onwards, which was when English became more widely propagated in secondary schools. That the three older cohorts did not practise with their secondary school classmates as much could simply be because prior to the late 1970s, the learning of foreign languages in secondary school was not widespread.

**Table 3.6  Using the foreign language with classmates outside the classroom in secondary school**

| Age group | Number of respondents (Percentage) | | | |
|---|---|---|---|---|
| | Usually | Sometimes | Not used | Total |
| 46 to 50 | 0 (0.0%) | 2 (12.5%) | 14 (87.5%) | 16 (100.0%) |
| 41 to 45 | 0 (0.0%) | 4 (13.8%) | 25 (86.2%) | 29 (100.0%) |
| 36 to 40 | 0 (0.0%) | 8 (23.5%) | 26 (76.5%) | 34 (100.0%) |
| 29 to 35 | 2 (4.1%) | 18 (36.7%) | 29 (59.2%) | 49 (100.0%) |
| 24 to 28 | 0 (0.0%) | 28 (41.8%) | 39 (58.2%) | 67 (100.0%) |
| Total | 2 (1.0%) | 60 (30.8%) | 133 (68.2%) | 195 (100.0%) |

Note: 'Usually' and 'Sometimes' were pooled together in the Loglinear Analysis because the number of respondents for some cells was too small.

No significant difference was found concerning their use of the foreign language with classmates outside the classroom at university, even though the youngest cohort seemed to do so a little more frequently; only 33.8% among the youngest cohort did not use the foreign language at all to converse with their classmates while on the average 47.8% of the four older cohorts did not.

Practising with tapes and materials (Table 3.7) seemed to be a crucial part of the foreign language learning experience of Chinese learners with an average of 96.5% reporting that they used such a learning method either very often (50.5%) or sometimes (46.0%). The general trend over time was an increase in frequency of use with 31.6% of the oldest group and 66.2% of the youngest group reporting that they used this method very often.

The most frequent television watchers (Table 3.8) were the youngest respondents though the second youngest group also did so more than the three older groups. A significant effect was found when the percentages of respondents who did not watch any television (6.3% and 16.7% for the two younger cohorts as compared to 33.3%, 23.3% and 33.3% for the three older groups) were compared to those that did (93.8% and 83.3% for the two younger cohorts and 66.7%, 76.7% and 66.7% for the three older ones).

**Table 3.7 Learners practising on their own with tapes and materials in the foreign language**

| Age group | Number of respondents (Percentage) | | | |
|---|---|---|---|---|
| | Very often | Sometimes | Not at all | Total |
| 46 to 50 | 6 (31.6%) | 11 (57.9%) | 2 (10.5%) | 19 (100.0%) |
| 41 to 45 | 15 (42.9%) | 18 (51.4%) | 2 (5.7%) | 35 (100.0%) |
| 36 to 40 | 12 (36.4%) | 19 (57.6%) | 2 (6.1%) | 33 (100.0%) |
| 29 to 35 | 25 (52.1%) | 22 (45.8%) | 1 (2.1%) | 48 (100.0%) |
| 24 to 28 | 43 (66.2%) | 22 (33.8%) | 0 (0.0%) | 65 (100.0%) |
| Total | 101 (50.5%) | 92 (46.0%) | 7 (3.5%) | 200 (100.0%) |

**Table 3.8 Watching television to learn the foreign language**

| Age group | Number of respondents (Percentage) | | | |
|---|---|---|---|---|
| | Very often | Sometimes | Not at all | Total |
| 46 to 50 | 2 (13.3%) | 8 (53.3%) | 5 (33.3%) | 15 (100.0%) |
| 41 to 45 | 6 (20.0%) | 17 (56.7%) | 7 (23.3%) | 30 (100.0%) |
| 36 to 40 | 1 (3.3%) | 19 (63.3%) | 10 (33.3%) | 30 (100.0%) |
| 29 to 35 | 4 (9.5%) | 31 (73.8%) | 7 (16.7%) | 42 (100.0%) |
| 24 to 28 | 5 (7.8%) | 55 (85.9%) | 4 (6.3%) | 64 (100.0%) |
| Total | 18 (9.9%) | 130 (71.8%) | 33 (18.2%) | 181 (100.0%) |

Note: 'Very often' and 'Sometimes' were pooled together in the Loglinear Analysis because the number of respondents for some cells was too small.

The pattern of seeing movies and watching video tapes (Table 3.9) over time also indicates that the two younger groups were more privileged in the use of such a method of learning. Respondents that did this the least (51.9% not doing so) were six years old or younger at the start of the Cultural Revolution in 1966 (aged 36 to 40 in 2000).

**Table 3.9 Seeing movies or watching video tapes in the foreign language**

| Age group | Number of respondents (Percentage) | | | |
|---|---|---|---|---|
| | Very often | Sometimes | Not at all | Total |
| 46 to 50 | 1 (7.7%) | 8 (61.5%) | 4 (30.8%) | 13 (100.0%) |
| 41 to 45 | 3 (11.5%) | 12 (46.2%) | 11 (42.3%) | 26 (100.0%) |
| 36 to 40 | 0 (0.0%) | 13 (48.1%) | 14 (51.9%) | 27 (100.0%) |
| 29 to 35 | 2 (4.8%) | 31 (73.8%) | 9 (21.4%) | 42 (100.0%) |
| 24 to 28 | 10 (15.6%) | 46 (71.9%) | 8 (12.5%) | 64 (100.0%) |
| Total | 16 (9.3%) | 110 (64.0%) | 46 (26.7%) | 172 (100.0%) |

Note: 'Very often' and 'sometimes' were pooled together in the Loglinear Analysis because the number of respondents for some cells was too small.

The increase in use of songs (Table 3.10) as a self-learning activity was fairly steady over time with 61.5% of the oldest learners and 93.8% of the youngest learners doing so. This pattern is most obvious in terms of the percentages of learners not using such a method; 38.5% of the two oldest groups did not listen to or sing songs to learn the foreign language while only 6.3% of the youngest age group did not do so.

The pattern of reading newspapers and magazines (Table 3.11) is less straightforward. Two low periods for using such a method were found; the oldest group probably did not have much access to such materials as they were educated at a time soon after the People's Republic was established after a period of civil strife and the general population was not well off. It was therefore not surprising that 31.3% of this age group did not read newspapers or magazines in the foreign language at all while they were learning it. Another period of low use of such a method was the early part of the Cultural Revolution. The group (aged 36 to 40) that was six years old or younger when the Cultural Revolution started used this learning method less often than the other three age groups.

**Table 3.10  Listening to songs or singing songs in the foreign language**

| Age group | Number of respondents (Percentage) | | | |
|---|---|---|---|---|
| | Very often | Sometimes | Not at all | Total |
| 46 to 50 | 2 (15.4%) | 6 (46.2%) | 5 (38.5%) | 13 (100.0%) |
| 41 to 45 | 2 (7.7%) | 14 (53.8%) | 10 (38.5%) | 26 (100.0%) |
| 36 to 40 | 5 (18.5%) | 14 (51.9%) | 8 (29.6%) | 27 (100.0%) |
| 29 to 35 | 3 (7.1%) | 31 (73.8%) | 8 (19.0%) | 42 (100.0%) |
| 24 to 28 | 11 (17.2%) | 49 (76.6%) | 4 (6.3%) | 64 (100.0%) |
| Total | 23 (13.4%) | 114 (66.3%) | 35 (20.3%) | 172 (100.0%) |

**Table 3.11  Reading newspapers or magazines in the foreign language**

| Age group | Number of respondents (Percentage) | | | |
|---|---|---|---|---|
| | Very often | Sometimes | Not at all | Total |
| 46 to 50 | 4 (25.0%) | 7 (43.8%) | 5 (31.3%) | 16 (100.0%) |
| 41 to 45 | 0 (0.0%) | 24 (92.3%) | 2 (7.7%) | 26 (100.0%) |
| 36 to 40 | 3 (10.3%) | 18 (62.1%) | 8 (27.6%) | 29 (100.0%) |
| 29 to 35 | 6 (13.0%) | 34 (73.9%) | 6 (13.0%) | 46 (100.0%) |
| 24 to 28 | 25 (37.9%) | 38 (57.6%) | 3 (4.5%) | 66 (100.0%) |
| Total | 38 (20.8%) | 121 (66.1%) | 24 (13.1%) | 183 (100.0%) |

Respondents' pattern of reading books to learn (Table 3.12) is similar to their use of newspapers and magazines. The oldest group (aged 46 to 50) and the one most affected by the Cultural Revolution (aged 36 to 40) had higher percentages of learners not using such a method to learn foreign languages (23.5% and 17.2%). The second oldest group (aged 41 to 45) and the youngest cohort (aged 24 to 28) made greater use of learning through books.

**Table 3.12  Reading books in the foreign language**

| Age group | Number of respondents (Percentage) | | | |
|---|---|---|---|---|
| | Very often | Sometimes | Not at all | Total |
| 46 to 50 | 7 (41.2%) | 6 (35.3%) | 4 (23.5%) | 17 (100.0%) |
| 41 to 45 | 7 (23.3%) | 21 (70.0%) | 2 (6.7%) | 30 (100.0%) |
| 36 to 40 | 3 (10.3%) | 21 (72.4%) | 5 (17.2%) | 29 (100.0%) |
| 29 to 35 | 7 (15.9%) | 31 (70.5%) | 6 (13.6%) | 44 (100.0%) |
| 24 to 28 | 22 (33.8%) | 38 (58.5%) | 5 (7.7%) | 65 (100.0%) |
| Total | 46 (24.9%) | 117 (63.2%) | 22 (11.9%) | 185 (100.0%) |

Perhaps because they experienced better learning conditions, more of the respondents among the two younger cohorts reported less difficulty in learning some of the less demanding aspects of the foreign language such as: listening to news broadcasts ($\chi^2 = 11.43$, df = 4, p = 0.0221), reading simple instructions ($\chi^2 = 16.5$, df = 8, p = 0.0358), reading newspaper articles ($\chi^2 = 19.94$, df = 8, p = 0.0106) and writing a simple letter ($\chi^2 = 33.22$, df = 12, p = 0.0009). They also rated their ability to converse ($\chi^2 = 13.69$, df = 4, p = 0.0083), to make a speech ($\chi^2 = 15.68$, df = 8, p = 0.0472), to listen to news broadcasts ($\chi^2 = 10.48$, df = 4, p = 0.0331), to read simple instructions ($\chi^2 = 15.67$, df = 8, p = 0.0474) and to write a simple letter ($\chi^2 = 33.64$, df = 12, p = 0.0008) in the foreign language a little more highly. The group aged 36 to 40 is an occasional anomaly to this general trend, which could be related to the fact that anything foreign was largely disallowed during the Cultural Revolution.

To summarize, the experience of different age groups reflects the increasing policy emphasis on learning the first foreign language. The survey statistics indicate that English has been the most important foreign language in China from around 1960, except during part of the Cultural Revolution, and the post-1978 years have been particularly conducive to learning. In the light of the slight increase in confidence in using their foreign language among the younger learners, the policy is bearing fruit. It is encouraging that 45.6 % of the respondents in the youngest cohort were even ready to use the foreign language when conversing with their friends even after the completion of their education ($\chi^2 = 13.74$, df = 4, p = 0.0082). This percentage suggests a promising picture for future cohorts from similar backgrounds.

## *Dialect effects in learning the first foreign language: Non-foreign-language specialists*

While the effects according to the age of the respondents were expected since there were changes in the foreign language policy over a period of time, the few differences relating to the respondents' first dialect were less expected. Respondents with a northern dialect as their first dialect seemed to be slightly more open to learning their first foreign language in some ways.

Northern dialect respondents were more willing to use the foreign language when conversing with their classmates at university, at least sometimes ($\chi^2 = 4.64$, df = 1, p = 0.0312); 62.5% of them did so as compared to 45.8% of southern dialect speakers doing so (Table 3.13). Such readiness extended to their interaction with unspecified conversational partners ($\chi^2 = 7.07$, df = 1, p = 0.0078). This openness might be related to the fact that northern dialect speakers inhabit a greater area of China and Putonghua, the national dialect with an assured status, is a northern dialect. Hence, northern dialect speakers might not feel the threat to their own dialects in the face of competition from other languages (Wardhaugh, 1987; Robins & Uhlenbeck, 1991) as much as southern dialect speakers do. They may also have more language learning energy to spare as their own northern dialect is more similar to Putonghua. In the southern dialect region, there are several groups of southern dialects and their speakers are more likely to cling to their dialects as a mark of identity.

**Table 3.13  How dialect affected respondents' use of the foreign language with classmates outside the classroom at university**

| First dialect | Number of respondents (Percentage) | | | |
|---|---|---|---|---|
| | *Usually* | *Sometimes* | *Not at all* | *Total* |
| Northern dialect | 7 (5.1%) | 78 (57.4%) | 51 (37.5%) | 136 (100.0%) |
| Southern dialect | 2 (2.9%) | 30 (42.9%) | 38 (54.3%) | 70 (100.0%) |
| Total | 9 (4.4%) | 108 (52.4%) | 89 (43.2%) | 206 (100.0%) |

Note: 'Usually' and 'Sometimes' were pooled together in the Loglinear Analysis because the number of respondents for one cell was too small.

More northern dialect respondents also practised by themselves more often with tapes and materials than southern dialect speakers when learning the foreign language ($\chi^2 = 6.83$, df = 2, p = 0.0329) (Table 3.14).

More of them watched television in the foreign language more often when learning the foreign language ($\chi^2 = 3.93$, df = 1, p = 0.0474); 86.3% of them did so as compared to 73.4% of southern dialect speakers engaging in such an activity (Table 3.15).

**Table 3.14 How dialect affected respondents' use of tapes and materials in the foreign language**

| First dialect | Number of respondents (Percentage) | | | |
|---|---|---|---|---|
| | *Very often* | *Sometimes* | *Not at all* | *Total* |
| Northern dialect | 72 (55.8%) | 55 (42.6%) | 2 (1.6%) | 129 (100.0%) |
| Southern dialect | 29 (40.8%) | 37 (52.1%) | 5 (7.0%) | 71 (100.0%) |
| Total | 101 (50.5%) | 92 (46.0%) | 7 (3.5%) | 200 (200.0%) |

**Table 3.15 How dialect affected respondents' television watching in the foreign language**

| First dialect | Number of respondents (Percentage) | | | |
|---|---|---|---|---|
| | *Very often* | *Sometimes* | *Not at all* | *Total* |
| Northern dialect | 13 (11.1%) | 88 (75.2%) | 16 (13.7%) | 117 (100.0%) |
| Southern dialect | 5 (7.8%) | 42 (65.6%) | 17 (26.6%) | 64 (100.0%) |
| Total | 18 (9.9%) | 130 (71.8%) | 33 (18.2%) | 181 (100.0%) |

Note: 'Very often' and 'Sometimes' were pooled together in the Loglinear Analysis because the number of respondents for one cell was too small.

Perhaps because the northern dialect respondents were more open to speaking the foreign language and made more use of tapes and television, more of them expressed confidence about learning the pronunciation of the foreign language ($\chi^2 = 4.92$, df = 2, p = 0.0854); 37.7% of them rated the learning of foreign language pronunciation easy while only 24.7% of the southern dialect speakers did so (Table 3.16).

**Table 3.16 How dialect affected respondents' rating of difficulty in learning pronunciation**

| First dialect | Number of respondents (Percentage) | | | | |
|---|---|---|---|---|---|
| | *Easy* | *Neutral* | *Difficult* | *Did not use the foreign language in this way* | *Total* |
| Northern dialect | 50 (37.0%) | 60 (44.4%) | 25 (18.5%) | 0 (0.0%) | 135 (100.0%) |
| Southern dialect | 18 (24.7%) | 33 (45.2%) | 21 (28.8%) | 1 (1.4%) | 73 (100.0%) |
| Total | 68 (32.7%) | 93 (44.7%) | 46 (22.1%) | 1 (0.5%) | 208 (100.0%) |

Note: 'Difficult' and 'Did not use' were pooled together in the Loglinear Analysis because the number of respondents for some cells was too small.

As a result, more northern dialect respondents rated their pronunciation ($\chi^2 = 11.43$, df = 2, p = 0.0033) slightly better. Whether northern dialect speakers rated themselves better in pronunciation because they were more confident or whether they became more confident because they really achieved better results needs further investigation; the truth probably goes both ways as the relationship between attitude, motivation and achievement is probably interactive (Ellis, 1994, pp. 514–515).

## Location effects in learning the first foreign language: Non-foreign-language specialists

Respondents who grew up in the coastal region experienced better conditions in learning their first foreign language in a few ways.

More respondents in the coastal region began learning to speak the foreign language in primary school than those residing in the interior ($\chi^2 = 7.53$, df = 2, p = 0.0232). A similar pattern was found for learning the written form of the foreign language ($\chi^2 = 8.41$, df = 2, p = 0.0149) (Table 3.17).

**Table 3.17  How location affected the time respondents began learning the foreign language**

| Language ability learnt | Birth-place location | Number of respondents (Percentage) | | | | |
|---|---|---|---|---|---|---|
| | | From primary school | From secondary school | From university | At work | Total |
| Speaking | Coastal | 12 (14.1%) | 62 (72.9%) | 10 (11.8%) | 1 (1.2%) | 85 (100.0%) |
| | Interior | 6 (4.7%) | 99 (78.0%) | 18 (14.2%) | 4 (3.1%) | 127 (100.0%) |
| | Total | 18 (8.5%) | 161 (75.9%) | 28 (13.2%) | 5 (2.4%) | 212 (100.0%) |
| Writing | Coastal | 13 (15.3%) | 57 (67.1%) | 14 (16.5%) | 1 (1.2%) | 85 (100.0%) |
| | Interior | 5 (3.9%) | 103 (80.5%) | 17 (13.3%) | 3 (2.3%) | 128 (100.0%) |
| | Total | 18 (8.5%) | 160 (75.1%) | 31 (14.6%) | 4 (1.9%) | 213 (100.0%) |

Note: No respondents began learning before primary school. 'From university' and 'At work' were pooled together in the Loglinear Analysis because the number of respondents for some cells was too small.

Another interesting location effect relates to whether anyone at home would speak the foreign language with the respondents when they were learning the language. Only a small percentage from both groups (9.5% and 8.1%) had someone at home using the foreign language with them. But the two groups differed in the reasons for non-use of the foreign language at home. For respondents from the interior, the main reason (67.5%) was that no one at home knew the foreign language while they were learning it ($\chi^2 = 7.66$, df = 2, p = 0.0217) (Table 3.18).

More respondents growing up in the coastal region also rated their ability to make a speech ($\chi^2 = 6.32$, df = 2, p = 0.0424), to listen to news broadcasts

**Table 3.18  How location affected the home support respondents had**

| Birthplace location | Number of respondents (Percentage) | | | | Total |
|---|---|---|---|---|---|
| | Foreign language used | | Foreign language not used because | | |
| | Quite often at home | Occasionally with at least one family member | Family members preferred Chinese | No family member knew the foreign language | |
| Coastal | 0 (0.0%) | 8 (9.5%) | 35 (41.7%) | 41 (48.8%) | 84 (100.0%) |
| Interior | 0 (0.0%) | 10 (8.1%) | 30 (24.4%) | 83 (67.5%) | 123 (100.0%) |
| Total | 0 (0.0%) | 18 (8.7%) | 65 (31.4%) | 129 (59.9%) | 207 (100.0%) |

Note: 'Quite often' and 'Occasionally' were pooled together in the Loglinear Analysis because the number of respondents for some cells was too small.

($\chi^2 = 11.46$, df = 2, p = 0.0032) and to read academic and technical materials ($\chi^2 = 9.28$, df = 3, p = 0.02579) in the foreign language a little more highly. Location effects for more interactive or writing abilities were not found. Respondents from the coastal region also reported more current use of the foreign language in informal contexts such as conversing with their friends ($\chi^2 = 4.64$, df = 1, p = 0.0312), writing letters to their friends ($\chi^2 = 8.67$, df = 1, p = 0.0032) and interaction at shops or restaurants ($\chi^2 = 11.38$, df = 1, p = 0.0007 for oral interaction; and $\chi^2 = 7.71$, df = 1, p = 0.0055 for the use of the written form). Location effects for current use of the foreign language in more formal contexts were not found.

To summarize, for non-foreign-language specialists, the most notable differences in learner experience are differences relating to their age corresponding to the changes in policy though a few effects relating to the learners' first dialect or where they were born were also found. On the whole, younger learners experienced better learning conditions. Northern dialect speakers did a few independent oral learning activities a little more and more learners from the coastal region began learning the foreign language from primary school.

Table 3.19 is an overview of how non-foreign-language specialists rated their first foreign language abilities. Most of them thought their abilities were either 'Not good' or just 'Passable'. More respondents rated themselves at least 'Passable' or better on the less demanding tasks such as pronunciation (72.1%), reading simple instructions (81.4%), reading newspaper articles (66.3%) and writing a simple letter (69.2%) but few were satisfied with their other abilities. Only very few respondents not specializing in the foreign language considered themselves 'Passable' or better on skills like: making a speech (15.5%), listening to news broadcasts (15.5%) and writing academic and technical papers (14.8%) but then about a third of them did not seem to have to perform these activities in the foreign language.

**Table 3.19  Respondents' ratings of their abilities in their first foreign language**

| Ability | Number of respondents (Percentage) | | | | | |
|---|---|---|---|---|---|---|
| | Excellent or Very good | Good | Passable | Not good | Did not use this ability | Total |
| Pronunciation | 8 (3.8%) | 32 (15.4%) | 110 (52.9%) | 54 (26.0%) | 4 (1.9%) | 208 (100.0%) |
| Conversation* | 5 (2.4%) | 10 (4.8%) | 73 (35.1%) | 114 (54.8%) | 6 (2.9%) | 208 (100.0%) |
| Making a speech* | 0 (0.0%) | 7 (3.4%) | 24 (11.6%) | 110 (53.1%) | 66 (31.9%) | 207 (100.0%) |
| Listening to news broadcasts* | 3 (1.4%) | 7 (3.4%) | 71 (34.1%) | 112 (53.8%) | 15 (7.2%) | 208 (100.0%) |
| Listening to academic/ technical lectures* | 2 (1.0%) | 6 (2.9%) | 24 (11.6%) | 116 (56.0%) | 59 (28.5%) | 207 (100.0%) |
| Reading simple instructions | 17 (8.1%) | 54 (25.6%) | 100 (47.4%) | 31 (14.7%) | 9 (4.3%) | 211 (100.0%) |
| Reading newspaper articles* | 6 (2.8%) | 25 (11.8%) | 109 (51.7%) | 57 (27.0%) | 14 (6.6%) | 211 (100.0%) |
| Reading academic/ technical materials* | 5 (2.4%) | 15 (7.1%) | 57 (27.1%) | 90 (42.9%) | 43 (20.5%) | 210 (100.0%) |
| Writing a simple letter | 6 (2.8%) | 31 (14.7%) | 109 (51.7%) | 38 (18.0%) | 27 (12.8%) | 211 (100.0%) |
| Writing academic/ technical papers* | 0 (0.0%) | 6 (2.9%) | 25 (11.9%) | 102 (48.6%) | 77 (36.7%) | 210 (100.0%) |

* No respondents rated themselves 'Excellent' on this ability.

## Foreign language specialists learning the first foreign language

An analysis of the learning experience of foreign language specialists shows that their experience was largely similar to that of non-foreign-language specialists, particularly in secondary school. However, more foreign language specialists started learning the foreign language earlier; 18.7% of them learnt how to speak and 16.6% of them learnt how to write the foreign language in primary school or earlier as compared to 8.5% of the non-foreign-language respondents who did so. As expected of foreign language majors, more of their foreign language teachers at university used the target language in class. The most interesting differences are found in what the learners did outside the classroom to learn better (Table 3.20).

Except for talking with classmates during secondary school-days, which both groups did not do very much, foreign language specialists engaged in all the learning activities outside the classroom (as listed in Table 3.20) more

**Table 3.20  Relative use of different activities to learn outside the classroom**

| Learning activity in the foreign language outside the classroom | Non-foreign-language specialists n = 214 | | Foreign language specialists n = 193 | |
|---|---|---|---|---|
| | Learners using this activity* | Ranking of relative use | Learners using this activity* | Ranking of relative use |
| *Language comprehension and practice with tapes* | | | | |
| Checking the dictionary | 98.5% | 1 | 98.9% | 3 |
| Practising with tapes and materials | 96.5% | 2 | 98.9% | 3 |
| Listening to the radio | 88.1% | 3 | 98.9% | 3 |
| Reading books | 88.1% | 3 | 99.5% | 2 |
| Reading newspapers or magazines | 86.9% | 5 | 100.0% | 1 |
| Watching television | 81.8% | 6 | 87.6% | 11 |
| Listening to songs and singing songs | 79.7% | 7 | 94.3% | 8 |
| Seeing movies/watching video tapes | 73.3% | 8 | 92.7% | 10 |
| *Language production* | | | | |
| Conversing with unspecified others | 66.5% | 9 | 96.6% | 7 |
| Talking with classmates at university | 56.8% | 10 | 97.9% | 6 |
| Writing letters | 50.6% | 11 | 93.7% | 9 |
| Talking with classmates at secondary school# | 31.8% | 12 | 34.7% | 12 |
| Talking with a family member at home | 8.7% | 13 | 14.8% | 13 |

\* Including percentages from 'Very often' and 'Sometimes' categories. See Table 3.21.
# Not significantly different on this activity.

often ($p < 0.0004$ for talking with someone at home and $p < 0.0001$ for all other activities). The differences between non-foreign-language specialists and foreign language specialists are particularly salient in language production activities such as conversing with unspecified others (66.5% for non-foreign-language specialists and 96.6% for foreign language specialists), talking with classmates at university (56.8% and 97.9% respectively) and writing letters (50.6% and 93.7% respectively). That the two groups should be so different in talking with classmates at university is particularly interesting when they both did not do so very much during secondary school (31.8% and 34.7% respectively, which are not statistically different).

Even on the language comprehension activities and practice with tapes, for which the total percentages of learners using an activity are less obviously different between the two groups, there are still significant differences in the finer details ($p < 0.0001$); more foreign language specialists did these activities more often (Table 3.21).

That foreign language specialists seem to have engaged in more learning outside the classroom than non-foreign-language specialists concurs with the

**Table 3.21  Use of language comprehension activities and practice with tapes**

| Learning activity in the foreign-language outside the classroom | Non-foreign-language specialists n = 214 | | Foreign language specialists n = 193 | |
|---|---|---|---|---|
| | Using this activity very often | Using this activity sometimes | Using this activity very often | Using this activity sometimes |
| Checking the dictionary | 69.5% | 28.9% | 87.4% | 11.6% |
| Practising with tapes and materials | 50.5% | 46.0% | 78.1% | 20.9% |
| Listening to the radio | 22.7% | 65.4% | 58.3% | 40.6% |
| Reading books | 24.9% | 63.2% | 76.5% | 23.0% |
| Reading newspapers or magazines | 20.8% | 66.1% | 56.7% | 43.3% |
| Watching television | 9.9% | 71.8% | 27.0% | 60.7% |
| Listening to songs and singing songs | 13.4% | 66.3% | 27.8% | 66.5% |
| Seeing movies/watching video tapes | 9.3% | 64.0% | 27.0% | 65.7% |

current emphasis on learner responsibility in successful learning. As expected, upon graduation, foreign language specialists rated their own abilities more highly and used the language more frequently, except in the domain of interaction at shops and restaurants.

## Learning a second foreign language

Learning the first foreign language, which was English for over 90% of the respondents, has been the focus for the last forty years. But the time will come when more attention will be given to other foreign languages. Even now, Chinese students at university level may take an *er⁴wai⁴* (second foreign language). If they are majoring in foreign languages, they are required to do so. Those majoring in other subjects may still choose to do so as the second foreign language is useful for their disciplinary studies or their future work, for example, in international trade.

   Of the 222 respondents who did not specialize in foreign languages, whose experience is more indicative of the learning experience of the average university graduate in China, 179 (80.6%) of them did not learn a second foreign language. Of those who did so among this group, 29 (80.5%) of them learnt it only after secondary school (70.7% at university and 9.8% when they started working). The languages commonly learnt as second foreign languages by this group were Japanese (42.9%), German (16.6%), Russian (16.6%), English (11.9%) and French (7.1%). Most of the non-foreign-language specialists rated their competence in their second foreign language as 'Not good' and no longer used their second foreign language.

Of the 193 foreign language specialists surveyed, 169 (87.6%) of them learnt a second foreign language (with 95.9% of the youngest cohort doing so). The choice of the second foreign language appears to have changed through the cohorts ($\chi^2 = 37.56$, df = 24, p <0.0384) (Table 3.22). For the oldest group, the most popular languages were French (38.5%), Japanese (23.1%) and English (11.5%). At that time, most of them would have been required to learn Russian as their first foreign language. French became particularly popular for a while (54.5%) in the cohort aged between 36 and 40. For the cohort aged 29 to 35, Japanese and French were just as popular (35.8% and 34.0% respectively). For the youngest cohort, French and Japanese were also popular (39.6% and 27.1% respectively) but the third most popular language was German (18.8%), because English had become the first foreign language by then; in fact, this was the case even for an earlier cohort aged 41 to 45. It is also interesting to see a small percentage of the two younger cohorts (7.5% and 8.3% respectively) learning Russian again, perhaps reflecting the mending of relations between China and Russia from the mid-1980s.

The apparent difference in the most popular second foreign language between non-foreign-language specialists and foreign language specialists is interesting. For the non-foreign-language specialists, it was Japanese, perhaps because of its instrumental value in computer science and trade. For the foreign language specialists, the most popular second foreign language was French, perhaps because it is useful for foreign relations with Europe, the diplomatic track being one of the target career paths for foreign language specialists in China.

Table 3.22  Choice of second foreign languages by foreign language specialists

| Age group | French | Japanese | German | Russian | English | Another language | No second foreign language | Total |
|---|---|---|---|---|---|---|---|---|
| 46–50 | 10 (38.5%) | 6 (23.1%) | 0 (0.0%) | 1 (3.8%) | 3 (11.5%) | 1 (3.8%) | 5 (19.2%) | 26 (100.0%) |
| 41–45 | 11 (37.9%) | 4 (13.8%) | 6 (20.7%) | 1 (3.4%) | 1 (3.4%) | 1 (3.4%) | 5 (17.2%) | 29 (100.0%) |
| 36–40 | 18 (54.5%) | 3 (9.1%) | 1 (3.0%) | 1 (3.0%) | 1 (3.0%) | 2 (6.1%) | 7 (21.2%) | 33 (100.0%) |
| 29–35 | 18 (34.0%) | 19 (35.8%) | 7 (13.2%) | 4 (7.5%) | 0 (0.0%) | 0 (0.0%) | 5 (9.4%) | 53 (100.0%) |
| 24–28 | 19 (39.6%) | 13 (27.1%) | 9 (18.8%) | 4 (8.3%) | 1 (2.1%) | 0 (0.0%) | 2 (4.2%) | 48 (100.0%) |
| Total | 76 (40.2%) | 45 (23.8%) | 23 (12.2%) | 11 (5.8%) | 6 (3.2%) | 4 (2.1%) | 24 (12.7%) | 189 (100.0%) |

Most foreign language specialists (86.3%) began learning their second foreign language at university. They were not impressed with their own second foreign language competence; self-ratings of their various skills fell mostly in the 'Not good' or 'Passable' categories. But unlike the non-foreign-language specialists, about a third of them still used their second foreign language at work; 33.9% did so sometimes and 2.4% did so very often. A smaller number even used their second foreign language when conversing with friends; 10.4% did so sometimes and 0.6% did so very often.

## Summary and discussion

The main results on the survey of 415 learners can be summarized as follows:

**Non-foreign-language specialists**: While it must be emphasized that the survey sample of university graduates represents the best possible learning scenario, the results as a whole do indicate that the experience of learners kept pace with language education policy trends. Many more learners learnt English rather than Russian as their foreign language from around 1960 and cohorts entering secondary school from 1978 onwards did experience more favourable learning conditions for learning their first foreign language both in terms of classroom support as well as the learning activities outside the classroom. Within these broad historical trends, northern dialect speakers seem to have a slightly easier time in terms of mastering the pronunciation of the foreign language. There must be a host of reasons behind this phenomenon such as phonological differences between native dialects and the target foreign language, the northern dialect speakers' general openness to the foreign language and their readiness to use certain kinds of technical support a little more. But it is also possible that because their native dialect is more similar to Putonghua, the standard dialect, they have less learning to do on that front. How many phonological systems an average learner can handle concurrently during a learning period with ease and confidence is worth further investigation. In addition to age and dialect effects, some coastal effects were also observed. Learners growing up in coastal areas seem to have an advantage because coastal areas are more readily exposed to international interaction and hence there are more opportunities to use the foreign language upon completion of learning, which tends to be motivating.

**Foreign language specialists**: The most exciting finding in the comparison of the learning experience of foreign language specialists with other learners in China is that, in addition to much greater class time during the university curricula as foreign language majors, foreign language specialists tend to do a lot more learning in the foreign language in various ways outside the classroom as well. This argues for the perspective that there is a certain degree of self-selection in the development of successful language learners. Because they choose to do more learning on their own, they achieve better results and because they achieve better results, they do more learning; in other words, achievement, investment of learner energy and motivation are interactive (Ellis, 1994, pp. 514–515). This perspective is empowering in the sense that whether learners can succeed in language learning depends, to some extent, on whether they choose to do so.

**A second foreign language**: While the learning of English as a first foreign language is accepted as being necessary and useful by learners in China, the requirement for foreign language specialists to learn a second foreign language has been questioned. During my field trips, some students expressed their doubts about the usefulness of such an undertaking, particularly in the interior regions. I am also humbled by the fact that university teachers in foreign language departments in China have to pass a second foreign language test before they can be promoted, a feat I am unable to perform. Unless students intend to choose international diplomacy or trade as their career, a second foreign language may not be necessary. It is worth recommending that for those who intend to be teachers, it is more feasible for them to undergo training integrating the learning of the target foreign language with language pedagogy, rather than requiring them to devote precious learning time and energy to acquire limited competence in a second foreign language, so limited that they are likely to abandon it upon completion of the requirement.

## Four Case Histories

To complement the survey presented in the last section illustrating the overall experience of Han Chinese learners, case interviews of thirty-five Han Chinese learners were conducted on their total language experience (see Chapter 1, 'The Language Education in China Project', pp. 10–17). Interviewees were selected according to their age, first dialect and birthplace location. This section presents excerpts from four learning histories selected from different age groups (Lam, 2002): three with a northern dialect background and one with a southern dialect as his first dialect; two from the coastal region and two from the interior; two from the foreign language profession and two from other teaching posts. The learners were interviewed in Putonghua. Each interview took about an hour. In the following excerpts, the interviewee's age was that in 2000. All names are pseudonyms. The interviewer's comments are in square brackets.

The main issue in reviewing these learning biographies is whether individual experiences were consistent with policy trends and survey findings: that younger learners and those growing up in coastal regions experienced more favourable learning conditions. What else contributed to differences in individual experiences? Secondly, although the focus of this discussion is

English language learning, it is useful to consider the learning of English in the context of the total multilingual experience of learners (see Chapter 1, 'A Multilingual Approach to Language Education', pp. 17–18). To this end, some information about the interviewees' experience of other languages is also included. We could consider, for example, how important the learning of English was even to learners not intending to be English teachers.

The four learners to be considered are:

1. Deng: Southern Chinese from the coastal region, male, aged 45, a logic/philosophy teacher
2. Xue: Northern Chinese from the interior region, female, aged 44, an English teacher
3. Ling: Northern Chinese from the coastal region, female, aged 37, an English teacher
4. Hua: Northern Chinese from the interior region, female, aged 25, a Chinese teacher

## Deng (Southern Coastal Chinese Interviewee 10, male, aged 45, a logic/philosophy teacher)

**Background**: I was born in 1954 in Shanghai. I grew up speaking Shanghainese and Putonghua. In 1961, I started studying in a primary school. When I finished primary school in 1966, the Cultural Revolution broke out and new students were not admitted to secondary school. In 1967, I was admitted to secondary school but, in those days, school did not mean many classes. We worked in a factory and then a village. When I was sixteen, they sent me to Guangde where I worked as a farmer. In 1978, I went to university in Anhui and graduated in philosophy in 1982. I then taught at a secondary school. In 1983, I went to Wuhan to do my master's. I came to Beijing in 1986. I have been teaching logic and Putonghua at this university [in Beijing] ever since.

**English learning history**: From Primary 4, I already had English at school, two or three lessons a week. After primary school, my education was interrupted. Though lessons were unsystematic in secondary school, I was still learning by myself. I did some reading but I did not learn much. Later, in graduate school, I also studied English. But when I watch English television or read an English newspaper now, my comprehension is very bad. My listening is especially poor. When I was at university, we did not have cassette tapes. We had the big reels, the type used in showing movies. In 1980, we had the new tape recorders but I did not use them. When I became a graduate student, I used them but not frequently. There were very few foreign teachers; they hardly ever taught us, the non-English majors; they usually taught the English majors.

**Another foreign language**: I chose to study a second foreign language, Russian. Since I was learning English and Russian at the same time, my energies were not focused. I did not learn either language well.

**Time spent outside class**: I have been learning English for almost thirty years. I am very ashamed I have not learnt it well. In primary school, I learnt mostly in class. Outside class, I spent very little time — about fifteen to thirty minutes a day. After primary school, I would pick up an English dictionary or textbook often but each time, I only read it for a little while. So I did not improve much. At university, I definitely spent more time learning English. When I became a graduate student, I spent at least two hours every day, reading and listening to English broadcasts. It was partly because I had to sit for examinations.

**Learning materials**: It is very important when learning a language that we should use the books from that country. The textbooks in China in those days were written by Chinese people. Though we were trying to learn English, the content was about China — that was a huge problem. For example, there was a question about what newspapers we read and the answer was *People's Daily* [a direct translation from *Ren² Min² Ri⁴ Bao⁴*]. You should say instead, 'I am reading *New York Times*.' Even if you want to make it more Chinese, you should still say, 'I am reading *China's Daily*'. You should not say 'I am reading *People's Daily*' because there is no such English newspaper. In secondary school, some passages in the English textbook were just newspaper articles on the Cultural Revolution; the speeches of Chairman Mao were translated into English. Of course, we learnt some words from those passages but when you translate Chairman Mao's words into English, it is not everyday English.

**Environment**: A language environment is very important. If you let me go to London now, I may 'think half a day' before I know how to ask for directions. Perhaps people can understand me eventually but they may think 'Aiyah, your English is very bad.' But students here can learn everyday Chinese in half a year. So if you let me go to London or Hong Kong for half a year, I can improve my oral English a lot.

## Xue (Northern Interior Chinese Interviewee 30, female, aged 44, an English teacher)

**Background**: I was born in 1956 in a city in the Inner Mongolia Autonomous Region near Yinchuan. From birth, I was speaking the local Chinese dialect at home but from primary school, the teacher was speaking Putonghua. I went to primary school in 1962 and secondary school in 1973. From 1973 to 1975, I was 'sent to the village'; I taught in three or four village schools simultaneously. From 1975 to 1978, I came here [a university in the northern interior] to study English as my major. I stayed to teach in the Foreign Languages Department. In 1990, I was sent to England for my master's. I returned in 1991.

**Late start**: I learnt English in the classroom formally and rather late. In secondary school, what I learnt was Russian but I have forgotten all of it. From university at nineteen, I started learning English, every day in the classroom. In those days, the 1970s, conditions were not good. There were no learning materials. There was nothing. The tape recorder was the largest. Fifteen people shared one recorder. We looked at the reel turning. The teaching materials were written by Chinese people. We practised sentence structures, memorized them, memorized grammar, memorized the reading passages. No books to read. At last, my teacher lent me a book, *English 900*. I treated that like a rare treasure. Every day, I memorized those nine hundred sentences almost until I graduated in 1978.

**Economic reforms and books**: Then the economic reforms came and books also came in around that time. After that, I came across materials like *Essential English*. The earliest materials from overseas that I came across were *Linguaphone* materials. Both sets of materials were from England. After that, it was *English For Today*, American materials.

**First foreign teachers**: In 1979, the first batch of foreign teachers (*wai¹ jiao¹*) came to our university — two Americans. They came to teach the teachers. I was the youngest teacher then. The old professors with white hair all went to that class. Every day, we had class. I felt that was the time when my English, especially my listening and speaking, improved especially quickly. The foreign teachers stayed for two years. I studied under them all that while. Before that, I had not seen foreigners; I had not listened to them; I had not spoken to them.

**Short courses at Xian**: Then I was sent to Xian for further training. The British organized those short courses. They just started then — in 1982. I was there from February to July for half a year. I felt I learnt a lot. In the morning, we had lessons. In the afternoon, we sang English songs. My English improved quite fast. In 1986, I was sent to Xian again. This time, I taught listening, extensive reading, intensive reading and I learnt on my own.

**Sino-British exchange**: In 1989, there was a joint project between the Chinese and the British. Two British teachers came every year and they recruited two Chinese teachers to be sent to England as their counterparts. The project was to organize training in applied linguistics for young teachers from the northern interior. All over the country, there were twenty-odd such projects. The five-year project was called the Advanced Teacher Training Course. I worked with the British for a year. Then I was sent to England. In England, I stayed in a house with a Malaysian, a South American ... We could only communicate in English. After a year, I returned to work with the British again. Because the British teachers did half the teaching and I did half, we had a lot we needed to discuss. Almost every day, we had to discuss the progress of the students, the development of the course ... and I had to write the reports on our project. So my English improved. It was a lot of work but I felt happy.

## Ling (Northern Coastal Chinese Interviewee 4, female, aged 37, an English teacher)

**Background**: I was born in 1963 in a village in Hebei not too far from Beijing. My home Hebei dialect is very like Putonghua, almost identical. So I did not have to learn Putonghua in the classroom. The only language I had to study formally was English. I also learnt a little French and German when I went to university.

**Teachers' College**: Before university, I was first trained to teach science subjects in a teachers' college in Hebei. At the college, I listened to radio a lot. The channel I listened to most often was *Voice of America*. I also listened to *BBC* [British Broadcasting Corporation]. Upon graduation, I taught English at a junior secondary school for three years. I think those years were very crucial for my improvement in English because I was learning as I was teaching.

**English at university**: From 1984 when I went to university in Hebei, I have been exposed to English every day. During my undergraduate days, I read many books — *The Woman in White* and *Treasure Island*, the simplified versions. My character is an advantage in my learning. I have never been afraid to speak up. When I went to university, many of us were not good at speaking. In secondary school, they did not teach oral English. Most of my university classmates could not speak up. But I definitely could. I just tried my best to say what I could. From the beginning, I have liked this English language. I could have chosen another major but I felt English was good, so I chose English. It was not because I thought that in future a foreign language would be useful or would get me a job. After university, I did my master's in Heilongjiang and worked for a year before I did my PhD in Beijing.

**First contact with foreigners**: The first time I spoke to a foreigner I was 22. I could not understand anything. After that, I decided to make use of opportunities to communicate with native speakers. That was how I differed from other learners. For others, whatever the teacher taught in class, if there were any tapes, they would listen to them. But I asked myself, 'I had already listened to that so many times in class. Why couldn't I understand?' I realized it was not enough to listen to tapes or to the teacher. I needed exposure to foreigners and communication with them. When I realized that, I felt good. I had found my bearings and knew what I should do.

**Giving up overseas training**: But I did not go abroad. There was an opportunity to go to Harvard for a year but I was also offered a PhD place at [a university in Beijing]. I told myself there would be other opportunities for me to visit Harvard but if I did not take the PhD place then, I might never get another chance. So I gave up Harvard. When I graduated with my PhD in 1997, I came here [another university in Beijing] to teach in the Department of Foreign Languages. Last year, I had another chance to go abroad but I could not leave because of some family matter.

**Talk like a book**: When I first came to this university to teach, I wanted to make sure my foundation was good. Because I am teaching English, I use it all the time but I still feel I have a problem. It is not that I am not fluent and I do not feel I am intermediate but I talk like a book.

## Hua (Northern Interior Chinese Interviewee 29, female, aged 25, a Chinese teacher)

**Background**: Born in 1975, I grew up in a city in Guangxi. From 1992 to 1996, I went to university in Nanning. In 1996, I moved to Lanzhou to do graduate studies. I now teach in the Chinese department here [a university in the northern interior]. I spoke the Guiliu dialect from birth at home but because our home was in a factory compound and there were many workers from other provinces, I started speaking Putonghua from very young.

**English in school-days**: I started learning English in class from Secondary 1. (I also studied Japanese for a year in graduate school.) Teachers of English varied in how much English they used in class. Some, especially the university graduates, used English for the full lesson. Others, like those in Secondary 1, could not teach in English. When I was in Secondary 1, conditions for exposure to English were not very good. The opportunities I had came from cassette tapes from my family. I remember too that on CCTV Channel 4 [a government television channel], there were some news and travel programmes in English. I watched them often but did not understand much.

**Campus radio**: Before university, I did not focus on improving listening; the university entrance examination did not test listening. After I entered university, the Band 4 and Band 6 examinations [national examinations] would test listening. So in class, teachers would let us listen to some tapes. I bought some tapes too. The university also prepared some campus radio programmes in English. Each of us had a radio; it was not too expensive, about forty *yuans* [in Renminbi, the Chinese currency]. When we entered university, it was compulsory for us to buy it. We needed it for the Band 4, Band 6 examinations. I remember going to school in the morning — everyone was wearing earphones listening. At night around 8 or 9 pm, there was also a programme.

**English Corner, movies and books**: At university, there was more variety in the learning mode. We could go to the English Corner on Friday night. We could also see foreign movies quite often on campus. I also chose a course, 'English movie appreciation'. The subtitles were painted over to see how much you could understand. In comparison with secondary school, there were more reading materials.

**Examinations**: At university, I studied English for two years. After that, I was still learning by myself because I wanted to pass Band 6, not just Band 4. I passed Band 6 in my third year. It seems that we learn English to pass

**Photo 15** A lake at Guangxi Nationalities College. Behind the trees is the Department of Foreign Languages.

**Photo 16** An advertisement about an English drama competition at Guangxi Nationalities College.

examinations. In secondary school, it is to pass the university entrance examination. At university, it is to pass Band 4/Band 6. As a graduate student, it is to meet the graduate studies requirement. Since learning English is mainly for passing examinations, we do not read much. Near examinations, we do a lot of exercises.

**Motivated to learn**: In secondary school, I was not very aware of how I learnt English. At university, the English material I was exposed to enabled me to become more aware of my learning. The only time I really felt I wanted to learn English was when I was a graduate student; the pressure from English was not so great then. I had already passed Band 6. So the graduate English examination was easier. Around me, many classmates had very good English. Many of them wanted to go overseas and had to prepare for the TOEFL [Test of English as a Foreign Language] and the GRE [Graduate Record Examination]. So their English was very good. I felt I should also try harder. When I first went to university, I tried going to the English Corner but I was too shy. I cared very much about whether people would laugh at me. When the other person spoke, she too was very nervous. So after going twice, I stopped. But as a graduate student, I felt I should go to the English Corner because it was meaningless to learn English if I could not speak or understand it. So I went and I spoke.

## Discussion

The variation in experience in the four learning stories is consistent with policy changes and survey findings. They illustrate the growing importance of English competence in China, the different kinds of learner motivation and the interplay between learning effort and interactive opportunities. One wonders too about whether national goals in promoting English will always tally with individual purposes.

**Variation in experience and history**: The four learning histories reflect changes in policy and variation in policy implementation in different locations even within the same time period. First of all, conditions have definitely improved through the years. Younger learners, like Ling aged 37 and especially Hua aged 25, have experienced more favourable learning circumstances such as portable tape recorders, more books, campus radio, foreign movies and more openness to speaking English, for example, at English Corners. Secondly, a comparison of the experiences of the two older learners, Deng and Xue, aged 45 and 44 respectively, shows a difference between primary schooling in a coastal city and in the interior, at least for that period. Deng's exposure to English from Primary 4 testifies to the policy of introducing English from Primary 3 as a pilot scheme in some cities in the early 1960s (see 'Foreign Language Policy from 1949', pp. 71–84). Xue, one year younger, did not have any exposure to English in primary school or even secondary school, probably because she grew up in the interior while Deng grew up in Shanghai, a coastal city.

**Importance of learning English**: Though the four learners experienced different circumstances, their stories all testify to the growing importance of English in China. The two older learners, Deng and Xue, learnt Russian at some point. Xue learnt it in secondary school as her first foreign language (and did not learn English until her university days) and Deng chose to learn Russian as a second language (English being his first) at university. Xue reported having forgotten all her Russian and Deng did not learn it well. Ling, younger than Deng and Xue, learnt English as her first foreign language and a bit of French and German as well. Hua, the youngest, learnt English as her main foreign language and studied Japanese for a year as a graduate student. Their choices of foreign languages learnt are in line with the policy trends and survey statistics. Xue's university experience encapsulates particularly the sudden flurry of English Language Teaching exchange activities between China and other countries along with the economic reforms from around 1979, ushering in the period of English for modernization. Xue's and Ling's experience also point to the possibility of overseas visitorships in later years. By the time Hua, the youngest, was at university, many of her classmates wanted to go overseas and so took the TOEFL and the GRE in preparation for such. What is interesting is that all four of them, regardless of whether they intended to be teachers of English, reported caring about their English learning and competence. Deng, a teacher of logic and philosophy, expressed shame at not having learnt English well. Xue, an English teacher, treated the English book borrowed from her university teacher 'like a rare treasure'. Ling, also an English teacher, was not pleased that she 'talked like a book' in spite of her fluency and Hua, though a teacher of Chinese, set herself the goal of passing the national examination at a higher level (Band 6) although she was only required to pass the Band 4 test.

**Various kinds of motivation**: Deng and Hua both mentioned the effect of examinations, a type of extrinsic motivation, on their learning. When Deng was a graduate student, he spent at least two hours every day reading and listening to English broadcasts partly because he had to sit for examinations. Hua's experience shows a mixture of motivations. Though she said, 'It seems that we learn English to pass examinations,' she experienced a change at a time when she felt less pressure. During her graduate student days, she became interested in using English because she felt it was meaningless to learn it if she could not use it. So she went to the English Corner. She could also have been affected by her peers because around her, many 'classmates had very good English'. Hua's case shows that different kinds of motivation could affect a learner at different stages of her learning. Ling's story is interesting in that she specifically pointed out she was not instrumentally motivated in that she did not choose English because she thought that in future the language would be useful or would get her a job. She just liked the language from the beginning; in other words, she had intrinsic motivation though it appears that qualifications were not unimportant to her; between choosing to spend a year as a visiting scholar in Harvard and getting her PhD in Beijing, she chose the PhD. As for Xue, the fact that she was happy when her English improved while doing the project with the British exchange teachers shows that one of her motivations could well be resultative motivation. (See Ellis, 1994, pp. 508–517, for a review of the various types of motivation.) In learning stories not presented here, there are also other purposes for learning English. There was, for example, a monk in Xiamen who wanted to learn English to translate Buddhist sutras into English so as to convert

**Photo 17** A young monk from the monastery and temple next to Xiamen University. He was learning English to translate Buddhist sutras into English.

more people to Buddhism. Another learner from the Mulao minority group was writing a PhD dissertation in a top university in England on the social and cultural anthropological issues in the southern interior region. (See Chapter 4, 'Seven Case Histories' (pp. 155–173), for the story on his learning experience.) Among the younger English professionals, there are also those working in news agencies and international trade. How we categorize these various purposes is probably not that important since in reality learners can be affected by more than one type of motivation. It is worth noting, however, that if you ask Chinese learners the question, 'Why are you studying English?' nowadays, you will no longer get the common response of 'To serve the Revolution', which Lehmann (1975) traced to a textbook dialogue (pp. 76–77). The social psychology of English learning in China is now much more complex and kaleidoscopic and worthy of further research (Gao, 2004).

**Learning effort and interactive opportunities**: Whatever their purposes, learners in China have to invest a lot of time and effort within and outside the classroom to learn English. When they do, it is possible to learn successfully in China though English is not widely used in everyday life. Breakthroughs

**Photo 18** Lu Xun Square at Xiamen University: The English Corner where people gather to converse in English every Friday night.

in learning seem to happen at times of intense exposure and use. For some, like Xue and Ling, having to use English in their work constantly seems to have provided the opportunity for rapid improvement. Hua also forced herself to go to the English Corner. That Deng did not learn English well, though he started learning from Primary Four, could be related in some way to his not spending much time on English outside the classroom, particularly in his early years (granted that his schooling was interrupted by the Cultural Revolution, as was Xue's). Yet, even he recognized the learning effectiveness of communicative language and felt he could improve his English quickly if he went to London. He pointed out such was the advantage students could have in learning Chinese in China. Because interactive opportunities in English are not easy to come by in China, learners have to create them for themselves by practising with each other outside class, in dormitories or at the English Corners. Unless they do so, it will be difficult to make progress even if they listen to tapes and see movies frequently.

**Intercultural tension**: China is at the stage when most learners are trying to achieve some competence in English and the most urgent issues seem to focus on how to support such fervent desires to learn. But in the years to come, as resources for learning English become more available to more learners in China, intercultural tension relating to learning English may become more apparent. English learning is certainly a priority both at the level of the state and from the individual's perspective but the national motivation and the individual ones may not always be the same. This may create tension in policy implementation. For example, the state may plan to have more highly proficient teachers of English but the highly proficient ones may prefer to join the multinational companies with better employment packages in the booming Chinese cities such as Beijing, Shanghai, Guangzhou and Shenzhen. Among Hua's classmates, many wanted to go abroad; how many would return like Xue? (I should mention though that not everyone nowadays wants to go abroad. A young English teacher I met in a southern coastal city mentioned that he had relatives in North America and he could go abroad if he wanted to but his parents were not young any more and he would like to stay behind to take care of them; he also felt China was undergoing change and there would be opportunities in China too.) The state planned expansion in English learning to modernize and strengthen China but some of the learners who become good at English may love themselves more than their country. That is not to suggest, however, that learning English will make anyone a traitor to the national cause; many native English speakers also love their own country as well as the citizens of other countries. But when a foreign language assumes that much importance in a country, there are issues of inter-nationality, inter-culture and inter-identity that need to be addressed, both as a matter of policy by the state and as a matter of conscience in individuals. Between xenophobia and the worship of anything foreign, there are many viable resting points in between and it is for educators to help learners find them.

## Foreign Language Teaching in China Today

The survey results and the case histories have provided a general understanding of how English, and, to a much lesser extent, other foreign languages have been learnt in China. To find out how English and other foreign languages are now taught, discussions with heads of English or foreign language programmes at each educational level were held in four cities (not to be named to protect the privacy of the informants) from different regions:

1. Northern coastal region
2. Southern coastal region
3. Northern interior region
4. Southern interior region

The institutions visited for this purpose were the same institutions as those for finding out how Chinese is now taught (see Chapter 2, 'Teaching Chinese in China Today', pp. 59–69). The findings are now presented according to the three levels of education: primary, secondary and higher. The focus is on the teaching of English. It must be emphasized that the programmes described below are only examples, probably of the best scenarios, and so should not be taken as typical of circumstances all over China, particularly not of rural areas which tend to enjoy less advantageous conditions.

## English in primary education

All the four primary schools visited offer two semesters in a year with eighteen to twenty-two weeks in each semester, often inclusive of assessment. Lessons are forty minutes long. About 5% of the class time in primary school is devoted to learning English. On the basis of eighteen teaching weeks per semester, the total number of class hours spent on studying English in primary school ranges from 288 to 360 lessons or 192 to 240 hours. Table 3.23 provides an overview of the circumstances.

There is much variation in the delivery of the primary school English curriculum. Schools are only provided with curriculum guidelines rather than an official syllabus. Among the nine schools that provided information during my field trips or by correspondence, one starts teaching English as early as Primary 1 and two begin as late as Primary 5. The number of lessons also varies from one lesson per week to three lessons per week for different grades, with the higher grades attracting more class time for English and, in some schools, for the primary curriculum as a whole.

On the basis of discussions with primary English teachers, the following observations can be made. First, most evident is the shortage of teachers at this level. One school I visited in the southern interior only had one young teacher teaching English to all five grades from Primary 2 onwards. This shortage has to be addressed because parents are requesting schools to begin English lessons earlier. Secondly, teachers also need more support in terms of suitable reading materials; this inadequacy seems to be felt both in the coastal region and the interior. Thirdly, an interesting point mentioned by one teacher is that the school cannot start offering English from Primary 1 because students also learn *hanyu pinyin*, the alphabetical script for representing Putonghua, also from Primary 1 and will get confused if they have to attach different sounds to the same letters (Data source code: 11-024-001). Finally, according to another teacher, students are very enthusiastic in their first year of learning English but lose interest as they get older (Data source code: 222-734-007), perhaps because it is difficult to make much progress with so little class time and little support in terms of reading materials and other resources.

**Table 3.23 Teaching of English in four primary schools**

| Location of school | Coastal region | | Interior region | |
|---|---|---|---|---|
| | Northern city | Southern city | Northern city* | Southern city |
| No. of English teachers | 3 | 5 | 2 | 1 |
| Adequacy of English teachers+ | Serious shortage | No shortage | Serious shortage | Slight shortage but manageable |
| Equipment | Fully equipped# | No English library and no internet access | No language learning software or internet access | No compact disk player, compact disks, video projector or internet access |
| No. of students | 1,500 | 1,308 | 1,500 | 300 |
| No. of students per class | 44 | 52 | 50 | 35 |
| No. of lessons per week | 30 | 27 | 29.3 | 31 |
| No. of English lessons per week | 3 from Primary 4 onwards | 1 in Primary 3 and 4; 3 in Primary 5 and 6 | 2 from Primary 3 onwards | 2 from Primary 2 onwards |
| Textbooks used are published by | Education Commission of the City | Ministry of Education | Ministry of Education | Ministry of Education and commercial publishers |
| Assessment before entry | No entry test | No entry test | No entry test | No entry test |
| Assessment at the end of Primary 6 | District examination | City examination | No public examination | No public examination |
| Students' level upon graduation+: | | | | |
| Pronunciation | Passable | Excellent | Good | Passable |
| Conversation | Not too good | Very good | Good | Not too good |
| Writing letters | Not able to | Passable | Passable | Not too good |
| Listening to news broadcasts | Not able to | Not too good | Teacher does not know | Not too good |
| Reading newspapers | Not able to | Not too good | Not too good | Not too good |
| Data source code | 11-024-001 | 21-174-008 | 122-304-006 | 22-884-009 |

\* The response from the school visited was incomplete. The information for this column was provided by another school in the same region.

\# 'Fully equipped' means 'With: library, cassette recorder and tapes, video recorder and tapes, overhead projector, compact disk player and compact disks, computer and language learning software, video projector and internet access.'

+ According to the head of department.

## English in secondary education

The four secondary schools visited offer two semesters in a year with eighteen to twenty-two weeks in each semester, often inclusive of assessment. Lessons are forty-five minutes long. On the basis of eighteen teaching weeks, the total number of class hours spent on studying English in the six years of secondary school ranges from 1,080 to 1,210 lessons or 810 to 908 hours. Table 3.24 provides an overview.

From discussions with the heads of departments in the four secondary schools visited and other communication with those in five other secondary schools, it is evident that instrumental motivation to learn English is high by the time students reach secondary school. As one teacher in Beijing observed, 'Nowadays, when companies recruit new staff, the three requirements are: computer knowledge, English and a driving license.' (Data source code: 11-025-001). In the internal syllabus of the senior secondary school where he taught, teachers are reminded to help graduates attain a vocabulary of four thousand words so that 'passing the College English Band 4 Test should not be a problem' (Data source code: 11-025-001); students only have to pass this test at the end of their English course at university. Even in the interior, there is awareness of the importance of learning English well. 'Parents are especially supportive of their children learning English. Nowadays, where private tuition is concerned, the most fiery [in demand] tutors are those teaching English.' (Data source code: 12-252-005) In fact, 'because English can help students get a higher salary, they may neglect the learning of their mother tongue. So the Chinese teacher may complain.' (Data source code: 11-025-001) Unfortunately, in some secondary schools, particularly in the interior, the number of students in a class is often fifty-plus and may even be as high as seventy (Data source code: 12-252-005), which makes it difficult for students to have much opportunity for interactive practice. While the new syllabus does have English for interaction as an objective, students' vocabulary seldom goes beyond the domains of school life, family or everyday activities; so when they get to university, they have difficulty with academic and technical materials in English (Data source code: 112-035-004). To help students, teachers must be better trained. Several teachers I spoke to felt that if they could have short attachments overseas, it would be beneficial (Data source code: 111-025-001).

## English and other foreign languages in higher education

The English and/or foreign languages departments in the four universities visited offer two semesters in a year with eighteen to twenty weeks in each semester, often inclusive of two weeks of assessment. (Occasionally, a third semester of four weeks long might be offered as well.) Lessons are forty-five

**Table 3.24 Teaching of English in four secondary schools**

| Location of school | Coastal region | | Interior region | |
|---|---|---|---|---|
| | Northern city | Southern city | Northern city | Southern city |
| No. of English teachers | 13 | 18 | No information | 4 |
| Adequacy of English teachers[+] | No shortage | No shortage | Slight shortage but manageable | No shortage |
| Equipment | Fully equipped[#] | Fully equipped | No internet access | No overhead projector, compact disk player, compact disks, language learning software, video projector or internet access |
| No. of students | 1,000* | 1,200 | 1,800 | 300 |
| No. of students per class | 50 | 50 | 63 | 49 |
| No. of lessons per week | 32 | 33 | 35 | 35 |
| No. of English lessons per week | 5.6 | 5 | 5 | 5.2 |
| Textbooks used are published by | Ministry of Education | Ministry of Education | Ministry of Education | Ministry of Education |
| Assessment before entry | City examination | No entry test | Provincial examination | No entry test |
| Assessment at the end of Senior Secondary 3 | National higher education admission examination | National higher education admission examination | National higher education admission examination | National higher education admission examination |
| Students' level upon graduation[+]: | | | | |
|     Pronunciation | Passable | Passable | Passable | Passable |
|     Conversation | Passable | Passable | Passable | Passable |
|     Writing letters | Passable | Passable | Passable | Good |
|     Listening to news broadcasts | Passable | Passable | Passable | Passable |
|     Reading newspapers | Passable | Passable | Passable | Passable |
| Data source code | 11-025-001 | 21-175-008 | 12-255-005 | 22-885-009 |

\*  This school only offers three years of senior secondary school while the others offer three years of junior secondary school as well.

\#  'Fully equipped' means 'With: library, cassette recorder and tapes, video recorder and tapes, overhead projector, compact disk player and compact disks, computer and language learning software, video projector and internet access.'

[+]  According to the head of department.

to fifty minutes long. The total period of time spent on studying English as a major at undergraduate level ranges from about 800 to 2,800 lessons or 600 to 2,333 hours. All non-English-major students are required to complete a programme usually entitled College English, which is usually about 300 lessons or 250 hours long; among the twelve universities providing data, the minimum length was 180 lessons or 150 hours and the maximum length was 500 lessons or 417 hours. Apart from the difference in hours, English major students usually enjoy a smaller class size (around twenty-plus in each group) than non-English-major students (around forty-plus in each group). The total numbers of students in both groups are also vastly different since College English has to be offered to all students in a university, usually for four lessons per week for four semesters. Before entry into university, all degree level students must pass the examination for English in the higher education admission examinations. All of them are usually required by their university to sit for the national College English Test; English major students are expected to pass Band 6 (and preferably Band 8, the highest band) while non-English major students are expected to pass Band 4 (and preferably Band 6). Table 3.25 gives an overview of the circumstances.

Table 3.25  Teaching of English in four universities

| Location of university: | Coastal region | | Interior region | |
|---|---|---|---|---|
| | *Northern city* | *Southern city* | *Northern city* | *Southern city* |
| No. of teachers[@] | 88 | 122 | 65 | 67 |
| Adequacy of teachers[+] | Slight shortage but manageable | | | |
| Equipment | Fully equipped[#] | | | |
| No. of students | | | | |
| English as a major | 80 | 260 | 150 | 270 |
| English for non-majors | 6,000 | 5,500 | 4,000 | 8,000 |
| English major graduate students | 12 | 63 | 28 | 0 |
| Other students[*] | 3,508 | 1,377 | 708 | 505 |
| Average no. of students per class | | | | |
| English as a major | 20 | 22 | 25 | 28 |
| English for non-majors | 35 | 40 | 50 | 45 |
| Materials used are published/written by | Ministry of Education, other universities and teachers at this university | Commercial publishers and other universities | Ministry of Education and other universities | Ministry of Education |

*(continued on p. 119)*

*(Table 3.25 continued)*

| English major students' skills upon graduation[+]: | | | | |
|---|---|---|---|---|
| Pronunciation | Passable | Very good | Very good | Good |
| Conversation | Passable | Good | Very good | Good |
| Writing letters | Passable | Excellent | Excellent | Good |
| Listening to news broadcasts | Passable | Very good | Very good | Good |
| Reading newspapers | Good | Excellent | Very good | Good |
| Giving a speech | Not too good | Good | Very good | Good |
| Writing academic / technical essays | Passable | Very good | Good | Good |
| Listening to academic / technical talks | Not too good | Very good | Good | Good |
| Reading academic / technical materials | Passable | Very good | Very good | Good |
| Non-major students' level upon graduation[+]: | | | | |
| Pronunciation | Passable | Good | Good | Passable |
| Conversation | Not too good | Not too good | Passable | Not too good |
| Writing letters | Good | Passable | Very good | Passable |
| Listening to news broadcasts | Passable | Passable | Passable | Not too good |
| Reading newspapers | Passable | Good | Passable | Passable |
| Giving a speech | Not too good | Not too good | Passable | Not too good |
| Writing academic / technical essays | Not too good | Passable | Passable | Not too good |
| Listening to academic / technical talks | Not too good | Passable | Passable | Not too good |
| Reading academic / technical materials | Not too good | Good | Good | Passable |
| Data source code | 11-026-001 | 21-176-016m/n | 12-256-004 | 22-886-020 |

[@]  Including teachers of other foreign languages.
[*]  Students majoring in other foreign languages, non-English-major graduate students and non-degree students.
[#]  'Fully equipped' means 'With: library, cassette recorder and tapes, video recorder and tapes, overhead projector, compact disk player and compact disks, computer and language learning software, video projector and internet access.'
[+]  According to the head of the programme.

The estimation of students' level of skills in each location by the head of department must again be received merely as a rough indication; the head from the university in Beijing was probably being unduly humble about the performance of his students. In general though, the difference in achievement between students majoring in English and the non-English-major students is obvious.

Some universities also offer graduate level studies for English majors as well as non-majors. Graduate students majoring in English usually study around 550 lessons but there is a lot of variation ranging from 256 lessons to 1,000 lessons. Non-English-major students may also be supported by English courses ranging from 64 lessons to 240 lessons long. To enter a graduate programme, candidates have to pass an English test in the national admission examinations for graduate level studies. To exit from the programme, they only have to satisfy the requirements of their own university.

From discussions with heads of foreign language programmes, four developments appear to be particularly important. First, it is best if the English curriculum could be 'like a dragon' from primary to university so that there is no unnecessary overlap and assessment for different stages could be better planned. Secondly, the new syllabus for English majors allows for discipline-specific knowledge to be acquired along with English, which is welcome. Thirdly, some universities are experimenting with teaching other subjects in English. One university in the northern interior, for example, transferred a teacher from the English section to help teach journalism in English to students majoring in journalism as a pilot scheme. That university would have liked to teach economics and law in English as well but the economics and law teachers did not feel comfortable teaching in English (Data source code: 12-256-004). Fourthly, it is difficult to retain English majors in teaching, particularly in the interior, because they attract 'six or seven job offers' in the big cities on the coast such as Beijing, Tianjin, Shanghai and Guangzhou (Data source code: 12-256-004). This is detrimental to the teaching of English in the schools.

Besides English, other foreign languages attracting students are: Japanese, French, German, Russian and Spanish. In addition, in the northern interior, Arabic languages are also studied and, in the southern interior, Vietnamese and other languages in Indo-China are popular. A university in Beijing reported these numbers: 420 students studying Japanese, 180 studying German, 60 studying French and 45 studying Russian in programmes of 128 lessons long (Data source code: 11-026-001). Japanese is also popular in the southern coastal region with one university reporting eighty students studying Japanese as a major in a programme of about 800 lessons long and another thirty to forty studying it as a second foreign language in about 300 lessons over two years (Data source code: 21-176-016m). Not surprisingly, therefore, of the twenty heads of foreign languages departments providing data, half of them reported that Japanese now attracts the greatest number of students besides English. This is different from the learning experience of the last cohort of learners for whom French was still the most popular foreign language (Table 3.22).

### Teaching English as a commercial enterprise

Apart from the attention it receives within the educational system, English is also becoming 'big business' (Wang, 2001) in the commercial sector. For the last ten years or so, to supplement the income both for individual teachers and for the English academic unit, it has also been an accepted practice for foreign language teachers in the university sector to take on additional work outside the university. One head of department mentioned to me how difficult it was to keep the younger staff because salaries in joint venture companies were so much higher. Traditionally too, many of the teachers at university level live on campus, which makes it possible for students to consult them at their homes at all times (and they often do). Teachers are thus not expected to keep office hours in the department building, which often does not have individual offices for them to work in quietly anyway. Teachers who know me better jokingly refer to the teaching, translation or editorial work they do outside their university work as 'moonlighting' but there is nothing clandestine about such activities as it is accepted by the authorities. It has been possible for teachers in universities to do such outside practice because of the boom in English learning in the commercial sector. The cover story of the December 2001 issue of *Yanzhou Zhoukan* traces such development generally, citing examples like the New Oriental tuition centres and Li Yang's multi-million Crazy English programme in which learners may be taught in classes of a few thousand per class, a practice which has attracted much controversy (Bolton, 2003, pp. 253–258; Shen & Gao, 2004). There are many other enterprises of various scales, particularly in the coastal cities.

## Summary

In this chapter, I have presented the changes in foreign language policy in the light of China's relations with the world. Statistics from a survey offer an overall picture of the experience of learning English from primary school to university in the last few decades. Four case histories of learners, two older and two younger, make these statistics more meaningful in terms of individual experiences of the changes through time. Finally, information provided by heads of programmes of English and other foreign languages give an indication of some of the recent circumstances.

From all the data provided, it is obvious that English has been the most important foreign language in China since the late 1950s. Russian competence is still available among some of the older teaching staff though the most popular second foreign language among younger foreign language professionals now seems to be Japanese, perhaps because of the popularity of Japanese drama series, movies, songs and food and the similarity of Japanese to Chinese. With China's entry into the World Trade Organization, it is to be expected that other foreign languages such as French and German (for the European community), which have always had a following, or Spanish (for the Latin world) may also attract more learning fervour from students training to be foreign language professionals at university level. At the school level, it is likely that English will continue to be exclusively important, that is, in addition to the Chinese language.

In the last chapter and this one, I have focused on the experience of the majority ethnic group, the Han Chinese. In the next chapter, I shall present the experience of learners from the minority ethnic groups.

# 4

# Developing Minority Languages and Bilingualism

## Introduction

In spite of the published research about minority languages or minority education even in English (for example, Hansen, 1999; Lee, 2001; Zhou, 2003), the multilingual nature of the Chinese population is still not widely appreciated. To many people in the world at large, China is a monolingual country. The actual linguistic circumstances are much more complex. As indicated in Chapter 1, there are fifty-five ethnic minorities officially recognized by the central government. Even in the 1990s, it was already reported that over eighty languages were used among the minorities (State Language Commission, 1995, p. 159). More recently, it has been estimated that over 120 languages are used, even though only 60 minority languages are officially recognized (Zhou, 2003, p. 23). (See Downer, 1991, for a classification of the minority languages according to language families and Ramsey, 1987, for other details.) The total minority population is 106,430,000 or 8.4% of the total population of China (National Bureau of Statistics, 2001). This chapter is about the development of minority languages under the present government and the language learning experience of minority learners. There are four parts in the chapter. The language policy towards minorities at different times is first outlined. Secondly, more details on one of the policy measures, the codification of minority languages in China, are provided. Thirdly, some preliminary observations about the overall learning experience of minority learners based on a small-scale survey of sixty learners are made. Finally, seven case histories of learners from different minority groups are presented and discussed.

## Language Policy Towards Minorities

If minority languages are to be maintained at the national level, then the policy of the state has to support the development of the languages. Yet, if the minority groups in China are not proficient in Chinese — the national language, they cannot participate in the mainstream life of the country easily. For minority groups to maintain their own languages and cultures and, at the same time, have easy access to the national life and the associated economic benefits, bilingualism could be the answer. However, widespread bilingualism was not targeted as a policy goal for minority learners in the early years of the People's Republic.

If we look back in time, for centuries before 1949, the Han Chinese ethnic group, the majority population, had co-existed with the various minority groups residing mostly in the border areas and bilingualism among certain sectors (particularly, government officials, scholars and traders) of the dominant Han Chinese group as well as the minorities had made possible interethnic communication between the various ethnic groups for diplomatic and commercial purposes. (See He, 1998, pp. 3–69, for a discussion of pre-1949 bilingualism in China.)

Since the establishment of the People's Republic in 1949, the language policy towards the minorities could be largely demarcated into five phases:
1. Egalitarian respect for minority languages (1949–1956)
2. Unstable policy towards minority languages (1957–1965)
3. Suppression of minority languages and cultures (1966–1976)
4. Restoration of the status of minority languages (1977–1990)
5. Bilingualism as a policy goal (1991–the present)

This division into five phases is based on an analysis of Wang (1998), He (1998) and Zhou (2003). The first three periods are based on Wang's discussion, which covers only the years from 1949 to 1976. He (1998, p. 80) does not present a distinct list of periods; in her analysis, the years between 1957 to 1959 were presented as a period of extreme Han Chinese chauvinism, during which the development of minority languages suffered a severe setback but after those few years, bilingualism in Chinese and minority languages was revived until 1966 when conditions worsened again after the Cultural Revolution.

Zhou (2003), commenting on developments from 1949 to 2002, identifies three periods:
1. The first pluralistic stage (1949–1957)
2. The Chinese monopolistic stage (1958–1977)
3. The second pluralistic stage (1978–2002)

During Zhou's first and third periods of pluralism, the minorities were respected and accommodated but during Zhou's second period (which he calls 'the Chinese monopolistic stage'), from 1958 to 1977, they were suppressed. Zhou admits though that from 1962 to 1963, there was a brief reprieve from integrationism or the tendency to assimilate minorities into the Greater Han culture. This recognition, together with Wang's and He's analyses mentioned above, seems to suggest that it is more appropriate to separate Zhou's second period into two periods: a period during which the policy towards minorities was unstable (1957–1965) and another during which the minorities were certainly suppressed (1966–1976). During Zhou's third period (1978–2002), a policy shift also emerged in the early 1990s; from around the time when the Soviet Union disintegrated, China looked more carefully at the issue of nationalities within her own borders and from then on, bilingualism as a policy goal has become more evident. In recognition of this subtle change in policy, I have separated Zhou's third period into two periods: a period during which the status of minorities was restored (1977–1990) and another one with bilingualism as a policy goal (1991–the present).

However the periods are dated, what is evident is that, throughout the policy shifts, there has been constant tension between allowing minority languages to be used and developed and providing minority groups access to national life via Putonghua, as for other Chinese dialect groups in China.

## Egalitarian respect for minority languages (1949–1956)

It is consistent with the political ideology of the Communist Party to accord equality to all ethnic groups. Hence, even before the People's Republic was established, as early as in 1932, it was affirmed at the first national meeting of the worker and peasant soldiers that it was necessary to establish schools as well as publishing and printing houses in which minority languages would be used, to allow all government offices to use the ethnic languages, to bring worker and peasant cadres from local ethnic communities into the national administration and to firmly reject the tendency towards dominance of the Great Han Chinese ethnicity (Xie, 1989, p. 27).

This ideological position was explicitly announced in 1949, when the People's Republic was established, and incorporated into the first constitution of the Republic publicized in 1952, 'Every ethnic group has the freedom to use and develop its own language and script' (He, 1998, pp. 70–71). In the same year, the State Council issued 'Guidelines for Regional Autonomy for Minority Nationalities in the People's Republic of China', which required autonomous governments 'to adopt the languages of all minority nationalities within their jurisdiction for the development of these minorities' culture and education' (Zhou, 2003, p. 44). In 1954, this position was affirmed when the first constitution was passed by the first session of the First National People's Congress (Zhou, 2003, p. 44). In the early 1950s, the policy to codify the language scripts for ethnic groups that already had scripts and to create new scripts for those groups that did not have scripts but would like to have them was explicitly announced and systematically implemented (He, 1998, p. 71). (Details on this codification process will be provided in 'Codification of

Minority Languages' of this chapter; see pp. 130–139.) To ensure that there would be enough trained personnel for such linguistic work, the Chinese Academy of Sciences (2002) established the Institute of Linguistics in 1950 and the Central Institute of Nationalities (now the Central University of Nationalities) started the department of linguistics in 1951 (He, 1998, p. 79). In 1951, seven language teams of more than one hundred linguists were sent to Yunnan, Guizhou, Sichuan and Guangxi to do research on the minority languages in those places. In 1956, seven language survey teams of more than seven hundred linguists were sent from Beijing, six to survey minority languages in the south and southwestern regions and one to do so in the northwest (Zhou, 2003, p. 22).

In the spirit of such an ideological position, when the policy to teach Putonghua to all Han Chinese students in all primary and secondary schools was implemented from 1956, it was specifically mentioned that Putonghua propagation did not need to be implemented in minority ethnic group areas for minority learners (State Language Commission, 1996, p. 12). This meant that ethnic minority students did not have to convert to Putonghua. Yet, in such areas, if Chinese was already being taught in the minority schools or used for broadcasting, then it was specified that the dialect of Chinese to be used should be Putonghua (State Language Commission, 1996, p. 15).

### Unstable policy towards minority languages (1957–1965)

Ideals and realities, however, do not always match. What was upheld in the Chinese constitution of 1954 was not always implemented in reality (Zhou, 2003, p. 44). After the initial fervour of work on the codification of scripts, around 1957, the argument that minority scripts were useless started to surface; it was proposed that minority learners could transfer directly to Putonghua instead of via their own writing script (He, 1998, p. 80). In 1958, the same year that the *Hanyu Pinyin Scheme* to standardize Putonghua was completed (see Chapter 2, 'The Standardization of Chinese, pp. 33–43), an article published by the Culture and Education Department of the State Commission on Nationalities Affairs argued that while minorities had the right to use their languages, such use had to be for the benefit of the progress of their communities and the unity of the motherland. Two implications followed: first, the use of the minority writing systems might be limited to certain domains or might not even be officially affirmed; secondly, minority writing systems would be expected to aim for consistency with the *Hanyu Pinyin Scheme* for Chinese to work towards convergence of writing systems at some point in time (Zhou, 2003, pp. 111–112). The experimental use of some new writing scripts was halted (He, 1998, p. 80). In the late 1950s, on the socio-economic front, minority groups were also caught up in the reorganization of communities (whether Han Chinese or minorities) into communes in the Great Leap Forward and all the associated enforced labour. (See Zhou, 2003, pp. 60–77, for more discussion on how socialist construction eroded the policy respecting minorities in the late 1950s and how the tide turned towards egalitarianism again between 1962 to 1963 but reverted once more to integrationism from 1964.)

## Suppression of minority languages (1966–1976)

While the policy stance towards minorities was vacillating, at least for certain minorities, if not all, in the late 1950s and early 1960s, by the mid-1960s, the protected status of minority languages and minority learners was clearly undermined. During the Cultural Revolution from 1966 to 1976, minority languages were considered 'useless' and 'backward'. Many minority language administration offices were disbanded. The use of some minority languages was discontinued by force. That affected minority education adversely. Minority education organizations or teacher training colleges for minority teachers were disestablished (He, 1998, p. 81). Some interviewees in the present study reported that the prevailing mood at that time was so antagonistic towards minority languages and cultures that even the singing of folksongs in minority languages was forbidden in some places. In 1971, all ten institutes of nationalities were closed down and a great number of cadres in minority affairs and teachers were persecuted (Wang, 1998, p. 8).

In such a repressive climate, not surprisingly, some minority language parents would enrol their children in Han Chinese schools, regardless of whether the children had any knowledge of Chinese before entry to the school. Some managed to survive, albeit with hard work, and others ended up not achieving proficiency in their own minority language or in Chinese. Paradoxically, such a period of suppression of minority languages did result in a greater number of minority learners having some working knowledge of Chinese, at least, of spoken Chinese (He, 1998, pp. 81–82).

Towards the end of the Cultural Revolution, from around 1973, work on the minority languages of the Mongol group, the Zang (Tibetan) group, the Kazak group, the Chosen group and the Yi group was revived but the prevailing mood was still not too supportive of the development of other minority languages. In fact, in 1975, the 1954 constitution was amended so that while the minorities were still allowed to use their languages, they were no longer encouraged to 'develop' them (Zhou, 2003, pp. 77).

## Restoration of the status of minority languages (1977–1990)

The end of the Cultural Revolution brought a new day to education in China as a whole and also to minority language developments. In May 1978, the State Council reaffirmed the functions of the State Commission on Nationalities Affairs. In December 1978, this Commission and the Chinese Academy of Sciences held an academic forum that reasserted the restoration of rights to minority groups (Zhou, 2003, p. 78). In the 1982 constitution of China, it was reaffirmed in Article 4 that 'every ethnic group has the freedom to use and develop its own language and script and to maintain or change its own cultural practices' (Ministry of Education, n.d.a; He, 1998, p. 88; National People's Congress, 1999, p. 6). The right to pursue legal proceedings in one's own ethnic language was also provided for in Article 134 of the same constitution (Ministry of Education, n.d.a; National People's Congress, 1999, p. 41). Various pronouncements on minority language matters took place during the 1980s. Codification work on some minority languages was also renewed and some new writing scripts were recognized during this period.

## Bilingualism as a policy goal (1991–the present)

By 1991, in a note from the State Council, it was pointed out that, among the ethnic minorities, there were more people who were bilingual but there was insufficient guidance, personnel or financial support for minority language developments (State Language Commission, 1996, p. 35). The same note called for a renewed effort to continue work in the codification and design of orthographies, the encouragement of bilingualism among the cadres and the use of minority languages in education or bilingual education (State Language Commission, 1996, pp. 36–37). This bilingual policy stance could in part be motivated by the recognition that, without a good balance of accommodation and assimilation tendencies among its ethnic groups, a country with several nationalities might disintegrate into its component nationalities as in the case of the Soviet Union in 1991. From the early 1990s, the term 'nationalities' has been gradually replaced by 'ethnic groups' in the government rhetoric on minority matters. In 1997, at a forum held by the State Commission on Nationalities Affairs in Beijing (Zhou Qingsheng, personal communication, cited in Zhou, 2003, p. 94), it was agreed that the term 'ethnic group' would be a more appropriate translation for *minzu*. In 1998, the State Commission on Nationalities Affairs changed its English name to the State Commission on Ethnic Affairs (Zhou, 2003, p. 94).

In spite of the subtle change in policy emphasis towards bilingualism, the legal provisions have remained largely the same. 'The Law on Regional Autonomy for Minority Nationalities in the People's Republic of China' was first passed in 1984 and revised in 2001 (National People's Congress, 2001; Ministry of Education, n.d.a). Some relevant articles in this law are translated as follows:

**Article 10**. The autonomous offices in the autonomous ethnic areas are to safeguard the freedom of ethnic groups to use and develop their languages and scripts and to maintain or change their cultural practices.

**Article 21**. In executing their duties, the autonomous offices in the autonomous ethnic areas, according to the regulations in the autonomous areas, are to use one or more languages or scripts commonly used in that area; if several languages or scripts are used at the same time, they can use primarily the language or script of the ethnic group in that region.

**Article 37**. The schools (or classes) recruiting mainly minority learners should use textbooks in the minority language and teach in the minority language, if conditions allow for that; according to actual circumstances, in Chinese lessons starting from lower primary or upper primary, Putonghua and standardized Chinese characters should be taught.

**Article 47**. The peoples' courts and prosecuting offices should use the languages commonly used in the local regions to review documents or judge cases and should, within reason, provide interpreters who know the local minority languages. For those involved in legal proceedings but who do not understand the local minority languages, translation should be provided. One or more of the local languages or scripts should be used in legal documents, according to actual needs, to protect the rights of citizens from every ethnic group to use their own ethnic language and script in legal proceedings.

**Article 49**. The offices in the autonomous ethnic regions should educate and encourage all cadres to mutually learn the languages and scripts of each other. Han Chinese cadres should learn the local ethnic languages and scripts. Cadres from minority ethnic groups, while learning their own ethnic languages and scripts, should at the same time, learn Putonghua and standardized Chinese characters propagated throughout the country. National workers in autonomous ethnic areas who can use more than two of the local languages and scripts well should be encouraged with rewards.

Of the relevant legal provisions in the 2001 law, two of them are most instrumental towards promoting bilingualism among the ethnic minorities. They are Articles 37 and 49. Article 37 points explicitly to the use of Putonghua when teaching Chinese in minority schools. Although this policy position was stated as early as 1956, reaffirming this position in the revised constitution is itself a policy affirmation. Article 49 requiring cadres to be proficient in both Chinese and the local minority language(s) directly encourages the growth of a sector of bilingual personnel towards effective government and administrative communication on minority matters. Such bilingual personnel tend to be more easily found among native speakers of minority languages because there is little interest to learn minority languages among the Han Chinese.

## Summary

In sum, except during the Cultural Revolution, and perhaps a few sporadic years before that, the national policy towards minority languages, at least those that are officially recognized, has been generally supportive. The state provides linguistic researchers to codify a good number of minority languages and minority learners have not been forced by law to abandon their own languages to convert entirely to Putonghua. Yet, the real everyday circumstances of many a minority learner may not be as simple. For minority learners to succeed educationally, especially if they speak languages without a writing script or one that is widely used, proficiency in Putonghua is quite necessary. Before the learning experiences of minority learners are presented in 'The Overall Experience of Minority Learners' (pp. 139–154) and 'Seven Case Histories' (pp. 155–173), we now turn to the codification of the languages themselves, especially in terms of orthographic developments, in the next section.

# Codification of Minority Languages

Soon after the establishment of the present government in China, major ethnographic research was conducted to better understand the minority groups, mostly residing in the border regions. This was not purely a linguistic exercise or merely a pursuit of egalitarian ideals but was born out of the genuine need to communicate with the minority groups in the border areas to achieve and maintain national stability.

The specific tasks at hand were: the development of writing systems for the minority languages and research into the spoken forms of the languages and bilingual training of the cadres working on minority affairs (Ramsey, 1987, p. 162). Standardizing or designing the scripts for the minority languages was important to meet the government's objective of enhancing literacy. Without codification of the scripts, it was difficult to record the spoken languages or to teach them to the Chinese cadres or the minority groups themselves. Some of the minority languages had their own orthographies and some did not. The revision of existing scripts or the design of new ones was based mostly on the Chinese script or the Roman alphabet though the Cyrillic script was used as a basis for some languages in the early 1950s under Russian influence. What follows is a summary of their development (updated from Lam, 1998). It should be pointed out here that the facts presented below are highly simplified towards a general understanding of such developments as background for an appreciation of the learning experience of minority learners; as such, they may not be true of all the dialects or languages used by the ethnic groups. (See Zhou [2003], for a more detailed account of these developments.)

## Minority groups with scripts retained

Among the fifty-five ethnic minorities, the Hui and Man groups use the Chinese language like the Han people. They have undergone linguistic acculturation. Ten other ethnic groups (the Chosen group, the Dai group, the Kazak group, the Kirgis group, the Mongol group, the Russ group, the Sui group, the Uygur group, the Xibe group and the Zang group) have had their own orthographies established, some for quite a long historical period (Table 4.1). Some attempt to change the orthographies for some of these ethnic groups (the Kazak group, the Kirgis group, the Uygur group and the Xibe group) was made in the 1950s but the older orthographies were finally adopted again. According to Zhou (2003, p. 104), the Uzbeks also had their own writing script even then but it was not officially recognized.

**Table 4.1  Minority groups with scripts retained**

| Name of ethnic group | Summary history of script(s) | Basis of current script |
|---|---|---|
| 1. Chosen (Korean) | In 1441, the Chosen script was created with some Chinese characters borrowed. In 1446, the script was propagated. In 1895, using a mixed script with Chinese and Chosen forms was forbidden. In 1952, the Chosen people in China stopped using Chinese characters in the Chosen script. | Alphabet based on the shape of articulatory organs |
| 2. Dai | Four scripts are used for this language. The year 638 was the uncertain date of birth for one of the scripts, the origin of which was related to the spread of Buddhism. Other scripts were created later. In 1955, some attempt was made to revise two of these scripts but one group reverted to using the old script. | Indian alphabet |
| 3. Hui | The Hui people have acculturated to Chinese and most of them do not use a language of their own now. | Acculturation to Chinese |
| 4. Kazak | The tenth to the twelfth century saw the spread of the Islam religion to the Kazaks and the Arabic alphabet was gradually adopted. Between 1917 and 1924, the Arabic alphabet was modified for the Kazak language. In 1929, a Roman script was created. In 1941, a Cyrillic script was adopted instead. In 1959, a Roman script was created again. In 1965, the new Roman script was propagated but in 1982, the Arabic script was adopted once more. | Arabic alphabet |
| 5. Kirgiz | Before the tenth century, an old alphabet was used. With the spread of Islam, an Arabic script was adopted. Between 1954 and 1956, the Arabic script was modified. In 1957, the Cyrillic script was published but | Arabic alphabet |

*(continued on p. 132)*

*(Table 4.1 continued)*

| Name of ethnic group | Summary history of script(s) | Basis of current script |
|---|---|---|
| | in 1958, the Cyrillic script was abandoned and the Arabic script was adopted again. From 1959 to 1979, the Roman scripts of the Uygurs and the Kazaks were used by the Kirgiz people. But in 1979, the Arabic script was adopted again. By 1988, the standard Arabic script and dictionary were published. | |
| 6. Man (Manchu) | The Man people have acculturated to Chinese and most of them do not use a language of their own now. | Acculturation to Chinese |
| 7. Mongol | In the thirteenth century, the Mongol script was created based on the Uighur alphabet originally derived from the Aramaic script. | Uighur alphabet |
| 8. Russ (Russian) | The Russ people in China use the same Cyrillic script for the Russian language in Russia. | Cyrillic alphabet |
| 9. Sui | The Sui people had their own script even before 1949, made up of pictographic characters written from right to left. Some of them resemble Chinese written in reverse. So it is sometimes called 'reverse writing'. | Chinese script |
| 10. Uygur | From the seventh to the tenth century, the Tujue (突厥) and the Uighur alphabets were used. During the tenth and eleventh centuries, the Uygurs were exposed to the Arabic alphabet. By the fifteenth century, the Arabic script was used to replace older alphabets. In the 1950s, eight letters in the alphabet were discarded and six letters were added. In 1959, a Roman script was designed and in 1965, it was propagated. By 1976, the use of the Arabic script was forbidden. But in 1982, the Arabic script was adopted once again. | Arabic alphabet |
| 11. Xibe | In 1947, the Xibe script based on the Manchu script was codified. In 1955, the Cyrillic script was published. In 1958, the Roman script was designed but the work to propagate it was then discontinued. | Uighur alphabet |
| 12. Zang (Tibetan) | The script was created in the seventh century. | Indian alphabet |

Summarized from: Chinese Academy of Social Sciences, Research Institute on Nationalities, and the State Commission on Nationality Affairs (1992) and Ministry of Education of the People's Republic of China (n.d.b).

## Minority groups with scripts revised

Ten other ethnic groups who had their own orthographies even before 1949 were: the Bai group, the Jingpo group, the Lahu group, the Lisu group, the Miao group, the Naxi group, the Va group, the Yao group, the Yi group and the Zhuang group. These groups had their original orthographies modified or additional Roman orthographies created for them (Table 4.2).

Table 4.2 **Minority groups with old scripts revised or new scripts added**

| Name of ethnic group | Summary history of script(s) | Basis of current script |
|---|---|---|
| 1. Bai | The old script was based on the Chinese script. In the 1980s, the new phonetic Bai script was created. | Roman alphabet |
| 2. Jingpo | In 1899, one Roman script was created by an American missionary. Another variety propagated by French missionaries from 1934 was revised by the Chinese government from 1956 and finalized in 1983. | Roman alphabet |
| 3. Lahu | In the early twentieth century, the script for the Lahus in Burma was created; then missionaries brought it to China. In 1957, the Lahu script was revised and propagated. | Roman alphabet |
| 4. Lisu | There are two scripts for the Lisu language. From 1912 to 1914, a Roman script was created by Christian missionaries. In 1956, a new Roman script with some Cyrillic letters was incorporated. In 1957, Cyrillic letters were removed from the Lisu alphabet. In 1958, the Roman script was propagated. | Roman alphabet |
| 5. Miao | In 1905, a phonetic script using geometric symbols and diacritics was created for one Miao dialect by Samuel Pollard, a British missionary, with help from Miao and Han Chinese teachers. In 1956, the script for this dialect was reformed and scripts for three other dialects were also created. In 1957, the four scripts were propagated. But in 1958, they were revised to resemble *hanyu pinyin* in using Roman letters. In 1982, the Pollard script was revised again and standardized using symbols as in the original Pollard script. | Several scripts are in use but the 1982 Pollard script is officially promoted |
| 6. Naxi | Before 1956, three scripts were in use – two ideographic scripts and one syllabic script. In 1956, fieldwork began. In 1957, a Roman script was designed for the Naxi language but in 1958, the work was discontinued. In 1981, such work resumed. | Roman alphabet |
| 7. Va | In the early twentieth century, a Roman script was created by a missionary. In 1957, the script was standardized. | Roman alphabet |
| 8. Yao | The Yaos had been using the Chinese script to write their own language. In the 1980s, the present script was created. | Roman alphabet |
| 9. Yi | One theory claimed that 1485 was the date of the oldest Yi document. The old Yi script was based on the | A syllabary but with variation |

*(continued on p. 134)*

*(Table 4.2 continued)*

| Name of ethnic group | Summary history of script(s) | Basis of current script |
|---|---|---|
| | Chinese script using some characters as a syllabary. A Roman script created in 1951 and finalized in 1956 for the Yi language was later retained only as an aid to pronunciation. In 1975, a new syllabary was finalized and propagated from 1976. This was approved as the official writing system in 1980. But other scripts using only characters or a combination of characters and a syllabary have also be used. | in the use of Chinese characters as logographs |
| 10. Zhuang | Before 1952, the Zhuangs used a script created from radicals in the Chinese script mixed with Chinese characters. In 1952, a new Roman script was created based on the Laibing dialect but it was discarded in favour of another one created in 1955 based on the Wuming dialect and with some Cyrillic letters and International Phonetic Alphabet letters included. In 1982, this script was revised to use only the Roman letters. | Roman alphabet |

Summarized from: Chinese Academy of Social Sciences, Research Institute on Nationalities, and the State Commission on Nationality Affairs (1992), Ministry of Education of the People's Republic of China (n.d.b) and Zhou (2003).

## Minority groups with new scripts created

From the 1950s and as recently as the 1980s, new orthographies were developed for nine ethnic groups previously without a writing script (the Buyei group, the Derung group, the Dong group, the Hani group, the Jin group, the Li group, the Qiang group, the Tu group and the Tujia group) (Table 4.3). The adoption of the Roman alphabet for many of the new orthographies was in line with the guidelines for the propagation of Putonghua (State Language Commission, 1996, p. 16). Although the minorities, except for the cadres, have not been required to learn Putonghua, in recent years, they have been encouraged to become bilingual in their own language as well as Putonghua (State Language Commission, 1996, p. 37). The argument for using the Roman alphabet as a basis for the new scripts was that doing so might ease the burden of minority learners in learning Putonghua as well as maintaining their own ethnic language because a Roman script, *hanyu pinyin*, was already created for Putonghua to aid pronunciation.

**Table 4.3 Minority groups with new scripts created**

| Ethnic group | Summary history of script(s) | Basis of new script |
|---|---|---|
| 1. Buyei | Before 1956, the Buyei people used the Chinese script for writing their language. In 1956, a Roman script for their language was created. In 1957, the Roman script was propagated but the work was discontinued in 1959. In 1981, the script was revised and in 1985, it was finalized. | Roman alphabet |
| 2. Derung | In the 1980s, a Roman script was created. | Roman alphabet |
| 3. Dong | In 1956, a Roman script similar to *hanyu pinyin* was created. In 1958, the script was propagated. | Roman alphabet |
| 4. Hani | In 1957, a Roman script was created. | Roman alphabet |
| 5. Jino | The script was created in the 1980s. | Roman alphabet |
| 6. Li | In the 1950s, a Roman script was created for the Li language. | Roman alphabet |
| 7. Qiang | The script was created in the 1980s. | Roman alphabet |
| 8. Tu | In 1979, a Roman script was created and it was confirmed in 1988. | Roman alphabet |
| 9. Tujia | The script was created in the 1980s. | Roman alphabet |

Summarized from: Chinese Academy of Social Sciences, Research Institute on Nationalities, and the State Commission on Nationality Affairs (1992), Ministry of Education of the People's Republic of China (n.d.b) and Zhou (2003).

## The overall situation today

The total number of ethnic groups in China (including the Han Chinese and the Mans and the Huis who have adopted Chinese as their language) who now have officially recognized orthographies is thirty-two (Ministry of Education of the People's Republic of China, n.d.b) (Table 4.4).

The twenty-four ethnic groups still without an officially recognized writing script are: the Achang group, the Blang group, the Bonan group, the Daur group, the Deang group, the Dongxiang group, the Ewenki group, the Gaoshan group, the Gelao group, the Gin group, the Hezhen group, the Lhoba group, the Maonan group, the Monba group, the Mulao group, the Nu group, the Oroqen group, the Pumi group, the Salar group, the She group, the Tajik group, the Tatar group, the Uzbek group and the Yugur group. Some of these groups (the Blangs, the Daurs, the Dongxiangs, the Nus and the Pumis) have had writings scripts designed (Zhou, 2003, pp. 126–127) or in use even before 1949 (the Uzbeks) (Zhou, 2003, p. 104), but the official status of their scripts is uncertain. The total population of the twenty-four ethnic groups was 2,607,976 people or 2.9% of the total minority population in 1990 (based on the 1990 Census statistics in Downer, 1991, p. 78) but is now 2,731,000 people or 2.6% of the total minority population in 2000 (Population

**Table 4.4  Minority ethnic groups according to population size**

| Name of ethnic group | Population of at least 1 million | Name of ethnic group | Population between 100,000 and 1 million | Name of ethnic group | Population below 100,000 |
|---|---|---|---|---|---|
| Zhuang[R] | 16,178,811 | She | 709,592 | Blang[N?] | 91,882 |
| Man[C] | 10,682,262 | Lisu[O&N] | 634,912 | Tajik | 41,028 |
| Hui[C] | 9,816,805 | Gelao | 579,357 | Achang | 33,936 |
| Miao[O&N] | 8,940,116 | Dongxiang[N?] | 513,805 | Pumi[N?] | 33,600 |
| Uygur[O] | 8,399,393 | Lahu[R] | 453,705 | Ewenki | 30,505 |
| Tujia[N] | 8,028,133 | Sui[O] | 406,902 | Nu[N?] | 28,759 |
| Yi[R] | 7,762,272 | Va[R] | 396,610 | Gin | 22,517 |
| Mongol[O] | 5,813,947 | Naxi[O&N] | 308,839 | Jino[N] | 20,899 |
| Zang[O] | 5,416,021 | Qiang[N] | 306,072 | Deang | 17,935 |
| Buyei[N] | 2,971,460 | Tu[N] | 241,198 | Bonan | 16,505 |
| Dong[N] | 2,960,293 | Mulao | 207,352 | Russ[O] | 15,609 |
| Yao[R] | 2,637,421 | Xibe[O] | 188,824 | Yugur | 13,719 |
| Chosen[O] | 1,923,842 | Kirgiz[O] | 160,823 | Uzbek[O?] | 12,370 |
| Bai[O&N] | 1,858,063 | Daur[N?] | 132,394 | Monba | 8,923 |
| Hani[N] | 1,439,673 | Jingpo[O&N] | 132,143 | Oroqen | 8,196 |
| Kazak[O] | 1,250,458 | Maonan | 107,166 | Derung[N] | 7,426 |
| Li[N] | 1,247,814 | Salar | 104,503 | Tatar | 4,890 |
| Dai[O] | 1,158,989 | | | Hezhen | 4,640 |
| | | | | Gaoshan | 4,461 |
| | | | | Lhoba | 2,965 |

Based on 2000 Census statistics reported in Population Census Office (2002, pp. 18–46). For comparison with 1990 Census statistics, see Dai et. al. (1997, pp. 321–325), Downer (1991, p. 78) and Teng (2001, pp. 300–303), Chinaetravel (2000) and Ministry of Education of the People's Republic of China (n.d.b).
[C]  Use the Chinese language and script.
[O]  Use an old script that existed before 1949.
[R]  Use a script revised from an old script that existed before 1949.
[N]  Use a script newly created after 1949.
[?]  Use a script the official status of which is uncertain (Zhou, 2003, p. 104 on the Uzbek script and pp. 126–127 on other scripts).

Census Office, 2002, pp. 18–46). The slight drop in the percentage in spite of the slight increase in actual numbers suggests that populations of groups without a writing script (or one that is officially recognized) seem to grow at a slower rate than those with officially recognized writing scripts. Whether this is related to low literacy and low survival rates or whether some members of these groups have acculturated to Chinese or other minority languages is worth further thought.

In the 1990 census, the total population of the minorities was 91,200,000 and made up about 7.5% of the population of China (Dai et al., 1997, p. 10). But the minority population has been growing at a faster rate than that of the Han majority population. According to the results from the 2000 national census, the total minority population has become 106,430,000 or 8.4% of the total population of China, which is 1,265,830,000 on the China mainland alone or 1,295,330,000 in Greater China (inclusive of the populations in Hong Kong, Macao and Taiwan) (National Bureau of Statistics of the People's Republic of China, 2001).

A population of 106.43 million is not, by any measure, a small number. It is easily the total national population of many countries, which makes it not surprising that a name previously used for 'ethnic groups' in China was 'nationalities', perhaps also because some of them do share a common ethnicity with people in a country beyond Chinese borders. Examples are the Chosen (Korean) people, the Mongol (Mongolian) people or the Russ (Russian) people in China.

The eighteen minorities with at least a million people in the same ethnic group (except for the Man and the Hui groups who have adopted Chinese as their language) now all have their own officially recognized writing scripts. Ten out of the seventeen minorities (58.8%) with at least 100,000 people also have an officially recognized writing script. But for groups with a population smaller than 100,000, the development of writing scripts has been rather erratic; only three out of the twenty groups (15.0%) with this population size now have their writing scripts officially recognized. Yet, even those minority languages without officially recognized writing scripts have been studied by researchers and brief introductions to the phonology, grammar and vocabulary to these languages have been published. Some examples are introductions to the languages used by the She minority (Mao & Meng, 1986), the Gelao minority (He, 1983), the Dongxiang minority (Liu, 1981), the Pumi minority (Lu, 1983), the Achang minority (Dai & Cui, 1985), the Nu minority (Sun & Liu, 1986), the Gin minority (Ouyang, Cheng & Yu, 1984), the Hezhen minority (An, 1986), the Oroqen minority (Hu, 1986) and the Lhoba minority (Ouyang, 1985) published by the Central University of Nationalities Press in the 1980s. In addition to researchers from the academic world, missionaries or other organizations have studied some of these languages.

## *Motivation for orthographic reform*

Taken as a whole, the adoption, revision and creation of orthographies for the ethnic minorities in China have taken various routes for various languages, with some languages retaining non-Chinese scripts and others adopting the Chinese one. Those scripts created or revised since the establishment of the present government (Tables 4.2 and 4.3) have been mostly based on the Roman alphabet, in line with the adoption of *hanyu pinyin* for Putonghua.

Although there has been much direct government initiative involved in the orthographic changes in minority languages in the last half century, the resultant changes still have to be accepted by the users of the languages. That the new alphabets for the Kazak language, the Kirgiz language, the Uygur language and the Xibe language were rejected in favour of the older scripts shows that popular support is needed for this kind of policy change. The acceptance by the users of the language depends on a variety of factors such as: emotional attachment to the older script because of cultural or religious reasons, how easy it is for users to learn the new script, the degree of bilingualism in the community and the practical need for learning the new script.

The post-1949 developments in the minority orthographies must also be seen in the light of their earlier developments. For example, the openness to other cultures and languages in the vicinity to different degrees and at different times through military occupation or religious evangelism has been directly reflected in orthographic development. Some of the minority languages adopted the Arabic script because of conversion to the Islam religion. The Roman alphabet was adopted for some minority languages first by Christian missionaries coming from the West who were interested to develop orthographies for bible translation and evangelism. Apart from religious efforts, the spread of foreign languages through language learning both in China (Chapter 3 of this book) as well as during studies abroad could have contributed to the increasing openness of users of Chinese to the use of the Roman alphabet in *hanyu pinyin* for Putonghua. For the minority language groups, the impact is probably felt less through the learning of a Western language like English and more through their exposure to *hanyu pinyin* used for the Chinese language.

A final consideration is expediency. The propagation of the Roman alphabet in the new orthographies for the minority languages was made in the hope of easing the learning of the minority languages (and Putonghua) as well as to facilitate printing, and, in recent decades, electronic communication and computerization.

The codification in the scripts made it possible for linguistic analyses of some of the languages to be represented and disseminated. On the basis of these linguistic descriptions, teaching materials to teach these languages could be written for minority language classes. By one count, twenty-one minority languages have been used in primary and secondary schools in China (Zheng, 2003, p. 17). For the large minority groups such as the Zhuang people, minority language classes may even be held at the school level and bilingual education conducted partly in the minority language and partly in Putonghua may be available for some learners in some locations. For other minority groups with a small population, learning the minority language formally might only be more possible at the university level at the nationalities institutes located in provinces such as Yunnan, Guizhou, Guangxi and Hubei and, of course, at the Central University of Nationalities in Beijing.

## The Overall Experience of Minority Learners

Having reviewed the codification work in minority languages, we have a slightly better idea of the range of possibilities for language education of minority learners. The vast number of minority groups in China makes it difficult to conduct a comprehensive survey of all the minorities, particularly because many of them are still not literate in Chinese or even in their own languages because scripts do not exist for them. Although a survey on language learning experience was designed (see Chapter 1, 'The Language Education in China Project', pp. 10–17) and a total of 133 copies were sent to fifteen nationality institutions and universities in areas with large minority populations in several attempts, only 95 were returned. Of these, only 60 were valid. The Loglinear Analysis involving the Chi-square statistic ($\alpha = 0.05$), a robust test suitable for categorical data and unequal cell sizes, was used for analysing most of the data for age effects according to the respondents' age in the year 2000 (Table 1.3). The Analysis of Variance was also used for analysing some data ($\alpha = 0.05$). As respondents differed greatly in their native languages and the total number of respondents was small, little weight was put on the statistical analysis; the survey information was mainly used as preliminary data to guide the interviewing in eliciting the case histories. Nevertheless, some general observations based on the survey data are presented here in the hope that the issues raised by these preliminary results may interest researchers to pursue them in greater depth.

It must be emphasized again that the respondents were all university graduates. The occupational backgrounds of the respondents were: minority language teachers/researchers (21.7%), Chinese language teachers/researchers (5%), foreign language teachers/researchers (6.7%), teachers of other subjects (25%) and other occupations (40%); one respondent (1.7%) did not specify the occupation. Most (70%) were born in rural areas, 18.3% in urban areas and 11.7% did not specify their birthplace location. Two-thirds (66.7%) were male and one-third (33.3%), female.

Respondents were asked questions on their learning of their minority language, Chinese and their first foreign language. The most interesting aspects of their three learning areas are presented in the following sections. Differences in total sample sizes for various aspects were due to non-responses to some questions.

## Learning minority languages

Of the sixty minority respondents in the valid data pool, five (8.3%) did not know any minority language. Those that did learn a minority language specified various languages as the minority language they knew best (Table 4.5). The discussion that follows is based on responses from these fifty-five learners.

Most of the fifty-five respondents (81.8%) learnt how to speak their minority language at home from the time they were born but at least half (53.7%) never learnt how to write it (Table 4.6), even though about 85.5% of the respondents came from ethnic groups with a writing script for their language (Table 4.5). This suggests that in spite of all the work that went into the codification of the minority language scripts, the actual use of the writing scripts for some languages is not widespread. Some minority language learning may occur in primary school and another chance to study minority languages is at university. Secondary school seems to offer little opportunity for minority language learning. The number of minority language lessons at primary and secondary school was about six to seven lessons per week for the respondents who did study it as a subject while that at university ranged from three to about eleven lessons per week, depending perhaps on whether they were specializing in the minority language.

**Table 4.5  Minority language background of respondents**

| *Minority language* | *Number of respondents (Percentage)* |
|---|---|
| The Bai language[M] | 3 (5.5%) |
| The Chosen language[M] | 1 (1.8%) |
| The Dong language[M] | 1 (1.8%) |
| The Jingpo language | 2 (3.6%) |
| The Lisu language | 1 (1.8%) |
| The Man language[MC] | 1 (1.8%) |
| The Miao language[M] | 1 (1.8%) |
| The Mulao language* | 2 (3.6%) |
| The Uzbek language* | 1 (1.8%) |
| The Yao language[M] | 4 (7.3%) |
| The Yi language[M] | 4 (7.3%) |
| The Yugur language* | 4 (7.3%) |
| The Zang language[M] | 4 (7.3%) |
| The Zhuang language[M #] | 25 (45.5%) |
| An unspecified minority language | 1 (1.8%) |
| Total | 55 (100.0%) |

[M] With a population of at least a million.
[C] Acculturation to Chinese.
* No writing script available.
[#] The Zhuang minority is the largest minority group in China (15.2% of the total minority population).

**Table 4.6 Time respondents began learning their minority language**

| Time minority language learning began | Number of respondents (Percentage) | |
|---|---|---|
| | Speaking | Writing |
| At home from birth | 45 (81.8%) | 1 (1.9%) |
| From kindergarten | 0 (0.0%) | 0 (0.0%) |
| From primary school | 2 (3.6%) | 6 (11.1%) |
| From secondary school | 1 (1.8%) | 0 (0.0%) |
| At university | 6 (10.9%) | 14 (25.9%) |
| At work | 1 (1.8%) | 4 (7.4%) |
| Did not learn this aspect of the language | 0 (0.0%) | 29 (53.7%) |
| Total | 55 (100.0%) | 54 (100.0%) |

**Table 4.7 Use of the minority language as a medium of instruction**

| Subject/ Educational level | Number of respondents (Percentage) | | | |
|---|---|---|---|---|
| | All teachers taught in the minority language | Some teachers taught in the minority language | No teachers taught in the minority language | Total |
| *Teaching of the minority language* | | | | |
| Primary school | 2 (50%) | 2 (50%) | 0 (0.0%) | 4 (100.0%) |
| Secondary school | 1 (33.3%) | 1 (33.3%) | 1 (33.3%) | 3 (100.0%) |
| University | 3 (20.0%) | 9 (60.0%) | 3 (20.0%) | 15 (100.0%) |
| *Teaching of other subjects* | | | | |
| Primary school | 7 (16.3%) | 21 (48.8%) | 15 (34.9%) | 43 (100.0%) |
| Secondary school | 1 (2.4%) | 11 (26.8%) | 29 (70.7%) | 41 (100.0%) |
| University | 2 (4.7%) | 4 (9.3%) | 37 (86.0%) | 43 (100.0%) |

Note: That the total numbers reporting learning the minority language at each level do not match those in Table 4.6 exactly is due to inconsistency in the respondents' answers.

There seems to be greater use of the minority language in teaching both the minority language and other subjects in primary school than at other levels, probably as a matter of necessity as some minority learners at that age do not speak Chinese (Table 4.7). By the time they reach university, very few minority learners (only 14.0%) are taught other subjects in the minority language. The lesser use of the minority language as a medium of instruction for other subjects (from 34.9% of teachers not using it in primary school to 86.0% not doing so at university) as learners move up the educational ladder means that for them to have educational advancement, Putonghua competence is usually crucial.

In conversing with classmates, respondents also used their minority language less frequently as they progressed through the educational system

(Table 4.8). In primary school, 71.1% would use the minority language frequently as compared to 33.3% and 8.5% when they were in secondary school and at university respectively. Like the Han Chinese learners, for their secondary school education, minority learners might move to bigger counties or cities with a greater mix of students from different language or dialectal backgrounds, making it necessary for them to convert to a regional dialect or Putonghua in secondary school. At university where Putonghua is commonly spoken, their choice is obvious.

**Table 4.8  Use of the minority language when conversing with classmates**

| Educational level | Number of respondents (Percentage) | | | |
|---|---|---|---|---|
| | Usually | Sometimes | Not at all | Total |
| Primary school | 32 (71.1%) | 7 (15.6%) | 6 (13.3%) | 45 (100.0%) |
| Secondary school | 15 (33.3%) | 22 (48.9%) | 8 (17.8%) | 45 (100.0%) |
| University | 4 (8.5%) | 22 (46.8%) | 21 (44.7%) | 47 (100.0%) |

Most of the respondents (80.8%) had home support in the minority language when they were learning the language. For 66.0%, the minority language was used very often at home because everyone at home used it. Another 14.9% spoke it with at least one family member although not everyone at home used the minority language. This non-use might arise from acculturation to Chinese or intermarriage with Han Chinese (Table 4.9).

**Table 4.9  Use of the minority language at home when learning the language**

| Use of the minority language at home | Number of respondents (Percentage) |
|---|---|
| Very often because everyone at home used the language | 31 (66.0%) |
| At least one family member used the language with the learner | 7 (14.9%) |
| The minority language is not used because all family members preferred using Putonghua or a Chinese dialect | 4 (8.5%) |
| None of the family members knew the minority language | 5 (10.6%) |
| Total | 47 (100.0%) |

Apart from using the language in conversation (by 90.5% of the respondents) or listening to or singing songs in the language (by 50% of the respondents), only about 20% of the respondents did other learning activities outside the classroom (such as reading books and so on) to enhance their competence in the minority language. In fact, only about half the respondents gave answers to some of the questions about speaking and listening activities involving technical equipment outside the classroom; either such opportunities were not available or, if available, not taken advantage of, perhaps because minority learners felt their proficiency in the minority language was sufficient for their purposes. The response rate to questions about reading and writing activities outside the classroom was slightly better (about 65%) but the majority of those that responded mentioned that they did not learn the writing script or that there was no script for their minority language. Their very low use of independent learning activities in their minority language suggests that, for such learning to occur, the development of literacy in the language must be possible in the first place.

Table 4.10 is an overview of how minority respondents rated their minority language abilities. Their ratings for their speaking and listening abilities were higher than those for reading and writing but their overall abilities were rather weak or not developed; except for pronunciation and conversation which had 84.6% and 84.3% respectively giving ratings of 'Passable' or higher, less than 50% of the respondents rated their other abilities 'Passable' or higher.

**Table 4.10 Respondents' ratings of their abilities in their minority language**

| Ability | Number of respondents (Percentage) | | | | | |
|---|---|---|---|---|---|---|
| | Excellent or Very good | Good | Passable | Not good | Did not use/learn this ability | Total |
| Pronunciation | 16 (30.8%) | 19 (36.5%) | 9 (17.3%) | 8 (15.4%) | 0 (0.0%) | 52 (100.0%) |
| Conversation | 18 (35.3%) | 15 (29.4%) | 10 (19.6%) | 6 (11.8%) | 2 (3.9%) | 51 (100.0%) |
| Making a speech | 10 (19.6%) | 6 (11.8%) | 8 (15.7%) | 9 (17.6%) | 18 (35.3%) | 51 (100.0%) |
| Listening to news broadcasts | 8 (15.7%) | 9 (17.6%) | 7 (13.7%) | 11 (21.6%) | 16 (31.4%) | 51 (100.0%) |
| Listening to academic/ technical lectures | 6 (12.2%) | 5 (10.2%) | 4 (8.2%) | 6 (12.2%) | 28 (57.1%) | 49 (100.0%) |
| Reading simple instructions | 7 (13.2%) | 7 (13.2%) | 6 (11.3%) | 3 (5.6%) | 30 (56.6%) | 53 (100.0%) |
| Reading newspaper articles | 6 (11.3%) | 7 (13.2%) | 4 (7.5%) | 4 (7.5%) | 32 (60.4%) | 53 (100.0%) |
| Reading academic/ technical materials | 5 (9.4%) | 4 (9.4%) | 4 (7.5%) | 4 (7.5%) | 35 (66.0%) | 53 (100.0%) |
| Writing a simple letter | 5 (9.3%) | 8 (14.8%) | 4 (7.4%) | 3 (5.6%) | 34 (63.0%) | 54 (100.0%) |
| Writing academic/ technical papers | 4 (7.7%) | 3 (5.8%) | 6 (11.5%) | 2 (3.8%) | 37 (71.2%) | 52 (100.0%) |

Among the younger cohorts of minority learners, there is an indication that even the listening and speaking abilities may be in the process of being lost among some of them in some domains. The percentages of respondents not using the minority language to listen to news broadcasts rose from 14.3% for the oldest group to 55.6% for the youngest group ($\chi^2$=34.28, df = 16, p = 0.0050) (Table 4.11). These might have switched to listening to broadcasts in Putonghua.

**Table 4.11  Respondents' ratings of their ability to listen to news broadcasts in the minority language**

| Age group | Number of respondents (Percentage) | | | | | |
|---|---|---|---|---|---|---|
| | Excellent or Very good | Good | Passable | Not good | Did not use this ability | Total |
| 46 to 50 | 0 (0.0%) | 3 (42.9%) | 2 (28.6%) | 1 (14.3%) | 1 (14.3%) | 7 (100.0%) |
| 41 to 45 | 3 (37.5%) | 0 (0.0%) | 0 (0.0%) | 2 (25.0%) | 3 (37.5%) | 8 (100.0%) |
| 36 to 40 | 3 (21.4%) | 5 (35.7%) | 3 (21.4%) | 1 (7.1%) | 2 (14.3%) | 14 (100.0%) |
| 29 to 35 | 1 (7.7%) | 0 (0.0%) | 0 (0.0%) | 7 (53.8%) | 5 (38.5%) | 13 (100.0%) |
| 24 to 28 | 1 (11.1%) | 1 (11.1%) | 2 (22.2%) | 0 (0.0%) | 5 (55.6%) | 9 (100.0%) |
| Total | 8 (15.7%) | 9 (17.6%) | 7 (13.7%) | 11 (21.6%) | 16 (31.4%) | 51 (100.0%) |

In addition, while the use of the minority language has remained fairly steady at home for different age cohorts, there seems to be lesser use of the minority language with friends among the younger cohorts (Table 4.12).

**Table 4.12  Use of the minority language at home and with friends**

| Domain | Age group | Number of respondents (Percentage) | | | |
|---|---|---|---|---|---|
| | | Very often | Sometimes | Not at all | Total |
| At home | 46 to 50 | 1 (20.0%) | 4 (80.0%) | 0 (0.0%) | 5 (100.0%) |
| | 41 to 45 | 5 (62.5%) | 1 (12.5%) | 2 (25.0%) | 8 (100.0%) |
| | 36 to 40 | 6 (42.9%) | 5 (35.7%) | 3 (21.4%) | 14 (100.0%) |
| | 29 to 35 | 6 (40.0%) | 5 (33.3%) | 4 (26.7%) | 15 (100.0%) |
| | 24 to 28 | 5 (62.5%) | 2 (25.0%) | 1 (12.5%) | 8 (100.0%) |
| | Total | 23 (46.0%) | 17 (34.0%) | 10 (20.0%) | 50 (100.0%) |
| With friends | 46 to 50 | 3 (42.9%) | 4 (57.1%) | 0 (0.0%) | 7 (100.0%) |
| | 41 to 45 | 3 (37.5%) | 5 (62.5%) | 0 (0.0%) | 8 (100.0%) |
| | 36 to 40 | 4 (28.6%) | 7 (50.0%) | 3 (21.4%) | 14 (100.0%) |
| | 29 to 35 | 0 (0.0%) | 10 (66.7%) | 5 (33.3%) | 15 (100.0%) |
| | 24 to 28 | 0 (0.0%) | 5 (71.4%) | 2 (28.6%) | 7 (100.0%) |
| | Total | 10 (19.6%) | 31 (60.8%) | 10 (19.6%) | 51 (100.0%) |

Though 42.9% of the oldest group would use the minority language to converse with friends very often, no one among the youngest cohort would use the language for this purpose very often. Instead, the percentage of respondents not using the minority language when conversing with friends increased from 0% to about 30% for the two younger cohorts ($\chi^2$=16.91, df = 8, p = 0.0311).

To sum up, three features are particularly salient in the experience of minority learners learning their minority language. First, minority languages are more used in primary school than in higher levels of education. Secondly, the learning of minority languages is more for conversation than for literacy. Finally, its use at home is most stable and its use in other domains is uncertain or rather limited.

## Learning Chinese

All sixty minority respondents knew Putonghua. (As the questionnaire was administered in Chinese and the target sample was university graduates, this was a methodological requirement.) Minority learners from different age cohorts did not seem to have had very different experiences of learning Chinese, except in a few aspects, particularly for the youngest cohort aged 24 to 28.

By the end of primary school, 98.3% of the minority respondents would have been exposed to written Chinese but only 74.6% would have learnt Putonghua (Table 4.13). This suggests that some of them were taught written Chinese in another Chinese dialect in primary school. For the youngest cohort aged 24 to 28, more of them learnt Putonghua and written Chinese earlier but the difference that emerged was not statistically significant.

**Table 4.13 Time respondents began learning Putonghua and written Chinese**

| Time learning of Chinese began | Number of respondents (Percentage) | | | |
| --- | --- | --- | --- | --- |
| | Putonghua | | Written Chinese | |
| | For all age cohorts | Youngest cohorts aged 24 to 28 | For all age cohorts | Youngest cohort aged 24 to 28 |
| At home from birth | 7 (11.9%) | 3 (25.0%) | 6 (10.0%) | 4 (33.3%) |
| From kindergarten | 3 (5.1%) | 2 (16.7%) | 3 (5.0%) | 1 (8.3%) |
| From primary school | 34 (57.6%) | 5 (41.7%) | 50 (83.3%) | 7 (58.3%) |
| From secondary school | 8 (13.6%) | 2 (16.7%) | 0 (0.0%) | 0 (0.0%) |
| At university | 6 (10.2%) | 0 (0.0%) | 0 (0.0%) | 0 (0.0%) |
| At work | 1 (1.7%) | 0 (0.0%) | 1 (1.7%) | 0 (0.0%) |
| Total | 59 (100.0%) | 12 (100.0%) | 60 (100.0%) | 12 (100.0%) |

For the minority respondents, the amount of class time devoted to learning Chinese was more than that for the Han Chinese respondents (represented by the sample of non-Chinese-language specialists as discussed in Chapter 2) (Table 4.14). In primary school, it was about three lessons more per week; in secondary school, about five lessons more, and at university, about six lessons more. There was also more variation in the number of lessons minority respondents had, as indicated by the standard deviations. (As 5% of the minority respondents were Chinese language specialists, their experience would have contributed a little to this variance.)

**Table 4.14  Class time for learning Chinese**

| Educational level | Minority learners | | | Han Chinese learners | | |
|---|---|---|---|---|---|---|
| | Number of Chinese lessons per week | | Number of respondents | Number of Chinese lessons per week | | Number of respondents |
| | Mean | Standard deviation | | Mean | Standard deviation | |
| Primary school | 12.634 | 10.251 | 56 | 9.430 | 3.547 | 307 |
| Secondary school | 12.375 | 11.452 | 56 | 7.568 | 2.983 | 303 |
| University | 9.740 | 10.540 | 48* | 4.039 | 5.137 | 243* |

* Some respondents did not report that they studied Chinese as a subject at this level.

However, at the university level, an interesting age effect was found ($F = 3.092$, $df_1 = 4$, $df_2 = 43$, $p = 0.025$). The youngest age cohort, who only had 3.1 lessons per week with little variance, was found to be significantly different from the group aged 36 to 40, most affected by the Cultural Revolution. The corresponding cohort of young Han Chinese learners also had 3.2 Chinese lessons per week at university. This suggests that younger minority learners, if they succeed in entering university, are likely to experience similar learning circumstances as Han Chinese learners.

As for the use of Putonghua as a medium of instruction, the educational experience of minority respondents differed from that of the Han Chinese respondents basically in the lesser use of Putonghua in primary school, both in teaching Chinese and in teaching other subjects (Table 4.15). This is consistent with the finding of greater use of the minority language in primary school as presented earlier. The use of Putonghua in secondary school for both groups of respondents was similar. In fact, for minority respondents, the use of Putonghua to teach other subjects at university was even greater than that for the Han Chinese learners, perhaps because in some interior regions in China, for the Han Chinese learners, there was a regional Chinese dialect that their teachers of other subjects could resort to.

**Table 4.15  Use of Putonghua as a medium of instruction**

| Educational level | Subject | Number of respondents (Percentage) | | | |
|---|---|---|---|---|---|
| | | All teachers taught in Putonghua | Some teachers taught in Putonghua | No teachers taught in Putonghua | Total |
| *Minority respondents* | | | | | |
| Primary school | Chinese | 13 (22.4%) | 34 (58.6%) | 11 (19.0%) | 58 (100.0%) |
| | Other subjects | 10 (17.2%) | 25 (43.1%) | 23 (39.7%) | 58 (100.0%) |
| Secondary school | Chinese | 29 (50.0%) | 24 (41.4%) | 5 (8.6%) | 58 (100.0%) |
| | Other subjects | 22 (37.9%) | 24 (41.4%) | 12 (20.7%) | 58 (100.0%) |
| University | Chinese | 47 (88.7%) | 5 (9.4%) | 1 (1.9%) | 53 (100.0%)* |
| | Other subjects | 50 (84.7%) | 6 (10.2%) | 3 (5.1%) | 59 (100.0%) |
| *Han Chinese respondents* | | | | | |
| Primary school | Chinese | 167 (53.2%) | 98 (31.2%) | 49 (15.6%) | 314 (100.0%) |
| | Other subjects | 128 (40.8%) | 109 (34.7%) | 77 (24.5%) | 314 (100.0%) |
| Secondary school | Chinese | 171 (54.5%) | 110 (35.0%) | 33 (10.5%) | 314 (100.0%) |
| | Other subjects | 117 (37.3%) | 145 (46.2%) | 52 (16.6%) | 314 (100.0%) |
| University | Chinese | 202 (76.8%) | 60 (22.8%) | 1 (0.4%) | 263 (100.0%)* |
| | Other subjects | 183 (59.4%) | 118 (38.3%) | 7 (2.3%) | 308 (100.0%) |

* Some respondents did not report that they studied Chinese as a subject at this level.

The minority respondents also used Putonghua less often when conversing with their classmates outside the classroom in primary school than Han Chinese respondents; 69.5% of them did not use it at all as compared with 36.7% of Han Chinese learners who did not do so in primary school. This difference became less pronounced in secondary school and practically non-existent by the time they reached university (Table 4.16).

**Table 4.16  Use of Putonghua when conversing with classmates**

| Educational level | Number of respondents (Percentage) | | | |
|---|---|---|---|---|
| | Usually | Sometimes | Not at all | Total |
| *Minority respondents* | | | | |
| Primary school | 12 (20.3%) | 6 (10.2%) | 41 (69.5%) | 59 (100.0%) |
| Secondary school | 13 (22.0%) | 23 (39.0%) | 23 (39.0%) | 59 (100.0%) |
| University | 48 (80.0%) | 8 (13.3%) | 4 (6.7%) | 60 (100.0%) |
| *Han Chinese respondents* | | | | |
| Primary school | 121 (38.3%) | 79 (25.0%) | 116 (36.7%) | 316 (100.0%) |
| Secondary school | 126 (39.9%) | 105 (33.2%) | 85 (26.9%) | 316 (100.0%) |
| University | 267 (84.8%) | 44 (14.0%) | 4 (1.3%) | 315 (100.0%) |

The minority respondents were also asked if they engaged in independent learning activities outside the classroom to learn Putonghua better; most of them were rather enthusiastic in most of the independent learning activities (Table 4.17), which is a direct contrast to their little engagement in similar learning activities in their minority language. This difference shows that minority learners are not uninterested in or incapable of independent learning, provided that learning opportunities are available (given literacy in the language) and they feel the need to enhance their competence in the language.

**Table 4.17 Minority learners' learning activities in Putonghua outside the classroom**

| Learning activity | Number of respondents (Percentage) | | | |
|---|---|---|---|---|
| | *Very often* | *Sometimes* | *Not at all* | *Total* |
| Reading books | 46 (88.5%) | 5 (9.6%) | 1 (1.9%) | 52 (100.0%) |
| Reading newspapers/magazines | 39 (78.0%) | 8 (16.0%) | 3 (6.0%) | 50 (100.0%) |
| Checking the dictionary | 37 (71.2%) | 12 (23.1%) | 3 (5.8%) | 52 (100.0%) |
| Watching television | 35 (70.0%) | 12 (24.0%) | 3 (6.0%) | 50 (100.0%) |
| Conversing with others | 37 (68.5%) | 14 (25.9%) | 3 (5.6%) | 54 (100.0%) |
| Writing letters* | 32 (65.3%) | 15 (30.6%) | 2 (4.1%) | 49 (100.0%) |
| Listening to the radio | 32 (65.3%) | 14 (28.6%) | 3 (6.1%) | 49 (100.0%) |
| Listening to/singing songs | 28 (60.9%) | 14 (30.4%) | 4 (8.7%) | 46 (100.0%) |
| Seeing movies or video tapes | 26 (54.2%) | 16 (33.3%) | 6 (12.5%) | 48 (100.0%) |
| Practising with tapes/materials | 14 (36.8%) | 12 (31.6%) | 12 (31.6%) | 38 (100.0%) |

Note: Differences in totals arose from non-responses to some questions.
* The youngest cohort used this learning activity less frequently than the older groups ($\chi^2 = 15.67$, df = 8, p = 0.0474).

In spite of all their independent learning efforts (which, of course, could have continued even after secondary school), by the time the minority respondents left secondary school, 42.9% of them were still not satisfied with their level of competence in Putonghua, except for the youngest cohort, 91.7% of which felt their Putonghua was good enough for university education or their working life ($\chi^2 = 10.69$, df = 4, p = 0.0303) (Table 4.18). This difference according to age was not observed among Han Chinese respondents, the majority (79.1%) of which felt their Putonghua upon completion of secondary school was quite adequate. The confidence exhibited by the youngest cohort of the minority respondents could be interpreted as an indication that the bilingual orientation for minority learners in more recent years might be bearing fruit, at least for some learners. What effects this acquisition of Putonghua has on maintaining their own languages needs further investigation.

Table 4.18  Rating of Putonghua competence when leaving secondary school

| Age group | Number of respondents (Percentage) | | |
|---|---|---|---|
| | Felt Putonghua competence was good enough | Felt Putonghua competence was not good enough | Total |
| Minority respondents | | | |
| 46 to 50 | 3 (42.9%) | 4 (57.1%) | 7 (100.0%) |
| 41 to 45 | 2 (28.6%) | 5 (71.4%) | 7 (100.0%) |
| 36 to 40 | 6 (46.2%) | 7 (53.8%) | 13 (100.0%) |
| 29 to 35 | 10 (58.8%) | 7 (41.2%) | 17 (100.0%) |
| 24 to 28 | 11 (91.7%) | 1 (8.3%) | 12 (100.0%) |
| Total | 32 (57.1%) | 24 (42.9%) | 56 (100.0%) |
| Han Chinese respondents | | | |
| 46 to 50 | 30 (83.3%) | 6 (16.7%) | 36 (100.0%) |
| 41 to 45 | 41 (78.8%) | 11 (21.2%) | 52 (100.0%) |
| 36 to 40 | 41 (77.4%) | 12 (22.6%) | 53 (100.0%) |
| 29 to 35 | 63 (78.8%) | 17 (21.3%) | 80 (100.0%) |
| 24 to 28 | 64 (79.0%) | 12 (21.0%) | 81 (100.0%) |
| Total | 239 (79.1%) | 63 (20.9%) | 302 (100.0%) |

In summary, although the minority learners in this study had lesser exposure to Putonghua in primary school, by secondary school, they were experiencing more similar learning circumstances as their Han Chinese counterparts. In addition, most of the minority learners invested a lot of independent learning effort to enhance their competence in Putonghua. We have to remember though that this sample of minority respondents is not typical of the average minority learner in China. Many of the respondents were teachers, administrators, civil servants and information workers, occupations requiring competence in Putonghua; so they were likely to have undergone training in Putonghua with more than the usual seriousness, though the assumption that they made their career choice early on in life and learnt Putonghua so as to support such a choice might not hold for every one of them.

## Learning foreign languages

Only fifty-five of the sixty minority respondents had learnt a foreign language. The majority (85.2%) of the fifty-five respondents learnt English as their first (or most important) foreign language. This is quite close to the percentage of Han Chinese respondents learning English (90.7%). The other foreign languages learnt by the minority respondents were: Japanese (5.6%), Russian

(3.7%), German (1.9%) and an unspecified language (3.7%). Consistent with foreign language policy trends (see Chapter 3, 'Foreign Language Policy from 1949', pp. 71–84), the two learners of Russian were from the oldest cohort aged 46 to 50.

Unlike the Han Chinese respondents with 8.5% learning to speak and write the foreign language from primary school, none of the minority respondents learnt their first foreign language in primary school; forty-three of the respondents (78.2%) began learning to speak their foreign language from secondary school, eleven (20.0%) from university and one (1.8%) at work. Within this general pattern, the group aged 41 to 45 was aberrant with 75.0% of them learning to speak their foreign language only when they went to university. They could have been affected by irregular schooling during the Cultural Revolution. A similar pattern emerged for the time they began learning the written form of their foreign language.

**Table 4.19  Class time for foreign language learning in secondary school**

| Age group | Minority learners | | | Han Chinese learners | | |
|---|---|---|---|---|---|---|
| | Number of foreign language lessons per week | | Number of respondents | Number of foreign language lessons per week | | Number of respondents |
| | Mean | Standard deviation | | Mean | Standard deviation | |
| 46 to 50 | 3.800 | 0.447 | 5 | 4.727 | 1.8488 | 11 |
| 41 to 45 | 5.000 | 1.414 | 2 | 3.778 | 1.7172 | 27 |
| 36 to 40 | 4.222 | 1.202 | 9 | 4.310 | 2.4217 | 29 |
| 29 to 35 | 4.941 | 1.435 | 17 | 5.500 | 1.4477 | 48 |
| 24 to 28 | 6.900 | 2.514 | 10 | 6.500 | 2.3276 | 68 |
| Total | 5.116 | 1.905 | 43* | 5.383 | 2.2602 | 183* |

* Some respondents did not report that they studied a foreign language as a subject at this level.

Like for the Han Chinese learners, there was a statistically significant increase in class time for foreign language learning in secondary school for the youngest cohort of minority language learners (F = 4.397, $df_1$ = 4, $df_2$ = 38, p = 0.005) (Table 4.19).

At university level, excluding the data from the four foreign language specialists who had around twenty lessons per week in the foreign language, the average class time devoted to foreign language learning for the minority respondents was 6.1 lessons per week, comparable to 5.5 lessons per week for the Han Chinese respondents.

The degree of use of the foreign language as a medium of instruction in foreign language classes and in teaching other subjects to minority learners is, on the whole, similar to that for Han Chinese learners at both secondary and university levels. For minority respondents, only 60.0% of their secondary school teachers used the foreign language to teach it as compared to 64.4% of the teachers of Han Chinese respondents who did so. However, 21.8% of the minority respondents did not study the foreign language as a subject in secondary school, which is higher than the percentage of the Han Chinese respondents who did not have such an opportunity in secondary school (13.3%). At university level, both batches of respondents experienced more similar circumstances; only 7.4% of the minority respondents reported non-use of the foreign language by teachers in foreign language classes while 6.3% of the Han Chinese respondents reported such. The youngest cohort of minority learners all had foreign language lessons at university as compared to 33.3% of those aged 46 to 50 who had no such opportunity. For both minority and Han Chinese respondents, as expected, the foreign language was not used by their teachers in teaching other subjects in secondary school; at university level, about 9% of both batches of respondents reported that some of their teachers of other subjects used the foreign language in their non-foreign-language classes.

Similarity between the two ethnic groups was also found for other aspects such as the degree of home support and the extent to which minority learners would use independent learning activities outside the classroom to learn the foreign language. Both the minority respondents and the Han Chinese respondents experienced little home support for their learning of the foreign language; only 11.1% of the minority respondents had at least one family member to speak the foreign language with, as compared to 8.7% of the Han Chinese respondents who reported such. On the whole, the amount of work minority learners put into independent learning activities outside the classroom appears to be similar to the efforts made by Han Chinese respondents but there is one slight difference; Han Chinese learners seem to use the foreign language a little more when conversing with their classmates during secondary school; 31.8% of the Han Chinese respondents were ready to do so as compared with only 16.0% of the minority respondents who were. We could attribute this to the fact that among the Han Chinese respondents, there were some who learnt the foreign language from primary school and these would have been in a better position to act as catalysts for conversational practice in the foreign language in secondary school. A more likely explanation, however, is that for minority learners to switch to Putonghua in secondary school is already a step away from their native minority languages more used in primary school. For them to try to converse in the foreign language, which is the third language they learn, is more difficult, both psychologically and linguistically, at least in secondary school. By university, there is more readiness; 49% of the minority respondents were ready to use the foreign language at least sometimes when conversing with their classmates outside the classroom (as compared to 56.8% of the Han Chinese respondents who were).

In any case, upon completion of secondary school education, the two batches of respondents felt just as non-confident about their competence in the foreign language; only around 11% in both groups considered their level of competence adequate for university education or working life, although there is a slight suggestion that younger cohorts in the years ahead may be able to do a little better (Table 4.20).

**Table 4.20  Rating of foreign language competence when leaving secondary school**

| Age group | Number of respondents (Percentage) | | |
|---|---|---|---|
| | Felt foreign language competence was good enough | Felt foreign language competence was not good enough | Total |
| Minority respondents | | | |
| 46 to 50 | 0 (0.0%) | 5 (100.0%) | 5 (100.0%) |
| 41 to 45 | 0 (0.0%) | 6 (100.0%) | 6 (100.0%) |
| 36 to 40 | 1 (8.3%) | 11 (91.7%) | 12 (100.0%) |
| 29 to 35 | 3 (17.6%) | 14 (82.4%) | 17 (100.0%) |
| 24 to 28 | 2 (18.2%) | 9 (81.8%) | 11 (100.0%) |
| Total | 6 (11.8%) | 45 (88.2%) | 51 (100.0%) |
| Han Chinese respondents | | | |
| 46 to 50 | 1 (5.3%) | 18 (94.7%) | 19 (100.0%) |
| 41 to 45 | 1 (3.0%) | 32 (97.0%) | 33 (100.0%) |
| 36 to 40 | 1 (3.0%) | 32 (97.0%) | 33 (100.0%) |
| 29 to 35 | 8 (17.0%) | 39 (83.0%) | 47 (100.0%) |
| 24 to 28 | 11 (16.7%) | 55 (83.3%) | 66 (100.0%) |
| Total | 22 (11.1%) | 176 (88.9%) | 198 (100.0%) |

In summary, except for the fact that no minority respondents learnt the foreign language in primary school and slightly more of them did not learn it in secondary school, resulting in lesser use of the foreign language when conversing with their classmates in secondary school, they were largely similar to Han Chinese respondents in their foreign language learning experience.

## Summary and discussion

It must be emphasized that the sample of minority learners in this study were university graduates and not typical of the many minority learners who do not manage to enter university. The sample is also too small for the results to be given much weight. The preliminary results, however, do raise a few interesting issues about minority learners' experience of their native languages and their learning of Chinese and foreign languages.

**Learning minority languages**: Most minority learners seem to learn their language at home and use it mostly at home. About half the respondents never learnt how to write their minority language. Whether that is the case for all minority groups deserves more investigation. Although most minority learners do not seem very pleased with their abilities in their minority language, except in conversation and pronunciation, they do not seem too worried about it, perhaps because many of them do not have to use the minority language in education or their working life in future. The lack of a wide range of domains of use is probably what discourages minority learners from trying to acquire greater competence in the language. Codifying writing scripts is only a first step towards maintaining minority languages. If the languages have only a few functions to perform, learners will not be motivated to acquire a wide range of abilities in them; nor will they have the opportunity to do so. It seems that many minority learners in China usually go through a period of transitional bilingual education in primary school during which their native languages are used as a medium of instruction, along with a Chinese dialect, before they switch to Putonghua, mostly during secondary school. The dilemma for minority learners, and for the Chinese government, is that if they are educated entirely in their own languages, they cannot fit into university life as easily, unless university education and jobs are also widely available in minority languages, which, in view of the fact that there are fifty-five minority groups in China, is unlikely for most of them. Eventually, it is a matter of how much minority groups want to take advantage of the educational and economic advantages of achieving competence in Putonghua. So while the Chinese government does not suppress minority languages, in the sense that there is no stick to force minority learners to convert to Putonghua, there is certainly a carrot to attract them to do so. From a multilingual perspective, there is no harm in being able to acquire competence in more than one language and some minority learners in China seem motivated to do so, perhaps because the use of their own languages are upheld by Chinese law. Those who are willing to become bilingual may experience lesser use of their own languages in some domains. Even now, fewer minority learners who succeed in entering university are using their minority language with their friends. But that is essentially a matter of personal and pragmatic choice. Around the world, many people learn other languages all the time and when they do, inevitably they tend to lose some domains of use to the new languages they learn. Of course, whether different minority groups feel differently about the lesser use of their languages in some domains needs to be addressed, not least because the respondents in this survey were all fluent users of Putonghua.

**Learning Chinese**: During the Cultural Revolution when minority languages and cultures were suppressed, negative feelings about learning

Chinese would have been natural. But for the younger cohorts of minority learners, such historic memory may eventually fade away. As China becomes more established economically and internationally and learning Chinese becomes desirable even to the international community, national pride may make it easier for more minority learners to feel more positive about learning Putonghua. This is not to suggest that minority learners are negative about this now. On the contrary, minority learners (at least those who manage to enter university) seem ready to invest a lot of energy in learning Putonghua, even outside the classroom. Many of them learn written Chinese first through another Chinese dialect. As Putonghua becomes more and more used in the Chinese educational system, more minority learners may have a less difficult time acquiring Chinese because they may then be taught Putonghua along with written Chinese from the beginning. But it will take time for Putonghua to pervade through the entire educational system, particularly in the rural areas where most minority learners come from. It is also unlikely that the use of Chinese dialects by the Han Chinese population in informal situations will stop altogether; so even if Putonghua is used in all classes, minority learners may still have to deal with two Chinese dialects, Putonghua in class and another Chinese dialect for informal interaction with their classmates.

**Foreign language learning**: Since most minority learners already have to learn Chinese as a second language, one would expect that they would have less time and energy to learn a foreign language. If their acquisition of Putonghua in primary school could be facilitated by not having to learn it through another Chinese dialect first, then minority learners would be in a slightly more equal position to acquire foreign language competence during secondary school. The survey, limited as it is, also shows that if minority learners manage to enter university, their foreign language experience from then on is not that different from that of Han Chinese learners. Minority learners are just as prepared to invest time and energy into learning foreign languages as Han Chinese learners are and capable of as much success. In fact, some minority learners may even have an advantage in learning some foreign languages if their own minority language belongs to the same language family. Some language families represented by minority languages in China are: Sino-Tibetan, Altaic, Austronesian, Austroasiatic, and Indo-European (Zhou, 2003, pp. 23–26). Since China has set her heart on playing a major role in international affairs, the minority groups in China are actually an asset in foreign diplomacy as many of them have close ties with the cultural traditions all around China.

The comments made thus far have treated minority learners from different ethnic groups as if they were homogeneous, which is far from the truth. Since there are so many different ethnic groups, much cannot be said in generalizations. It is hoped that the case histories presented in the next section can be more illuminating.

# Seven Case Histories

Altogether, seventeen learners from different ethnic groups were interviewed. Here are excerpts from the learning histories of seven learners, each representing a different ethnic group. Their age ranged from 25 to 51. The learners were interviewed in Putonghua about their total multilingual learning experience. Each interview took about an hour. In the following excerpts, the interviewee's age was that in 2000. All names are pseudonyms. The interviewer's comments are put in square brackets.

The main issues in reviewing these learning biographies are: were individual experiences consistent with policy trends and survey findings? Did most of the interviewees use their minority language mainly at home and go through initial education partially in the minority language but convert to Putonghua during the course of education? Secondly, was their experience of learning Putonghua and their first foreign language different from that of Han Chinese learners?

The seven learners, from the oldest to the youngest, to be considered are:

1. Fang: a female nationalities expert aged 51 from the Zhuang minority (the largest minority group with a population of 16.2 million and a new script for the language created after 1949)
2. Ping: a male economics teacher aged 43 from the Man minority (with a population of 10.7 million and Chinese as its adopted language)
3. Mei: a female teacher of the Yao language aged 37 from the Yao minority (with a population of 2.6 million and a new script for the language)
4. Mong: a male cultural anthropologist aged 35 from the Mulao minority (with only 207,352 people and no script for the language)
5. He: a male computer scientist aged 29 from the Hui minority (with a population of 9.8 million and Chinese as its adopted language)
6. Dai: a male Chinese history teacher aged 27 from the Miao minority (with a population of 8.9 million using several varieties of the Miao language with new scripts created for these varieties)
7. Ma: a male foreign languages graduate student aged 25 from the Dong minority (with a population of 3.0 million and a new script for its language)

## *Fang (Zhuang Interviewee 9, female, aged 51, a nationalities expert)*

**The Zhuang language**: I was born in 1949 in a Zhuang village among the mountains of Guangxi [in the southern interior of China]. Before I went to school, I spoke only the Zhuang language. In 1956, I began my primary education at a very small village school. They also spoke the Zhuang language. There were only four grades in that primary school. Students from two grades

**Photo 19** The administrative building at Guangxi Nationalities College.

**Photo 20** Slogan on the campus of Guangxi Nationalities College: 'The blessing of the teacher is like a sea. The virtue of the teacher is like a mountain.'

studied in the same classroom. When the teacher was teaching one grade, students in the other grade would do exercises. In the whole school, we had about sixty students.

**Primary school in the Guiliu dialect**: In 1959, I left my village to study in another primary school. It was still a village school but a better one. My father was working as a cadre in a state farm. I was an only child so my father sent for me so as to improve my educational conditions. My mother remained at our village. My grandmother went with me to live with my father. I enrolled for Primary 3 in that school. The teachers spoke the Guiliu dialect [a Chinese dialect]. I also learnt that dialect from my classmates. When I visited my classmates' homes, sometimes we spoke the Zhuang language and sometimes the Guiliu dialect. I continued to speak the Zhuang language with my father and grandmother at home. When buying things on the street, I would use either the Zhuang language or the Guiliu dialect. No one spoke Putoughua with me then but $yu^3wen^2$ [Chinese] was taught in Putonghua at school. Other subjects were taught in the Guiliu dialect. There was one year when I failed my $yu^3wen^2$ [Chinese].

**Secondary school in Putonghua**: In 1962, I went to another place to attend junior secondary school. Everything was taught in Putonghua then. But outside the classroom, everyone spoke the Guiliu dialect. In 1965, I started studying in a senior secondary school. The teacher required us to read newspapers at night and we listened to radio broadcasts in Putonghua.

**From intellectual youth to cadre**: In 1969, I 'went down to the village' ($xia^4$ $xiang^1$). [During the Cultural Revolution, it was common to send educated people to work in the villages so that they would learn from the farmers.] The place I was sent to spoke the Zhuang language. I was first a farmer; then, in 1970, I was 'taken out' to be a worker in an orchard. We grew mandarin oranges, grapes and watermelons. After half a year, I was 'taken out' to be a primary teacher to teach the children of the other workers in that orchard by myself. I taught four grades and a total of fifty or sixty children but my identity was still that of a temporary worker. In 1973, I became a cadre in the same orchard and had a stable monthly income of twenty-one *Renminbi* [the Chinese currency]. I expanded the school to one with six teachers, one for each grade, and became the principal. We taught in the Guiliu dialect. I also took care of women matters in that compound — divorces, fights, quarrels. We also established a youth group and I was the deputy secretary. I started a broadcast programme in the orchard too. I wrote the scripts and did the broadcasts myself. I was the only one in the programme. At night, sometimes we organized Hanyu [Chinese] lessons for the workers because they could not even write notes to ask for leave.

**Nationalities studies in Beijing**: In 1979, I came to this nationality institute [in the southern interior] to work in the resource and information centre. In 1984, I was sent to Beijing to study. About twenty of us were preparing for the admission examinations. The university allotted one classroom for us to revise together for twenty days. Only two of us gained admission. In 1986, I returned to teach nationalities studies here.

**Russian forgotten**: The first foreign language I studied was Russian in junior and senior secondary school but because there has not been any opportunity to use it, I have forgotten all of it. I have never studied English.

**Wide repertoire:** My best language now is Putonghua, especially when it comes to writing because I learnt it systematically. My second best is the Guiliu dialect. The Zhuang language is my third best. Then comes Russian. I can also understand some Kejiahua [the Hakka dialect] and Yueyu [Cantonese] and speak a little of the Yao language because our neighbours are Yao.

## Ping (Man Interviewee 2, male, aged 43, an economics teacher)

**Background**: I was born in a village in Liaoning in 1957. For my primary and secondary education, I studied in the village school. But that was the time of the Cultural Revolution so classes were not very regular. In 1979, I came to this university [in the northern interior] to study economics and graduated in 1983. I taught at a school run by the party [Communist Party] from 1983 to 1987. In 1987, I returned to this university [in the northern interior] to teach economics.

**The Man language**: I cannot speak the Man language though that is my ethnic language. I speak Hanyu [Chinese]. In the Heilongjiang area, some older people can speak the Man language but I cannot.

**Dongbeihua and Putonghua**: During my primary and secondary school-days, classes were taught in Putonghua. There was no difference in my language environment between my school or my home when I was growing up. I did not have to learn Putonghua because my home dialect, Dongbeihua [the Chinese dialect in the northeastern region], is close to Putonghua, the standard dialect. So it was very easy for me to interact with others at school and university. However, though they are similar, Dongbeihua is not exactly like Putonghua. The word 'sun', for example, should be pronounced $ri^4$ in Putonghua but in Dongbeihua, we say $yi^4$. There are also some differences in vocabulary. In my own dialect, 'sun' is $ri^4tou^2$ but in Putonghua, it is $tai^4yang^2$. My best language now is Hanyu [Chinese]. Since I am a teacher, if my Putonghua is not good, other people, especially students from the south, cannot understand me.

**Other Chinese dialects**: Among my classmates, there were people from different provinces such as Fujian or Jiangxi. We imitated each other and it was very humorous. When I teach, dialectal differences are also a good source of humour in class. To understand the local economy, you have to understand local dialects. Students are interested in dialectal differences too.

**Japanese**: I studied Japanese as my first foreign language [of first importance]. I did not study a second foreign language [of secondary importance]. I think the best time to learn foreign languages is when we are young but before going to university, I had not learnt any Japanese. Japanese was spoken by some old people in the northeastern region where I grew up because of occupation by the Japanese earlier. I chose Japanese as my first foreign language because I did not know English was so important then. When I went to university, many of my classmates had already studied English at school but I had not. I did not want to be at a disadvantage. So I chose a new language that other students had not learnt before. I also thought Japanese was closer to Chinese because of the presence of *kanji*. I later found that I had to spend a lot of effort and still could not perform as well as I had wished. Japanese is not easy to learn. There are too many changes in vocabulary and morphology, which makes it difficult to master. Japanese is not the same as Chinese but Chinese culture has a great influence on Japanese. Studying Japanese makes me feel proud to be Chinese. In Japanese lessons, we listened to tapes in class and the teachers explained the grammar and vocabulary. The teachers spoke in front of the class. We just took notes. The teachers' competence in Japanese was not very high. Most of them were *ban⁴tu² chu¹jia¹* [learnt Japanese halfway in their career paths]. We did not listen to tapes outside class; we were not required to do so. Among our classmates, we practised simple Japanese among ourselves. At that time, it was not common to do so. I spent two-and-a-half years learning Japanese. We used a book published in Jilin and *Atarashi Nihongo* [New Japanese] published jointly by Chinese and Japanese publishers. We also used a set of four books published by the Shanghai Foreign Language Institute with an emphasis on grammar, oral interaction and vocabulary. I had to pass Japanese to get promoted. But there were no special classes organized by the university to help me improve my Japanese; there were too few people choosing Japanese as their foreign language for their promotion assessment. Since I passed my Japanese examination, I have given up studying Japanese. My research is on the Chinese economy. So I cannot use my Japanese.

**English**: I did not do my master's degree and did not study English. Since I was studying economics in China, English was not so important to me. But now, I think it would have been better if I had studied English instead of Japanese. Then I can use English to publish my research and find information. But I have no time. My research and teaching take a lot of time. If I have time, I would like to learn English. I do not wish to learn Japanese any more. I do not like to learn it any more. It would be best if there could be a simple language that everyone could learn and use for international communication.

## Mei (Yao Interviewee 4, female, aged 37, a minority language teacher)

**Background**: I was born in Lingui in Guangxi in 1963. I came here [a city in the southern interior] in 1989. After graduation, I left to teach in a secondary school for four years. Then I was transferred back here to establish Yao studies. I now teach nationalities studies, linguistic theory and the Yao language at this university [in the southern interior].

**The Yao language**: I started learning the Yao language at home from the time I was born. It was like a basic instinct. Everyone at home spoke the Yao language. I grew up in the Yao region and went to a primary school in a village where some Han Chinese lived. I did not have any Yao language classes in primary school, secondary school or university. I only learnt the written form of the Yao language when I started working. In primary school, some of the lessons for other subjects were taught in the Yao language. During primary school, I often used the Yao language to speak with my classmates; in secondary school, I still did so sometimes. But at university, I did not use the Yao language with my classmates because my classmates came from several different regions. So it was easier for all of us to communicate in Chinese.

**Ethnic pride**: Ever since I was young, I have felt very proud that I can speak my own language. Though I have been outside [my village] studying or working for twenty or thirty years by now, I still feel the same. If I meet my friends from my ethnic group, or my relatives, there is no occasion when I have the opportunity to use the Yao language that I do not. I am not like some people who have this attitude — if they speak the Yao language, they are afraid other people will laugh at them. I do not have this feeling. I feel very proud I know my language. After I started working, I found that there are also Yao people residing in countries outside China. I can communicate with them using our language. I often do interpretation. So I feel my language can cross national boundaries. I feel very proud. I do not feel any pressure.

**Hanyu in primary school**: At the time when I was growing up, there was very little opportunity for us to be exposed to Hanyu [Chinese]. Unlike nowadays, there was no television and no radio. Now, children in my home village are much better. At two or three years old, they know Hanyu. When I started primary school, I did not know Hanyu. I only knew my own ethnic language. During Primary 1 and Primary 2, my teacher was from my ethnic group. She taught us bilingually using the Yao language and Hanyu but she did not teach us the Yao script. She only taught us how to say 'Have a meal' and other phrases in Hanyu and in the Yao language. In that way, we could understand what she was saying. Even Hanyu lessons were taught partly in the Yao language and partly in Putonghua. For members from a minority language group, learning Hanyu was quite difficult. I remember the first week when I went to primary school, my grandmother gave me ten cents. In those days, ten cents could buy four pieces of candy. I did not know how to speak Hanyu.

When I went to the shop, the woman there could not understand my Yao language. I did not know how to speak with her. So for a whole week, I did not succeed in buying candy. Later, another student from a higher grade, who was also from my village, told me, 'Let me buy the candy for you. I know how to speak Hanyu.' So she went to buy it. After she bought it, I gave her half of it. I only got to eat half of it. In that way, little by little, after the teacher taught us bilingually in various ways, we also learnt Hanyu. Soon when I spent time with Han Chinese classmates, I could speak Hanyu. But we were speaking in the Guilin dialect though the teacher was speaking Putonghua in class.

**Putonghua at a later age**: In primary and secondary school, I had about eight lessons per week for Hanyu [Chinese] and at university, I still had six Chinese lessons per week. By secondary school, only Putonghua was used to teach Hanyu [Chinese] and other subjects. But my classmates and I still responded largely in the Guilin dialect. Only at university did we really use Putonghua to respond to the teacher and talk with each other. When I started working, I used mostly Putonghua. In the Yao language classes I teach now, I use both the Yao language and Putonghua. But for all other subjects I teach, I only use Putonghua to teach. We are required to do so at this university.

**Other minority languages or Chinese dialects**: I can also say a few sentences in the Zhuang language because there were some Zhuang people living in our region. When we were small, we played together. I also know some Chinese dialects like Baihua [Cantonese] because I studied and worked at different places.

**English**: Only in the last year of my senior secondary school did the teacher talk to us about learning English because we had to take an examination in English. But I really learnt English only when I went to university. It was a requirement. We had six lessons of English per week for two years. We only managed to go through Books 1 and 2 of Xu Guozhang's series. The lessons were partly taught in Putonghua. I never used English to speak with my classmates. Very few people in my region used English. So I did not learn it well and I was already rather old when I started learning it. I spent a lot of time purposely to memorize the vocabulary but I am not pleased with the results. I do not use English at all now.

**Japanese**: I began to learn Japanese from about a year ago because I had to pass my promotion assessment. I chose to study Japanese so that I could use it [to meet the foreign language requirement] for this assessment.

### Mong (Mulao Interviewee 10, male, aged 35, a cultural anthropologist)

**Background**: I was born in 1965 in a village in the Mulao Autonomous Xian [county]. In 1970, when I was five, I began studying in the village school. From 1976 to 1978, I attended my junior secondary school at the village. From 1978 to 1981, I did my senior secondary schooling in the city of the *xian* [county]. From 1981 to 1985, I studied archaeology in [a university in the southern coastal region]. I went on to do my master's in anthropology from 1985 to 1988 at the same university. In 1988, I was posted to do research at the nationalities research centre [in a university in the southern interior region]. From 1994 to 1995, I was sent to [a foreign languages programme in Guangzhou] to study English. In 1996, I was transferred to the State Education Commission in Chengdu to have further training in English. From October 1997 to October 1998, I was attached to the institute in social and cultural anthropology [at a top university] in England. I spent another year from November 1999 to October 2000 [at another university] in England and I am now back at this university [in the southern interior] to collect data for my PhD.

**The Mulao language**: My wife is also from the Mulao ethnic group but we do not speak the Mulao language at home. So my child does not speak the Mulao language. My first dialect is the Guiliu dialect. Although my father is from the Mulao group, my mother is from the Zhuang group. I can understand the Mulao dialect but I cannot speak it because even at home, my parents spoke the Guiliu dialect to each other. I only know the address terms for 'father, mother, grandfather, grandmother, elder brother, elder sister, younger brother, younger sister, uncle …' in the Mulao language. I use the Guiliu dialect for talking about other things. My mother sometimes told us folktales in the Zhuang language but we could not understand them. Sometimes, we also joked in the Zhuang language.

**Primary school and junior secondary school in the Guiliu dialect**: In primary school, my teacher used the Guiliu dialect to teach. Even Chinese lessons were conducted in the Guiliu dialect. From 1970 to 1976, there were three or four teachers from other provinces. They taught in Putonghua. From 1976, in junior secondary school, I was still taught largely in the Guiliu dialect, except for chemistry, which was taught in Putonghua.

**Putonghua in senior secondary schooldays**: From 1978, at senior secondary school, all my subjects were taught in Putonghua because that school was in the city of the *xian*. Outside class, we still conversed in the Guiliu dialect but I had no difficulty listening to Putonghua by then. In our village environment or even in the *xian*, there were many things we cannot write or think about in our dialect. But when we watched television or listened to the radio, we found that other people could talk about a lot of things in Putonghua and their vocabulary was much greater. So we felt there were many things we still did not know. Our Putonghua pronunciation also had to be accurate. If it is not accurate, it can become a different word. Two of my Chinese teachers were very talented and wrote very well. One of them encouraged us to keep editing our own essays. When an essay was good, we would be asked to recite it in front of the whole class. There were also essay competitions in my school. If you were good, they would praise you by name in front of everyone. I learnt well because it was a kind of self-respect.

**Putonghua at university**: At university [in the southern coastal region], we were taught entirely in Putonghua. I used Putonghua a lot. I did not use the Guiliu dialect as there were many students from other provinces. When I went home at the end of the semester, the moment I saw someone when I got off the train, I wanted to address that person in Putonghua. Then I remembered I should use the local dialect and reverted to the local dialect. Sometimes when I watched television during the holidays, I would comment on the programme in Putonghua. But after being at home for a few weeks, I would again use the Guiliu dialect to talk about the television programmes.

**Putonghua now**: My best language now is Putonghua. I still cannot distinguish between the /n/ sound and the /ng/ sound but I write and think best in this language. Now at home, sometimes I speak Putonghua with my wife and sometimes we use Putonghua with our child though most of the time, we use the Guiliu dialect.

**Other Chinese dialects**: I can also understand a type of Kejiahua [Hakka] because my aunt speaks it. I do not speak Baihua [spoken in the nearby region] but I can understand a little of it.

**English at school**: When I was twelve, when my brother came back from school, he would teach me English words like 'flower' or 'air'. I started learning English formally in senior secondary school. We had four to six lessons per week. During my last senior secondary year, we had eight to ten lessons per week. The teacher used Putonghua to teach us English. The teacher had a good teaching method and was very strict. The teacher also told us that if our English was good, we could act as interpreters or tourist guides and introduce our China and rich culture to foreigners. In our village, the thinking was that if we stayed behind to plow the land, at the most, we could only support ourselves. But if we could have contact with foreigners, we could have a better income and have a higher status. One of the teachers acted as an interpreter in the People's Liberation Army in the Assist Vietnam to Withstand America campaign [the Vietnam War]. In his classes, he would tell us some of his experiences, which we found very interesting. I was aware that I was from the village. My mathematics, physics and chemistry were very poor but my memory was very good. So what the teacher said in arts or social studies subjects, I could remember very well. I was not good at understanding the more abstract ideas and could not grasp political theory, for example. But among my classmates, I was still considered the best. My classmates and I were always testing each other. It was very competitive. I improved a lot in senior secondary school. I came first in class, except for mathematics, physics and chemistry.

**English at university**: For my undergraduate studies, the teacher used English. Our teachers were all from China and they used Chinese sounds to pronounce English. We could hear their very strong Chinese accent. So we all wanted to hear the real English pronunciation. During my third and fourth years at university, I bought a small radio to listen to BBC [British Broadcasting Corporation]. Tapes were very expensive. We could not afford them. When I was at university, my family was very poor. I had two brothers and one sister. Three of us were still studying at that time. So the financial burden in my family was very heavy. My classmates and I also tried to speak English in our dormitory at specific times. For example, they would say, 'Today, from 8 am to 12 noon, in our dormitory, not a single sentence in Putonghua is allowed. Whoever speaks Putonghua will be fined.' The penalty was to go and collect food from the canteen for all seven or eight of us at the dormitory. There was also the English Corner. During my undergraduate days, I did not go there but during my MA, I did. For my MA, my English teacher was a 'foreign expert' [guest researcher or teacher]; he could not understand Putonghua and so taught in English. When I was undergoing training in Chengdu, there were three or four teachers from overseas. Two teachers from America could not understand a word of Chinese and taught in English. When I went to England, I attended seminars, audited their courses conducted in English and interacted a lot in English. My reading in English has mainly been on materials in my discipline. I do not have energy to read novels or essays in English.

### He (Hui Interviewee 3, male, aged 29, a computer scientist)

**Background**: I am from the Hui minority group and was born in a village in the Ningxia Autonomous Region in 1972. I only attended one-and-a-half years of Primary 1 and 2. I did not go to Primary 3 because the school was closed at that time. Only after the Gang of Four was destroyed [a term to signify the end of the Cultural Revolution when four influential members lost their power] did I go to school again. I went straight into Primary 4. I completed my primary and secondary education in Ningxia. In 1989, when I was seventeen, I moved to Lanzhou to study mechanical engineering. I was the only one from my birthplace who could go to university. Upon graduation in 1993, I started working in the Computer Centre of this university [a key university in the northern interior]. From 1998, I have been teaching computer system maintenance here.

**Arabic and Islam**: Before I went to school, I learnt a little Arabic at home and mostly at the Muslim temple. All the Hui children went to the temple to learn Arabic. It was one big class, with ten to twenty children altogether. The master would give us individual work according to our levels. We memorized extracts from the Koran. When I started school, I learnt Arabic at the temple only intermittently. I learnt to write a little Arabic too but I have forgotten all of it. However, Islam is still my religion. The Hui people have adopted the Chinese language but language is language and religion is religion.

**Chinese dialect at home and Putonghua at school**: At home, most of the time, we spoke the local northern Chinese dialect. I also spoke it with my friends and classmates or when buying things. I started learning Putonghua only when I went to school at nine or ten. In secondary school, the *yu³ wen²* [Chinese] teacher would play tapes to us to train us to speak Putonghua. Almost all the teachers taught in Putonghua but the influence of the Chinese teacher was the greatest. He was always carrying the tape recorder just to play tapes to us. After school, I did not practise much because my family conditions were not so good. We could not afford a tape recorder or receive broadcasts. My classmates were in a better position. They had tape recorders, could receive broadcasts and had more books at home.

**From Chinese words to stories**: I felt my Chinese dialectal pronunciation was a hindrance to my learning of Putonghua; because my pronunciation was not accurate, I could not figure out the words. By Primary 3, my classmates already knew many words. I knew very few. Learning Chinese was very, very painful for me in my primary and junior secondary schooldays. I often failed my Chinese. In junior secondary school, I spent about two years reading books of folk-tales and fairy tales in our town library. Then I could link up the words into sentences and the sentences into texts. That was how I learnt Chinese — from memorizing words and from reading those stories. I did not consciously try to practise speaking Putonghua to learn it better. When I went to university, my Chinese dialect became Putonghua by and by though we had no Chinese lessons then. My best language now is Chinese.

**English**: I started learning English only in senior secondary school so I was weaker than other students in English when I went to university. They had learnt it for six years by that time but I had only studied it for three years. Outside class in my schooldays, sometimes I would do some exercises in English but not often. At university, studying English was also rather strenuous for me. The classes were very big. The teacher talked. A lot of people listened together. Outside class, there were some English activities, like the English Corner. Some people went to them but I did not because I felt my English was not good. I did pass the Band 4 Exam [a national English examination for university students]. I think my English is just average now. Reading and listening — I am okay. But speaking and writing — I cannot handle them.

**English on the Internet**: Before 1995 or 1996, we were not connected to the Internet. When we became connected, what we first did was to send e-mails. We did so in English. Now every day, I go onto the Internet. Sometimes, I come across some web sites in English. I am not afraid of reading web sites in English. I can read through them slowly.

## Dai (Miao Interviewee 6, male, aged 27, a Chinese history teacher)

**Background**: I was born in 1973 in a village in Hunan. In 1980, at the age of seven, I entered the primary school in our village. In 1984, I attended Primary 5 in the city of the county. In 1986, I began my secondary school education in the same city. In 1991, I went to Beijing to do my BA in Chinese history in the nationalities university there. In 1998, I graduated with my master's from the same university in Beijing and came [to a nationalities university in the southern interior] to teach.

**Repertoire**: I am most proficient in the Xiang dialect [a Chinese dialect]. [Xiang is the name of a river originating in Guangxi and flowing in Hunan.] My second best dialect is Xinan Guanhua [the southwestern branch of the northern Chinese dialect spoken in Chengdu, Chongqing and the surrounding area]. Then comes Putonghua. My first foreign language is English but I have not learnt it well. But my English is still better than my competence in the Miao language, at least for reading.

**The Xiang dialect**: Everyone at home spoke the Xiang dialect. So that is my real mother tongue from birth to senior secondary school. I learnt Xinanguanhua only when I started working.

**Putonghua**: From primary school, I learnt *hanyu pinyin*. By Primary 3 or 4, I already knew Putonghua. I could not speak it well but I did not have difficulty with listening to Putonghua. But after I learnt Putonghua, I did not use it in my everyday life. I only used it mainly for reading and writing. I also used it for listening to broadcasts and reading newspapers. I became fluent in Putonghua during my university days. Before that, most of the time I was speaking my dialect and I did not go to other places. During my primary and secondary schooldays, very few teachers used Putonghua to conduct lessons.

**English**: I learnt English from junior secondary school. But it was basically 'Dumb English'. My reading was not bad. My listening was passable but my speaking was very bad. This was because we had very little opportunity to use English for interaction. I read the *China Daily* and *The 21st Century* when I was studying English. I also listened to some broadcasts in English. There was an English Corner at my university but because I did not speak English well, I seldom went there. At university, we had to pass the Band 4 examination [a national examination in English]. If not, we could not get our degree.

**The Miao language**: After Liberation [establishment of the People's Republic], the new Roman script for the Miao language was designed. The ancient Miao script is hardly used now. I learnt the Miao language only at university. I studied it for one year in my second year at university. I only know some basic rules, some very simple phrases and some basic grammar. Whether it is reading or interaction, my ability is not too good. With the help of a dictionary, I can read a little. I did not try to do any self-learning activities when learning the Miao language. When my studies were over, I did not bother with it any more. I no longer use it. In the mountain areas, where the Miao people live, the language is used a little. But there are no broadcasts, no newspapers and no use outside those areas. In some places, there are teaching materials in the Miao language and Miao schools, Miao language classes, but the propagation of the Miao language in the society is not very strong and not very effective.

**Baihua**: I also learnt a little Baihua [Cantonese] after I came here [the university in the southern interior] through self-study and interacting with people. I cannot speak it but I can understand about 60 to 70 percent of what people say.

**Difficulty in learning new languages**: Different languages have different grammars. The modes of thoughts are also different and the sounds are not the same. To learn Putonghua after learning a Chinese dialect, there are some sounds not easy to pronounce. It is the same with English sounds. The Miao sounds are particularly difficult to pronounce. There are some queer sounds that cannot be produced. So if you want to learn them, you cannot learn very well.

**Putonghua policy and minority languages**: Standardizing a country's language and script is very important. It has great implications for a country's economic and social development. But if the policy is implemented in too extreme a manner, then there will be some negative effects on other Chinese dialects and minority languages. If these dialects or languages die, it is a great pity.

## Ma (Dong Interviewee 1, male, aged 25, a foreign languages graduate student)

**Background**: I was born in a mountain village in Guangxi in 1975. At the age of seven, from Primary 1 to Primary 4, I studied in the village school. After that, I went to the school in the *zhen*⁴ [town] to study for one year. In those days, primary school only consisted of five years. Then in 1988, I went to the city in the *xian*⁴ [county] to enter junior secondary school. In 1991, I went to Liuzhou for my senior secondary school education. In 1994, I entered the Guangxi Normal University to study English and graduated in 1998. In 1998, I came here [a key university in the northern interior] to do my master's degree in English.

**The Dong language and the Zhuang language**: My first language was the Dong language. It was spoken at home. I also learnt the Zhuang language because the next village was a Zhuang village. When we went over to play, whatever they said, we just tried to speak the way they did. I cannot write the Zhuang script because I did not study it formally. It is a new script, artificially created after Liberation [establishment of the present Chinese government].

I cannot write the Dong language either. [A Roman alphabetic script was actually designed for the Dong language but it may not have been widely propagated.]

**The Guiliu dialect**: From Primary 1 to Primary 4, I was taught in the Guiliu dialect. We also spoke it outside class. When I went to the school in the town for Primary 5, because there were people from different minority groups in the town, we needed a common language. The Guiliu dialect was used for interacting with people from different minority groups. It was also used in class by the teacher. Sometimes Putonghua was also used by the teacher.

**Putonghua**: When I went to the junior secondary school in the $xian^4$, Putonghua was used as the medium of instruction. Outside class, the teacher would also use the Guiliu dialect sometimes, for example, during meetings for the class. In the English lesson, he would also use Putonghua to teach. The $yu^3wen^2$ [Chinese] teacher would use Putonghua to teach. Other teachers sometimes used Putonghua and sometimes the Guiliu dialect. During my junior secondary school years, my Putonghua was still not passable. When I went to senior secondary school in Liuzhou, all the teachers used Putonghua to teach. By then, I was able to interact with others in Putonghua. But it was at university that I really used Putonghua frequently outside class because the classmates came from several different places in Guangxi. When I was learning Putonghua, I did not purposely listen to tapes. So sometimes, my pronunciation is not very accurate. Only at university did I watch television or listen to broadcasts in Putonghua. Sometimes, I found it difficult to differentiate between Putonghua and the Guiliu dialect. So I tend to use the Guiliu dialect when I am speaking more colloquially. But when I need to be more literary, then I speak Putonghua. I am now best at Putonghua and my Dong language. Both are just as good.

**English**: I started learning English from Junior Secondary 1 in the $xian^4$. I learnt it well mainly because I was very interested. At that time, I did not think I wanted to become an interpreter or something instrumental like that. I just felt it was good to learn so I wanted to learn it well. For example, when I read the books and there were some pictures and I wondered, 'Why does this person have yellow hair?' So I became interested and wanted to learn their language. In junior secondary school, the teachers sometimes played tapes to us. I also did some reading in English outside class. There was also an English Corner that I sometimes went to in senior secondary school. At university, I also went to the English Corner. In class at university, the teacher required us to only use English. So we did. Outside class, sometimes I watched television or listened to broadcasts. Because they were native speakers, their pronunciation was purer. So I kept wanting to imitate them, even their facial expressions. My Dong language has affected my pronunciation of both Putonghua and of English. But sometimes, I found some similarities between English and the Dong language. For example, the word for 'door' in the Dong language is *duo*, similar to English. So it was easy for me to remember.

**Influence of English teachers**: I think the influence of teachers is very important. When I was in junior secondary school, my first English teacher was able to develop our interest in learning English. At university too, the teacher's English was very good. He had been to America and he was never tired and very hardworking. He affected me a lot. So I set my heart on learning English well.

**Difference between learning Putonghua and English**: When we studied Putonghua in secondary school, at first, we did not think of using it to interact with others because we used the Guiliu dialect outside class to interact with each other. But when learning English, we were purposely looking for opportunities to use it so that we could improve our English. When I could use the new language I learnt to communicate with others, I felt very happy.

**Japanese and German**: My second foreign language [of secondary importance] is Japanese and I also know a little German.

**Learning languages**: I think classes are necessary but after learning in class, we should try our best to interact with others in the language we are learning. If we can interact with native speakers of the language, that is even better. Reading is also important because it can enhance our vocabulary and our cultural understanding. If the state can provide more facilities like language laboratories, television and opportunities for cultural understanding, that should help. But there is no need to cramp the learners with knowledge. Instead, we should develop the students' interest in learning.

## Discussion

It must be emphasized that these seven learners were all university graduates. So their experience may not always match that of minority learners in general. The following discussion focuses on: their wide linguistic repertoire, the variation in their mode of learning and attitudes towards their minority language, their experience in learning Putonghua, their foreign language learning and how such experiences suggest language loss for some and enhanced trilingualism for others in the decades ahead.

**Wide repertoire**: The seven learners all knew several languages or dialects, though to different degrees (Table 4.21). Some of them (Fang, Mei and Dai) could both speak and write their minority language. Others had less competence; Ma could only speak the Dong language but could not write it; Mong could understand the Mulao language but only knew how to address his relatives in the Mulao language. He from the Hui minority learnt a little Arabic but used mostly a Chinese dialect at home. Ping from the Man minority also used a northern Chinese dialect at home. In fact, about half of them spoke mainly a Chinese dialect from birth but none of them had Putonghua as a first dialect. Several picked up some knowledge of other minority languages

Table 4.21  **Languages/dialects learnt by seven minority learners**

| Name of learner (Age) | Ethnic group | Minority language(s) | Chinese dialect(s) | Foreign language(s) |
|---|---|---|---|---|
| Fang (51) | Zhuang | The Zhuang language[H] <br> The Yao language | The Guiliu dialect <br> Putonghua <br> Kejiahua <br> Cantonese | Russian |
| Ping (43) | Man | None | Dongbeihua[H] <br> Putonghua | Japanese |
| Mei (37) | Yao | The Yao language[H] <br> The Zhuang language | Putonghua <br> The Guilin dialect <br> Baihua | English <br> Japanese |
| Mong (35) | Mulao | The Mulao language <br> The Zhuang language | The Guiliu dialect[H] <br> Putonghua <br> Kejiahua <br> Baihua | English |
| He (29) | Hui | Arabic | A local northern dialect[H] <br> Putonghua | English |
| Dai (27) | Miao | The Miao language | The Xiang dialect[H] <br> Putonghua <br> Xinan Guanhua <br> Baihua | English |
| Ma (25) | Dong | The Dong language[H] <br> The Zhuang language | The Guiliu dialect <br> Putonghua | English <br> Japanese <br> German |

[H] Home language as a child

or Chinese dialects from the community. Fang, the oldest, learnt Russian as her first and only foreign language. The younger five all learnt English. Japanese was also learnt by three learners, two of whom (Ping and Mei) learnt enough of it to meet the foreign language requirement in a promotion exercise.

**Formal and informal learning of minority languages**: Fang, from the Zhuang minority, the largest minority in China, had the opportunity to begin her primary education in her minority language, even though her teacher would teach two grades simultaneously, with one grade working on their own while teaching the other. Ping never tried to learn the Man language though he was aware that some older people in the Heilongjiang area could speak it. Mei spoke the Yao language from birth 'like a basic instinct' but did not learn its written form until she started working. Mong, from the Mulao minority with only 207,352 people and no script, learnt very little of it. His mother also told him folk-tales in the Zhuang language. He from the Hui minority learnt a little Arabic at home and mostly at the Muslim temple through memorizing extracts from the Koran in one big class of ten to twenty children at different levels. Dai learnt the Miao language only at university. Ma learnt the Dong language at home but never studied it formally.

**Attitudes towards minority languages**: In addition to their learning mode, a range of attitudes towards their minority language was also found among these learners. MeiBC felt 'very proud' that she knew her language and said, 'I am not like some people who have this attitude — if they speak the Yao language, they are afraid other people will laugh at them.' That she could use the Yao language with Yao people outside China also enhanced her ethnic pride in her language. He's loss of his Arabic competence did not affect his ethnic identity; he stated unequivocally, 'The Hui people have adopted the Chinese language but language is language and religion is religion.' In contrast, Ping and Mong did not appear too concerned that they had no or little competence in their minority language. Dai showed some ambivalence; while he would not try to improve his competence in the Miao language and 'did not bother with it any more' when his studies were over, he did lament that if 'languages die, it is a great pity'.

**Learning Putonghua**: Though all seven learners went through the education system successfully, several reported some difficulty to different degrees in their acquisition of Putonghua. All of them began life either in their minority language or a Chinese dialect other than Putonghua. The only one that seemed to have little difficulty was Ping, from the Man minority, who reported, 'There was no difference in my language environment between my school or my home when I was growing up. I did not have to learn Putonghua because my home dialect, Dongbeijua, is close to Putonghua, the standard dialect.' But even Ping had to learn the vocabulary differences between Dongbeihua and Putonghua. Others like Fang and He had a more difficult time at some stage in their education. Fang failed her Chinese one year and He failed it often; he reported, 'I felt my Chinese dialectal pronunciation was a hindrance to my learning of Putonghua; because my pronunciation was not accurate, I could not figure out the words. By Primary 3, my classmates already knew many words. I knew very few. Learning Chinese was very, very painful for me in my primary and secondary schooldays.' Even the youngest of the learners, Ma, reported that during his junior secondary school-days, his Putonghua was still not passable; not until he went to senior secondary school did all his teachers use Putonghua to teach. University education seems to guarantee competence in Putonghua if minority learners did not achieve competence in it earlier; at this level, the experience of minority learners was like that of Han Chinese interviewees.

**Foreign language learning**: The learning of English by minority learners was like that of the Han Chinese learners in that the younger learners seemed to have experienced better learning conditions (such as the use of tapes or the Internet) and greater learning success. One of the most successful learning stories was told by Mong from the Mulao minority. During his last senior secondary year, he was already aware of the instrumental function of English; he reported, 'The teacher … told us that if our English was good, we could act as interpreters or tourist guides and introduce our China and rich culture to foreigners. In our village, the thinking was that if we stayed behind to plow the land, at the most, we could only support ourselves. But if we could have contact with foreigners, we could have a better income and have a higher status.' So from a village in the Mulao Autonomous Xian (County), he acquired enough English to do a PhD in a university in England. Such an astounding experience, however, is exceptional. Too often, minority learners do not manage to gain admission into mainstream graduate programmes because of their inadequate mastery of English. It is therefore not surprising that there is some despair about the first foreign language requirement among minority learners. In survey data not presented above, an older Bai learner commented, 'Our minority brothers bear a double task — Hanyu [Chinese] and English. We try to grasp at everything but grasp nothing.' (Data source: 027-966-0004) Another older Zhuang learner asked with some understandable bitterness, 'In China, to participate in the promotion assessment exercise, one must first gain a pass in a foreign language examination. In England and America, do they also have to be examined in Hanyu [Chinese] before they can get promoted?' (Data source: 557-889a-0028). Younger minority learners, though, might be more open. Ma, the youngest of the seven learners, felt that he learnt English well mainly because he was 'very interested' in the language from his junior secondary school-days. 'At that time, I did not think I wanted to become an interpreter or something instrumental like that. I just felt it was good to learn so I wanted to learn it well.'

**Language maintenance and loss**: Since Putonghua and English have more prominent roles to play in education in China, some minority learners may experience gradual loss of their own languages. One can almost work out a survival index for the minority languages taking into account the following variables: the size of the population, the stability of the script and the religious affiliation or other cultural connections with other parts of the world. The larger the minority population, the more stable the script, the stronger the religious or cultural affiliation with other populations in other parts of the world, the less likely it is that a minority language in China will be lost. This is because the larger the population size and the more stable the writing script, the more likely it is that some education in the minority language can be pursued. The stronger the religious or cultural affiliation with similar populations internationally, the stronger the collective cultural identity (and hence individual linguistic identity) can be. (See Huang, 2000, incorporating other variables such as whether the language is used in administration, law, education, the media and the economy in his permutation of a language vitality index.)

**Trilingualism**: It is to be expected that with greater educational opportunities for minority learners and the widening network of broadcasting and television in Putonghua, proficiency in Putonghua will become more widespread among minority learners, at least for those residing in the more developed areas. As Han Chinese learners become more proficient in English as a whole, minority learners are also likely to experience more opportunities for interactive learning in English. Some degree of trilingualism may then become more and more achievable as an individual goal for minority learners, even before university.

## Summary

In this chapter, the policy periods were first identified. Except during the Cultural Revolution and some sporadic years before it, the national policy as a whole has been protective towards minority languages and minority learners. Linguistic work on describing minority languages was then described in greater detail. To date, twenty-nine ethnic groups now have their own scripts. Another two groups, the Mans and the Huis, have converted to Chinese. There are still twenty-four ethnic groups without their own officially recognized scripts. In the light of this development work on minority language scripts, and hence the possibility or impossibility of education in minority languages, some preliminary results from a survey of sixty minority learners were analysed. Against this general picture, seven case histories of learners from different ethnic groups — the Zhuangs, the Mans, the Yaos, the Mulaos, the Huis, the Miaos and the Dongs — were presented. They represent the educationally more successful minority learners. Their very success underscores the linguistic and cultural dilemma faced by minority learners in China. Unless they can become effectively bilingual in their own languages and Chinese, they run the risk of losing their own languages and cultures or not being able to participate in the national life of China as conveniently. This dilemma is not only individual but also national. While the government wishes to protect minority languages and to provide education in minority languages as a matter of policy and ideology, resourcing issues aside, it also has the duty to provide for minority learners opportunities in the mainstream national life, opportunities which are largely available mostly in Chinese as a matter of everyday reality.

# 5

# Conclusion

## Introduction

In previous chapters, against the background of political and educational developments in China from 1949, the three major policies concerning the standardization of the Chinese language, the promotion of English and other foreign languages and the development of minority languages as well as the experience of all three policies by learners in China have been presented. In this final chapter, learner experience of these policies is summarized, the implications of the findings for the study of multilingualism are pointed out, the current language education trends in China are highlighted, and directions for further research in this area are suggested.

## The Experience of Learners in China from 1949

There are two main categories of learners in China: the majority Han Chinese group accounting for 91.6% of the population and the minority learners coming from fifty-five other officially recognized ethnic groups. The learning experiences of these two categories of learners have been considered separately in previous chapters.

### Han Chinese learning Chinese

In the initial phase of the policy concerning the propagation of Putonghua and the standardization of Chinese characters, only the Han Chinese learners were affected. The effects were studied through a survey as well as case interviews. The survey of 318 learners showed effects according to the age of the learner, the first dialect of the learner and the birthplace location of the learner. These effects were also found, to some extent, in the learning stories of individual learners.

**Age effects**: The age of the learner did not seem to make a difference on the age they started learning Putonghua, but did affect the time when they started learning how to write Chinese. More learners in the younger cohorts started learning how to write Chinese at home. For the youngest age group, as many as 65.1% had started learning how to write Chinese before they entered primary school. This in itself is indicative of higher literacy rates among parents as a result of educational expansion from the early years of the People's Republic. The overall increase in literacy is probably also partly responsible for the fact that younger learners seemed to do more letter writing in Chinese as a way to enhance their competence in Chinese. Younger learners also reported greater access to technical support such as tape recorders, radio and television in their learning of Putonghua. This is consistent with the better economic conditions for a greater number of Chinese people in recent years as well as the increasing spread of Putonghua in broadcasting and the public media in China. As Putonghua became more and more widely used, younger learners also reported less difficulty in learning *hanyu pinyin* as an aid towards accurate pronunciation.

**Dialect effects**: While age did not affect the time learners were introduced to Putonghua, their native dialects did have such an effect. This is understandable because Putonghua is a northern dialect. Respondents with a southern dialect as their first dialect began learning Putonghua later. Southern dialect speakers in the interior region seemed to start learning Putonghua latest with 47.4% of them learning from primary school and 31.6% of them learning Putonghua only when they entered university or when they started working. Learners with a northern dialect as their first dialect also had slightly more class time devoted to learning Putonghua when they were in secondary school than learners in the south. More teachers in primary schools in the southern interior also used a local dialect rather than Putonghua when teaching Chinese. Not surprisingly, therefore, southern dialect speakers did not use Putonghua as much as northern dialect speakers did when conversing with their classmates in primary school and secondary school. Such dialect effects were not found at university level. University education seemed to guarantee competence in Putonghua if it had not been achieved earlier. This is because universities are attended by learners from many dialect groups from various provinces and Putonghua serves as a common dialect for interdialectal communication. The patterns of current use of Putonghua are also illuminating. While speakers from a northern dialect background use Putonghua more often at home, with friends and when shopping, they are no different from southern dialect speakers in their use of Putonghua at work or at government offices. Speakers from both the north and the south use Putonghua frequently at work and at government offices.

**Birthplace location effects**: Birthplace location also had a little effect on learners' experience. As expected, those who grew up in coastal areas enjoyed better conditions than those born in the interior. More learners from coastal regions started learning Putonghua at home from birth; in contrast, among those growing up in the interior, there was still 22.2% who learnt Putonghua only after secondary school. More teachers of learners in the coastal region also used Putonghua to teach subjects other than Chinese.

**Case histories**: The case histories of learners are largely consistent with the trends found in the survey but also show some individual differences. Four case histories were presented: two older ones and two younger ones, one from the north and one from the south in each age group. Yan, the older Northern Chinese learner, first learnt the Xian dialect and was largely educated in that dialect until his junior secondary school years. But he did not seem to have much difficulty picking up Putonghua and several other northern dialects as well during his travels because his first dialect was similar to Putonghua. In contrast, Tian, the other older learner from the south, was exposed to Putonghua only at university and observed that his Putonghua was still considered non-standard by northerners, though his pronunciation was already thought to be very good in the south. The two learners educated more recently, Xin and Danny, experienced better learning circumstances, but Xin coming from the rural area in a northern coastal province also had some difficulty. Her story shows that the divide between urban and rural regions even nowadays is probably as significant as that between the coastal and interior regions, if not more.

From both the survey and the case interviews, it can be concluded that the policy to propagate a standard form of Chinese — Putonghua — has been largely effective but there have been and will continue to be differences according to the first dialect of the learner. Learners in the coastal areas are also in a more advantageous position than those in the interior.

## Han Chinese learning English

The policy changes in promoting English in China have been experienced differently by learners educated during different time periods. Another difference found is that between those specializing in English and those not specializing in English. A survey was conducted on 222 non-foreign-language specialists and 193 foreign language specialists. Case interviews were also used to illustrate the experience of learning English.

**Non-foreign-language specialists**: The learning experience of non-foreign-language specialists is more representative of the average university graduate in China and age effects were observed for this sample. Consistent with the change in policy, the choice of foreign language shifted from Russian to English for later cohorts of learners. Most older learners also learnt their foreign language only at university while younger cohorts did so mostly from secondary school. There has also been a steady increase in class time for learning English in secondary school. Foreign language teachers also used the foreign language more in teaching the foreign language to recent cohorts of learners both in secondary school and at university.

**Foreign language specialists**: Where age effects are concerned, the experience of foreign language specialists is largely similar to that of non-foreign-language specialists, except that slightly more of the former started learning the foreign language before secondary school. There is also another important difference. Foreign language specialists did a lot more work on their own to learn the foreign language outside the classroom. The differences between the two groups are particularly salient in terms of language production activities. For example, foreign language specialists talked with classmates more at university and wrote letters in English more frequently.

**Case histories**: Case interviews of four learners educated at different times and in different birthplace locations also reflect similar age and specialism effects. Deng, a philosophy teacher, did not succeed in learning English well but Xue, majoring in foreign languages, educated also around Deng's time, experienced a different fate and became a professor of English. The experience of another learner, Ling, illustrates the desire for learners in China to learn English from everyday interaction with foreigners; though her English was very good, she still felt that she talked like a book. Hua, the youngest of the four learners interviewed, had the benefit of more technical support and her experience demonstrates the great motivation to learn English well even among non-English majors in recent times.

The data taken as a whole reflect the policy trends in foreign language education. Learners in recent times are more open and enjoy better conditions for learning English.

## The experience of minority learners

It is difficult to generalize about the experience of minority learners as there are fifty-five minority ethnic groups in China. The overall policy of the state towards minority languages is protective, except during the Cultural Revolution and some sporadic years before it. Protective codification of minority languages is consistent with the egalitarian ideology of the Communist Party.

**Development of scripts**: To date, twenty-nine ethnic groups have official writing scripts, some of which were revised or created with support from the central government. Another two groups, the Hui people and the Man people, have adopted Chinese as their language. The twenty-four ethnic groups that still do not have officially recognized writing scripts have a total population of 2.6 million or about 2.9% of the total minority population of China. Six of them have populations of less than a million and the rest have populations less than 100,000. Minority learners from an ethnic group with a large population are more likely to have their writing script codified and some access to education in their own minority language. Other variables that come into play are religious affiliation or international currency of their language.

**Survey results**: A small-scale survey of sixty minority learners yielded some preliminary results concerning their learning of their native languages, Chinese and English. Most of them learnt their minority language at home and used it mainly at home. About half of them never learnt how to write their minority language. Many of them went through a period of transitional bilingualism in primary school and converted to Putonghua as a medium of education gradually during secondary school. At secondary school, they also differed from Han Chinese learners in that they used English less frequently when conversing with their classmates. If they managed to enter university, then their experience in the use of Putonghua and English would be similar to that of Han Chinese learners.

**Case histories**: The seven case histories presented illustrate the great range of circumstances depending on minority backgrounds, age and individual choice. Fang came from the largest ethnic minority, the Zhuang minority with a population of 16.2 million. Educated in the early years of the People's Republic, she converted quickly to Putonghua so that it became her best language but she could still speak her Zhuang language. Ping from the Man group could not speak the Man language and had undergone complete acculturation to Chinese. His experience seems little different from that of any Han Chinese learner going to school in the northeastern part of China in the 1960s and early 1970s. Mei, a Yao learner, is interesting as someone who could communicate with other Yaos in other parts of the world in her own minority language and felt ethnic pride in being able to do so. Mong, from the Mulao group with a population of only 207,352 people and no writing script for their language, illustrates well the endangered status of a language with a small population and no writing script. He hardly spoke the Mulao language but spoke Putonghua well and became sufficiently competent in English to pursue a PhD at a university in England. He from the Hui group, like Ping from the Man group, also converted to Putonghua but, different from Ping, still identified with his own ethnic group because of his religious attachment to Islam. To him, 'language is language and religion is religion'. As one of the younger learners, He is interesting in his openness to learning English. A computer scientist, he reported his English was just average but he could read English web sites slowly. Dai from the Miao minority grew up mostly in the Xiang dialect, a Chinese dialect used in Hunan. Dai only studied the Miao language when he went to university and no longer used it. He studied this language using one of the scripts created after 1949. Though he hardly used the Miao language, he still held the opinion that 'If … languages or dialects die, it is a great pity.' Ma, a foreign language major, from the Dong minority exemplifies the ideal multilingual learner who manages to retain his own language, functions well in Putonghua and English, and has some knowledge of other languages as well. How much this is related to his aptitude for or training in linguistics is hard to tell.

All the minority learners interviewed were proficient users of Chinese, though some of them might have had to struggle with it at an earlier age, and graduated from university. But many minority learners do not gain admission to university because of inadequate proficiency in Chinese. Having to learn English is yet another linguistic challenge.

### A total experience

Although policies have largely been planned and implemented separately from each other, so much so that there are different government departments dealing with the policies on the standardization of Chinese, the promotion of English and minority language matters, it is much harder to consider them as entirely separate from each other in the actual experience of individual learners. Often, the development of proficiency in one language can enhance the development of competence in another language. At the same time, if learning time is devoted to one language, learners may have less learning energy for another and achieve less competence as a result. The learning stories of learners in China presented in previous chapters have illustrated the everyday reality of such effects. It is therefore important to take an integrated multilingual perspective in language planning.

## Implications for the Study of Multilingualism

The multilingual and multidialectal circumstances in China offer immense opportunities for research in linguistic description, applied linguistics, the study of bilingualism or second language acquisition and curricular concerns. Specific to the research approach and findings in this study, there are three main implications:

1. the significance of a multilingual approach in the analysis of language policy
2. the usefulness of relating learner experience to policy implementation
3. the value of examining learner experience towards understanding the dynamics of becoming multilingual

### A multilingual approach to language policy

Most studies of language policy in China would focus only on one of the three policy areas: the standardization of Chinese, the promotion of English and the development and use of minority languages because trying to track developments in all three is not exactly an easy task. One runs the risk of being superficial or simplistic in analysis. Yet, adopting an integrated perspective seems to do more justice to the realities of a country with multilingual circumstances. The parallel analysis of all three policy areas in this book, it is hoped, can offer insights not conveniently available otherwise.

The impact of politics on language policy, for example, can be more readily appreciated if events in all policy areas in the same period are considered as a whole. In the early 1950s, when friendship with Russia was considered a foreign relations goal, Russian featured prominently in foreign language education in China. At the same time, some attempt was made to use the Cyrillic alphabet to codify the writing scripts of some minority languages. When Russian relations took a less fruitful turn in the late 1950s, English became more important in education and the Roman alphabet was adopted in the design of *hanyu pinyin* for Chinese as well as codifying the minority languages. From around 1956 to 1957, as propagation of Putonghua set in, the early fervour in codifying minority languages subsided in parallel and the policy towards minority languages went into unstable ambivalence. Then came the Cultural Revolution from 1966 to 1976 with its devastating effects on education which affected the implementation of all three policies adversely. The post-Cultural Revolution years saw renewed efforts in all three policy areas. The 1980s saw a full-scale return to pre-Cultural Revolution policy goals in all three areas. And the disintegration of the Soviet Union in 1991 was a direct impetus for China to step up on its English language education to realize its goal to be more active internationally, and simultaneously to introduce rhetoric towards greater promotion of Putonghua among minority learners in the mode of bilingual education. If the Soviet Union had not disintegrated, there would not have been as much political space for China to move as smoothly into the international arena requiring more foreign language competence. Neither would the fearful prospect of a similar disintegration have prompted China to take a more decisive stance on the issue of how to integrate the fifty-five nationalities without antagonizing them. The measure taken from 1991 onwards has been to recast the minorities (formerly referred to as nationalities) as ethnic groups. Such an ideological change is then supported overtly by the bilingual policy for minorities. It is interesting to see how the three language policies have been shaped by the same political forces. This is an insight not so easily arrived at without a multilingual approach to policy analysis.

To look into the future, in terms of policy orientation, probably too much emphasis has been placed on learning English in China for economic and scientific advancement in recent years. The time will come, perhaps in a decade or two, when this will be questioned and the humanities (normally studied in Chinese) will again be found to be important. When China has become richer and the people have more material comforts, some of them will question what life is all about and that will be the time when English, and all its associated benefits, will not be enough. Just as governments may move from a perspective of education as investment to one of education as a human right (Tomasevski, 2003, p. 41), learners in China may, in time to come, treat language learning less as their personal investment and more as their personal fulfilment.

In the same vein, the bilingual policy for minority learners needs to be closely watched because among the many minority learners who have converted or will convert to Chinese even of their own accord, questions of ethnic identity and language rights may also surface in future, perhaps in forty or fifty years' time. Just as there are benefits associated with English for both Han Chinese and minority learners, there are also academic and economic advantages tied to competence in Putonghua for the minority learners. But in time to come, when these benefits have accrued, they too will not be enough. If the bilingual policy for minorities is successful and minority learners do not lose their own native languages while acquiring Chinese, then China can achieve a period of stable societal multilingualism using these generations of bilingual individuals from the minority ethnic groups as foci. That will be the best scenario both for the minority ethnic groups and for China as a whole. To achieve that, it is imperative that minority learners should not feel threatened by the learning of Chinese; to minimize such a threat, it is vital that minority language rights continue to be protected by the Chinese constitution, whether minority learners take advantage of them or not.

## *Relating learner experience to policy implementation*

It has never been easy to evaluate how successful a language policy is, particularly because there is usually some time lag and regional variation in policy implementation. In this study, two instruments were employed: surveys of learners and narratives of learner experience. Both have been found to be useful as windows to understanding policy implementation. Surveys provide a general picture while learning narratives illustrate nuances in individual circumstances. Of the two, conducting surveys is more labour-intensive and demands co-operation from a lot more informants. It takes a long time (about two and a half years in this study) to gather a sufficient data pool of learners from backgrounds that meet the requirements of the research design. Yet, surveys do provide an overall picture not available otherwise. The use of variables such as age, first language/dialect and childhood location seems to have proved useful in identifying informants, and these variables can probably be used in similar studies of other countries. Age is particularly important as a variable to track changes over time. The advantage of using learner narratives is that they provide more psychological insights about learners' motivation and other affective variables not so easily quantifiable. As they narrate their experience, learners are likely to identify for themselves, and hence the researcher, the relative importance of different languages and learning experiences in their learning psyche. Occasionally, learners may even point to specific historical circumstances which have an impact on their learning and thus play the role of informants for the construction of oral history. Whenever possible, using both instruments in combination is best because it allows the researcher to integrate sociological and psychological perspectives on the experience of language policy more readily.

## Understanding the dynamics of becoming multilingual

The findings as a whole have also contributed to a better understanding of the dynamics of becoming multilingual or multidialectal. These insights are discussed below in relation to the experience of the three policies.

**Insights from learning Chinese**: With reference to the analysis of the experience of learning Chinese, a number of observations may be made. First, the gradual change in attitude towards Putonghua over the age cohorts suggests that it takes at least two or three generations for a language policy like that to mature in a large country. Secondly, the positive attitude towards learning Putonghua suggests that, where there is a national identity and a social role still to be played by one's own dialect, acquiring the standard dialect can be perceived positively. Bidialectalism or multidialectalism is considered desirable and useful by most Chinese learners. Thirdly, learners seem to have a definite advantage when learning another linguistic system very similar to their native language or dialect. Compared with native speakers of Southern Chinese, native speakers of Northern Chinese dialects have less difficulty in learning Putonghua, a Northern dialect, and picking up other Northern Chinese dialects because the Northern Chinese dialects are more similar to each other. Fourthly, even if learners are competent in the other aspects of a language, a perfect accent seems to feature in some way in learners' perception of their competence, at least in a society like China's. Some learners from rural or southern areas in China seem rather conscious that they do not have the perfect Putonghua accent. This measuring of oneself against an ideal linguistic standard of the native speaker might be partly related to the fact that most of the informants in this study were in the teaching profession.

**Insights from learning foreign languages**: The analysis of foreign language learning experience in China has also yielded some insights. First, the comparison of the experience of non-foreign-language specialists with that of foreign language specialists indicates that when the foreign language is not widely used in the society, learners need to do a lot more work outside the classroom on their own if they wish to learn well, particularly in terms of interactive language production activities. This is certainly in line with the current emphasis on learner independence, learner autonomy and interactive language input for successful learning to occur. Secondly, in foreign language learning, the range of motivations (Gao, 2004) is usually as great as the variation in competence achieved, sometimes even at different times in a learner's life; the actual type of motivation, though not insignificant, does not seem as important as the intensity of motivation, at least not in China. Thirdly, in planning foreign language education, the ideological element cannot be ignored because learning a foreign language will create intercultural tension that needs to be resolved; the castigation of foreign language learning during the Cultural Revolution or, conversely, the propagation of the slogan of 'learning English to serve the Revolution' are extreme manifestations of such a concern, but it is one that cannot be disregarded in foreign language curricular design, materials development, classroom interaction and teacher development. Teacher educators need to consider how foreign language teachers can be better prepared to foster in their students a sense of 'intercultural rights and responsibilities' (Kramsch, 2001, p. 206). Essentially, that is an issue of ethnic and national identity and can be related to current studies of learner identity.

**Insights from minority learners' experience**: The study of minority learners has illustrated some aspects of multilingualism too. First, the better survival prospects of some minority languages over others point to population size, the existence of a writing script and a range of domains of language use as significant factors towards maintaining a minority language in a community. Secondly, the ethnic pride shown by some minority learners in their ability to use their minority language in some way suggests that any knowledge of one's ethnic language, no matter how incomplete in terms of domains of use, is still considered valuable. Such an attitude can be taken as support for the communicative perspective on bilingualism and multilingualism, in which a learner's deployment of all the languages or dialects in his/her total linguistic repertoire is more important than whether he/she can speak each language or dialect as perfectly as monolingual native speakers of the respective languages or dialects (Grosjean, 1992). Thirdly, the fact that minority learners may begin to learn their minority language at home, in primary school or at university suggests that ethnic languages of minority groups tend to be learnt in erratic modes. Fourthly, the educational patterns of minority learners in China seem to imply that it is best that learners should only be expected to deal with two linguistic systems during any one period of their learning. When minority learners in China had to learn three linguistic systems (their own language, a Chinese dialect and Putonghua) simultaneously, they seemed to experience some difficulty. Once two languages were stabilized within them (for example, their own language and Putonghua), they were then in a better position to learn a third language (English). This suggests that trilingualism

**Photo 21** A student takes his turn to clean the classroom in the Primary School at Lanzhou University.

**Photo 22** Slogan 'Care about the country. Look beyond to the world.' on a map at the Primary School at Tsinghua University

or multilingualism can be better achieved through successive stages of bilingualism involving two languages at each stage, one already acquired at a previous stage. How long each stage should be or would be probably depends on the aptitude of the learner and the quantity and type of language they are exposed to, among other factors.

**Multilingual openness**: As a whole, competence in more than one language or dialect in China was considered desirable by learners in this study. Learners in China, particularly the younger ones, appear to be very open about learning Putonghua and English, perhaps because the social use of their own dialects or languages is not legislated against or officially discouraged. Such openness to Putonghua and English is not surprising if we remember that until the early decades of the twentieth century, education in China was considered a privilege, not a right, especially for women. Because learning Putonghua and English can give access to education, particularly higher education, such learning is usually perceived positively, rather than as a threat to the maintenance of the learners' own dialects or languages. Only when we understand the great inadequacy of educational opportunity prior to 1949 can we appreciate why, for younger Han Chinese learners and a good number of younger minority learners, there seems to be such readiness to learning Putonghua, and later, English. If educational empowerment is not available in their own Chinese dialects or minority languages, having the opportunity for empowerment in Putonghua is still better than having no opportunity at all. Having gone through the historical traumas of foreign aggression, civil war and the Cultural Revolution, most Chinese learners nowadays just want to study in peace. This seems to imply that it is important to take the historical circumstances of a country into consideration before arguing for an ideological position that originated from another multilingual setting.

## Current Language Education Trends in China

In this new millennium, what are the current language education issues and trends in the three language policy areas: the teaching of Chinese, the promotion of English and other foreign languages as well as the language education of minority learners?

### Teaching of Chinese

Recent trends in the teaching of Chinese are in the following areas: the standardization of the language, materials development and assessment in the school curriculum, double degrees at university level, Teaching of Chinese as a Foreign Language (TCFL) and legislation.

**Language codification**: The teaching of Chinese to Han Chinese learners is inextricably tied to the propagation of Putonghua, the standardization of the Chinese writing script and the use of *hanyu pinyin*. The spread of Putonghua is evident, particularly in urban areas. The standardized Chinese writing script is now fully used all over the country. Younger learners are all familiar with *hanyu pinyin*, which has also become an acceptable way of recording Chinese characters in international communication, such as communication over e-mail and writing bibliographic references, though it will never be accepted as the only script for Chinese by Chinese people. Current developments evolve around ensuring high standards in pronunciation for broadcasting personnel and teachers as they are perceived as models of good pronunciation for learners all over China. Proficiency tests, such as the Putonghua Shuiping Ceshi (PSC or Putonghua Proficiency Test), are likely to achieve greater prominence in such quality assurance. As for the Chinese writing script, recent attention has centred around computerization and standardization in technical representations of Chinese characters as well as *hanyu pinyin*. For example, whether a stroke should have a rounded corner or an angular corner needs standardization in such representation as it affects machine readability of Chinese characters. The use of diacritics such as a level stroke or a slanted stroke above alphabetical letters to mark the tones in Putonghua has now been replaced across the board by the use of superscript numbers.

**The Chinese curriculum at schools**: While higher standards are aimed for in the pronunciation of Putonghua and the standardization of the orthographies is keeping up with the modern demands of computerization, in the actual teaching of the Chinese language and Chinese literature, much more can be done. Teachers of Chinese in China have been dissatisfied with the materials and the nature of the assessment of Chinese at the end of the schooling years. The time is ripe for more diversity in the materials, for the incorporation of various types of writings in keeping with the times, not only those that are politically correct, and for greater emphasis on mastery of the language and literature rather than discrete grammar or pronunciation points. It is to be expected that more than one set of materials for teaching Chinese can be a curricular goal and through the learning of Chinese, learners in China will not only learn to love their country, but also to critically examine the ways of other countries around the world as well.

**Double degrees in universities**: Language is not learnt in a vacuum and can never be taught effectively without content sufficiently interesting to the learners. As China opens up and the Internet becomes more and more available, young people in China are increasingly called upon to be able to interact with other ways of thinking. This is not just a matter of coming to terms with foreign cultures or the global context, but is also a matter of being able to use Chinese along with new developments in various academic

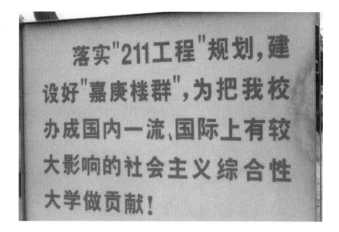

**Photo 23**  Slogan on Xiamen University campus on making the 211 plan a reality so that the university can be first-class in the country and also make a contribution internationally.

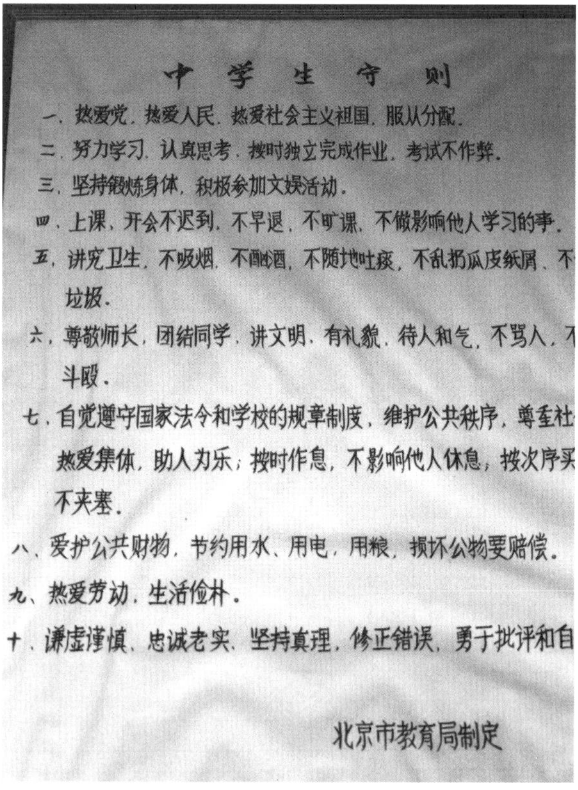

中 学 生 守 则

一、热爱党、热爱人民、热爱社会主义祖国、服从分配。

二、努力学习、认真思考、按时独立完成作业、考试不作弊。

三、坚持锻炼身体、积极参加文娱活动。

四、上课、开会不迟到、不早退、不旷课、不做影响他人学习的事。

五、讲究卫生、不吸烟、不酗酒、不随地吐痰、不乱扔瓜皮纸屑、不
     垃圾。

六、尊敬师长、团结同学、讲文明、有礼貌、待人和气、不骂人、不
     斗殴。

七、自觉遵守国家法令和学校的规章制度、维护公共秩序、尊重社
     热爱集体、助人为乐；按时作息、不影响他人休息；按次序买
     不夹塞。

八、爱护公共财物、节约用水、用电、用粮、损坏公物要赔偿。

九、热爱劳动、生活俭朴。

十、谦虚谨慎、忠诚老实、坚持真理、修正错误、勇于批评和自

北京市教育局制定

**Photo 24**  Regulations for Secondary School students posted at the Secondary School at Tsinghua University.

disciplines and professional operations. Chinese departments in universities in China have therefore been experimenting with double degrees such as Chinese and electronic publishing or Chinese and business.

**Chinese for foreigners**: With China's entry into the World Trade Organization in 2001 and the successful bid to host the Olympics in Beijing in 2008 and the World Expo in Shanghai in 2010, much of the attention has focused on the interest on the part of the Chinese people to learn English so as to serve all the international businessmen and tourists flocking to China in the next decade. As many as 22 million foreigners were reported to enter and exit China during the year of 2003 (Jiang, 2004). In Beijing, for example, it has been reported that the official target is to have 5 million people in the city, or one in three Beijing residents, speaking English by 2008 (Jen-Siu, 2002, p. 1). Yet, given these international developments, more foreigners are interested to learn Chinese as well. In July 2002, the number of foreigners learning Chinese abroad was estimated to be nearly 25 million (*People's Daily*, 24 July 2002, cited in China Internet Information Center, 2002); by the end of 2002, another estimate put it at close to 30 million (Xinhua News Agency, 8 February 2003, cited in China Internet Information Center, 2003). Over 2,100 universities in 85 countries offer courses in Chinese; foreigners from 114 countries have also registered for Chinese language courses over the Internet (*People's Daily*, 24 July 2002, cited in China Internet Information Center, 2002). By the end of 2002, as many as 540,000 people had taken the Chinese Proficiency Test (HSK) and more than one hundred test centres had been set up in twenty-seven countries around the world (China Education and Research Network, 2004). Within China, the 'Chinese for foreigners' programmes at various universities in China have also been faring well, particularly in cities like Beijing, Shanghai and Guangzhou. At major universities in several coastal cities, some of the newest and best-looking buildings on campus house the international students (mostly from other Asian countries) studying the Chinese language or Chinese studies, often on intensive programmes. These foreigners will eventually graduate from skill-based courses to courses in Chinese studies such as Chinese politics or the Chinese economy. The Teaching of Chinese as a Foreign Language (TCFL) will continue to grow in importance and is directly monitored by the State Office for Teaching Chinese as a Foreign Language (SOTCFL), which also provides assistance to the work of the World Chinese Language Teaching Society (Consulate General of the People's Republic of China in San Francisco, n.d.). The expansion in TCFL programmes presents a challenge to Chinese language teachers. They are increasingly called upon to incorporate an understanding of second language acquisition or applied linguistics into their teaching. Opportunities for related teacher training will be welcome.

**Legislation**: Reviewing the policy after half a century in the light of all the recent developments, it is evident that the national commitment to the propagation of Putonghua and the use of standardized simplified Chinese characters in all areas of the use of Chinese is unabated and clearly spelt out in the legislation on this matter announced on 31 October 2000 to be effective from 1 January 2001. In Article 3 of *Zhongguo Renmin Gongheguo Guojia tongyong yuyan wenzi fa* (The law on the commonly used language and script in the People's Republic of China), it is reaffirmed that Putonghua and standardized characters are to be propagated by the state. Article 9 states that government offices will use Putonghua and standardized characters, unless specified otherwise by law. The same is expected in schools (Article 10). Article 14 specifies the same requirements in broadcasting, movies, television, public facilities, signboards, advertisements, the names of enterprises and the packaging of products sold in China. The use of dialects is allowed when it is necessary to do so in the execution of public duty, in programmes approved by broadcasting authorities by state or provincial departments as well as in opera and certain modes of television art (Article 16). Traditional complex characters or non-standardized variant forms can be used in historical sites, surnames, calligraphic art, handwritten signboards, in publishing, teaching or research only as necessary and any other special circumstances approved by relevant state departments (Article 17). Even foreigners learning Chinese in China in the Chinese for foreigners programmes should be taught Putonghua and standardized characters (Article 20). What is interesting is that, as in the 1950s, the minority language learners are still not required to convert to Putonghua, in spite of the current goal of bilingualism for the minorities. Their rights to use and develop their own languages and scripts are protected in Article 8 of this law. Details of this law and a list of the 144 policy documents at national and provincial levels on this matter from November 1954 onwards are available on the web site of the Ministry of Education of the People's Republic of China (n.d.).

The national policy to propagate the standard dialect, Putonghua, and the use of simplified characters has been implemented along with nine years of compulsory education. This has resulted in a more educated and more literate population. Though the interior regions still suffer from poorer educational conditions, the educational advancement of the country as a whole is evident. This is almost a prerequisite for China's positioning in the international arena.

## Promotion of English and other foreign languages

The learning of foreign languages in China has always been linked with foreign policy, and foreign policy has always been shaped by the philosophy that for China to remain at peace with other nations, China must be strong and modern. In this age when China is increasingly recognized as an important player in international diplomacy and trade, the learning of English as a global language is emphasized more than ever from primary school to university, for English majors and non-majors, for civil servants and for personnel in private enterprises.

**The new school syllabus**: In May 1990, the official recommendation was only to teach English from Primary 5 and Primary 6 for 102 and 96 lessons respectively (Liu, 1994, pp. 2–3). Now, the requirement is to start from Primary 3. Some schools in the coastal area even start teaching English from Primary 1 because that is popular with parents. In the new syllabus published in July 2001, it is specified that the teaching of English should be organized on a high frequency pattern of at least four times a week. Teaching in Primary 3 and 4 should be organized on a short lesson format while teaching in Primary 5 and 6 could be delivered in a combination of short lessons and long lessons. Long lessons should not be longer than two class periods. This new syllabus not only specifies the standards to be aimed for in primary school but also in secondary school. The intention is to arrive at continuous learning throughout the school years. In secondary school, the teaching of English is not to be less than four class periods per week (Ministry of Education, 2001, p. 31). The target competence is divided into nine levels. At the end of Primary 6, learners should achieve Level 2. At the end of nine years of compulsory education, or the end of Junior Secondary 3, learners should achieve Level 5. Upon graduation from Senior Secondary 3, learners should achieve Level 7 (Ministry of Education, 2002, pp. 41–42). This attempt to have a continuous curriculum for the twelve school years is commendable. The syllabus also incorporates current ideas such as task-based learning, collaborative learning, the development of learner strategies or the inculcation of learner independence (Ministry of Education, 2002, p. 36).

**Diversity in textbooks**: A few sets of textbooks have been developed in line with the new syllabus. An example is that published by the Foreign Language Teaching and Research Press in collaboration with Macmillan Publishers which provides a 'one-dragon' (continuous) series from Primary 1 onwards for all twelve years of schooling in China. People's Education Press, in collaboration with Heinle and Heinle and Thomson Learning 2000, has also adapted David Nunan's (1999–2000) *Go for it* series for use in junior secondary school in China. Some foreign language specialists at Tsinghua University are working on two other series (Z-S. Lu, personal communication, 22 September 2003). Diversity is certainly the new trend in textbook development in China. With diversity comes the openness to collaboration with overseas publishers and the acceptance of overseas writers and all that it entails culturally and pedagogically.

**Implementation concerns**: From discussions with colleagues in China, it seems that while the new syllabus is up-to-date, teachers in schools feel the need for more training to meet the demands of the new syllabus. Publishers are often called upon to provide such training and can often afford to do so since they sell copies in the region of millions. Another problem, harder to solve, is that the new syllabus specifies that the class size should not exceed forty students per class (Ministry of Education, 2001, p. 31). With the declining birth rate and the lower enrolment in primary school (see Chapter 1, 'Education in China', pp. 6–8), that might be easier to achieve in the lower grades of primary school but in secondary school, at least for the next few years, that is quite an impossible target in some parts of China. Classes of sixty students each in some schools in the interior are not unheard of. Trying to get sixty students to do interactive small-group discussion within the same classroom with rows of tables is an immense challenge.

**Changes at university level**: Teaching at the university level is also experiencing rapid change both in the teaching of English majors as well as the teaching of English to other students.

**English majors**: The latest English syllabus for students majoring in English (English Team, Steering Committee for Foreign Language Teaching in Higher Education, 2000) has three main components:

1. English skills such as listening, speaking, reading, writing, interpretation, translation
2. English knowledge such as English linguistics, English literature, English and American culture
3. Related knowledge of a profession such as foreign relations, trade, law, management, journalism, education, technology, culture, military affairs

The first two components had always been emphasized in China in previous syllabi, but the last component is explicitly specified only in this syllabus. This innovation is in line with the current emphasis on content-based instruction, which allows learners to learn the language in parallel with learning the concepts in a particular discipline. While some educators in China feel that this is a good step forward and will make English major students more 'marketable', there are others who feel that soon there will not be enough 'pure' English specialists to serve future cohorts of students in such interdisciplinary studies in future.

**Non-English-major students**: For students not majoring in English, the revised syllabus as publicized in 1999 requires students to study College English (CE) for four semesters, two in the first year and two in the second year, about seventy hours in each semester, with not less than four hours per week. Students can enter at different levels. If students enter at College English Band 1, then they should try to achieve Band 4 at the end of the two years. If they enter at Band 3, then they should exit at Band 6 (Revision Team for College English Syllabus, 1999, p. 7). After this basic four-semester programme, they are also all required to take not less than one hundred hours of Subject Based English (SBE), two hours per week during their third or fourth year. These SBE lessons can, in principle, be largely taught by subject specialists from the relevant academic departments. Foreign language departments can provide support as appropriate. A sample unit from books designed to teach SBE, such as the series published by the Foreign Language Teaching and Research Press in 2001 to 2002, may contain five parts: reading and comprehension (seventeen pages including bilingual glossaries), listening training (one and a half pages), speaking training (one page), writing training (one page) and translation training (one-and-a-half pages). After meeting the two requirements in CE and SBE, non-English-major students may also elect to take other courses in Advanced English (AE) (Revision Team for College English Syllabus, 1999, p. 8). The two key features of the current syllabus are: first, it is more demanding on university entrants as a result of higher standards achieved by secondary school students; secondly, it provides a longer composite programme so that students will not stop learning English halfway through their university career.

**English-medium instruction at university**: Changes are still being considered. One idea that has been floated will require universities to provide 30 percent of the academic curriculum in English. Some universities are trying to achieve that by providing additional English training to teachers of academic disciplines (such as law and business), particularly those whose English has already achieved a certain standard. Those who have returned from graduate studies overseas are in a better position to undergo such training, after which, they will then teach their academic disciplines to non-English-major students in English. This seems to be the reverse of the standard English for Specific Purposes (ESP) mode of operation, in which English teachers try to learn enough of a subject such as law or medicine to teach Legal English or Medical English.

**Teacher education**: Now that most of the syllabi for different levels have been updated, another issue that is being given increasing attention is teacher education. In this connection, it will be useful to consider not only the education of English teachers but of language teachers as a whole. Knowledge transfer from ELT to other areas of foreign language teaching or even to the Teaching of Chinese as a Foreign Language (TCFL) to foreigners or to the ethnic minorities in China may occur. Cross-fertilization of ideas from different language education sectors can only benefit the language teaching profession in China as a whole.

**International input**: Further professionalization of language teachers in China is likely to involve more international discourse. In 2000, the International Association of Teachers of English as a Foreign Language (IATEFL) endorsed the establishment of a China branch. In parallel, China joined AILA (International Association of Applied Linguists) in 2002 in the form of CELEA (Chinese English Language Education Association). There is increasing openness to utilizing the scholarship from outside China. Copyright permission from major publishers for classics in linguistics and applied linguistics has been obtained by the Foreign Language Teaching and Research Press for developing a series of China editions for the training of language majors. In the list found in one of these books published in 2001 (Leech), there are already 112 books in this series. These are much more affordable for Chinese university students; a copy of Leech (2001) in China, for example, only costs twenty-five Renminbi (US$3).

**Other foreign languages**: As China establishes more relations with the rest of the world, she will need more people competent in more foreign languages. China already joined the World Trade Organization in 2001. In June 2003, the Closer Economic Partnership Agreement (CEPA) was signed between China and Hong Kong, through which multinational companies based in Hong Kong can enjoy trade terms hitherto unimaginable. This is viewed as a first step towards free trade between China and the rest of the world through the WTO. Beijing will host the Olympic Games in 2008 and Shanghai will host the World Expo in 2010. Amidst the excitement of all these circumstances, other foreign languages such as Russian and the major European languages may also enjoy a revival in China. The fact that there are now more than fifty research and university centres of Chinese studies in Russia as compared to just a dozen in the late 1980s (Yian, 2004) is an indication of Russia's current interest to understand China. In turn, the new leadership in China is careful to reckon with Russia. For example, at the end of May 2003 to early June 2003, on his first official trip abroad, Hu Jintao, the President of China, stopped first in Russia to meet with Vladimir Putin, the President of Russia, to discuss co-operation in energy supply and regional security among other issues. On the European front, the rapid increase of interest in learning Chinese in France even at high school level (China Education and Research Network 2004) may attract a corresponding growth in the number of Chinese learners taking up French. The year 2004 is also the year of 'France in China', culminating in an awe-inspiring exhibition of Picasso's famous painting, 'Parade', declared open by Jacques Chirac, the President of France, visiting Hong Kong at the end of his visit to the China mainland in October 2004. International diplomacy requires international language learning. The Beijing Foreign Studies University (2001, p. 11), for example, provides training in at least thirty other languages in addition to English: Russian, German, French, Spanish, Arabic, Polish, Slovenian, Czek, Rumanian, Albanian, Hungarian, Bulgarian, Serbian, Croatian, Korean, Kampuchean, Burmese, Singhalese, Thai, Vietnamese, Hausa, Swahili, Turkish, Laotian, Malay, Indonesian, Finnish, Japanese, Italian and Portuguese.

As the teaching of English begins earlier and earlier in the education system, more and more learners will achieve higher levels of competence before they reach secondary school or university. More than ever, it is necessary to consider the teaching of English at all levels as one total phenomenon. Otherwise, teachers at higher levels may be repeating teaching already conducted at lower grades. Children in primary school are keen to learn English, but enough teachers have to be provided for them and the salary has to be attractive enough for them to want to remain at that level, particularly in economically underdeveloped areas.

## Language education of minority learners

There are several current concerns in minority language education: the continuing work in the development of writing scripts, the enhancement of bilingualism, the teaching of English to minority learners and the maintenance of minority languages in the face of competition from Putonghua and English.

**Development of scripts**: With twenty-four minority languages still without official writing scripts, there is still work to be done in the area of codification. Although it is uncertain whether some scripts already developed have been approved (Zhou, 2003, pp. 126–127), the official rhetoric is calling for more consolidation in this area (State Council, 2002). Meanwhile, the education of learners from minority groups without writing scripts as yet has to go on. It is probable that they will become literate in Chinese or that of a larger minority group in the vicinity if they enter school. This means that if the codification work is not completed fast enough, even if pursued in good faith, it may become redundant later because minority learners may have acculturated to Chinese by then.

**Bilingualism**: Much research attention among specialists in minority language education has been given to models of bilingualism or bilingual education among minority learners. This is in keeping with enhanced levels of bilingualism among the minority learners. Although they have not been required to become proficient in Putonghua, except during the Cultural Revolution and some years before it when minority languages were repressed, some minority learners have converted to Putonghua or have developed bilingual competence in their own language and Putonghua. This trend is likely to continue, particularly in the light of the official rhetoric encouraging bilingual education from around 1991. A new syllabus for teaching Chinese to minority learners from Primary 1 onwards is now in place and the call for bilingualism is stronger than ever (State Council, 2002).

**The learning of English**: In fact, as Han Chinese learners are now required to learn English from Primary 3, there is a diffusing effect of this policy on minority learners as well. English programmes for minority learners are being piloted among different minority populations. Since several of the new writing scripts for minority languages were designed using the same Roman alphabet as English, there are both positive and negative transfer effects, in that though the English script is not unfamiliar to them, the differences in sounds represented by the letters in the alphabet may cause some confusion, particularly because their learning of Chinese is already aided by *hanyu pinyin*, also based on the Roman alphabet.

**Maintenance of minority languages**: With Chinese and English competing for learning time and effort, some minority learners may have difficulty maintaining their own minority languages. In the small-scale survey with valid responses from sixty minority learners (see Chapter 4, 'The Overall Experience of Minority Learners', pp. 139–154), there is some indication that, among the recent cohorts of minority learners, fewer of them conversed frequently with their friends in their minority languages. Most of them still did so sometimes but there were some who did not use their minority languages to converse with their friends at all. Another interesting pattern is that the number of Chinese lessons at university level for minority learners had become fewer for the younger cohorts (only three lessons per week for the youngest cohort in the survey). These two trends can be explained with reference to the fact that Putonghua has been successfully propagated through broadcasting and other channels and is now more widespread; it is therefore highly probable that more minority learners have achieved competence in Putonghua earlier on in their education. The motivation to learn the first foreign language (English in most cases) has also apparently changed through the age cohorts; the oldest cohort reported that they did not learn the foreign language well because they were too old to learn or the language was not much used in their region while most learners in the youngest cohort reported that they were motivated to learn the first foreign language because they were interested in it or because they felt they should learn it as an international language. We have to bear in mind though that the minority learners in the survey were all university graduates. Many minority learners do not gain admission to university and may not have the same minority language use patterns or motivation to learn English.

To sum up, minority language learners have become more open to bilingualism in Putonghua and their own language. Some of them are also more interested in acquiring some competence in English.

## Directions for Further Research

Language education in China is an extremely rich area of research because policy is still evolving in all three policy areas. Just tracking the policy shifts in the years ahead demands careful research work. To follow up on the present study, three projects can be conducted. First, in a year or two, another cohort of learners will have graduated and it might be fruitful to compare the new cohort's experience with that of the youngest cohort in this study to see if they are different. Such work will enable us to consider whether policy implementation has stabilized for one or more policies. Secondly, as this study was focused on university graduates, most of whom were in the teaching profession, it would seem useful to conduct a parallel study on non-university graduates and/or non-teachers. Thirdly, the survey of minority learners in this study was too limited in sampling; it might be fruitful to conduct the survey on a larger scale with more minority groups involved or to do more interviews of learners from other ethnic groups.

Related to this study but going beyond it will be new studies in the developing areas in this field such as:

1. the Teaching of Chinese as a Foreign Language (TCFL) as a phenomenon in its own right and as related to teacher preparation
2. the implementation of various curricula in English language teaching at various levels, particularly in primary school and for the non-English-majors at university, because these are sectors most prone to curricular change at this point
3. the teaching of foreign languages other than English in China
4. the various modes of bilingual and multilingual education that can be adopted for the education of minority learners in relation to their patterns of language maintenance (retaining knowledge and use of their language) and language shift (losing their own language and converting to another language) (Nunan & Lam, 1998, p. 121)
5. the dynamics of intercultural identity or multicultural identity or identities among learners in China as they become multilingual
6. the biscriptal (Lam, 2002) or multiscriptal behaviour of minority learners who learn two or three languages (their own language or Putonghua and English) using the same Roman alphabet
7. the further professionalization and internationalization of language teaching in China
8. the development of applied linguistics as related to multilingual language education in China

While there are still many issues awaiting further exploration, this study has demonstrated, to some extent, the usefulness of a multilingual orientation to the analysis of a country's language policy and the value of using learner experience to track policy implementation. The multilingual interactions in China in the next half century promise to be very interesting. To appreciate this excitement requires a readiness to keep all the multilingual circumstances in view, rather than to focus only on the developments in one of the language policies or on only the majority Han Chinese group or the ethnic minorities.

## Summary

In this final chapter, the major findings on learner experience in the last half century in China have been summarized and the implications for the study of multilingualism have been discussed. Some current trends in language education in China in the teaching of Chinese, the promotion of English and the development of minority education have been highlighted and a few areas for further research have been pointed out. It remains for me to hope that a multilingual orientation in studying language education in China can continue to be adopted, not only because that is a more fruitful approach to understand the circumstances in China but also because a multilingual outlook to linguistic developments around the world is more culturally enriching. In modern human history, the language that spreads to other nations is often the language that has economic and political power. When the English-speaking world loses its pre-eminence by those yardsticks, other European languages and Asian languages may return to their former positions in the world. Hopefully, no single language will predominate over the globe ever again and the world will be truly multilingual.

# Appendix I
# Questionnaire for the Survey of Han Chinese Learners

An adapted version of this questionnaire was used to survey minority learners.

## Survey on learners' language experience, February 2000

Part I      Background information
Part II     Putonghua
Part III    Other Chinese dialects
Part IV    Minority languages in China
Part V     First foreign language
Part VI    Second foreign language
Part VII   Other comments

Subject ID: ☐☐☐–☐☐☐–☐☐☐☐ 1–10

## Part I   Background Information

FOR OFFICE USE

1.  Place of birth: _____ (place) _____ (nearest big city) _____ (province)      ☐☐☐☐ 11–14
    How would you classify your place of birth?      ☐ Rural     ☐ Urban      ☐ 15

2.  Sex:            ☐ Male            ☐ Female      ☐ 16

3.  Occupation:      ☐ 17
    ☐ Chinese language teacher/         ☐ Foreign language teacher/
       graduate student                     graduate student
    ☐ Teacher of other subjects
    ☐ Another occupation (please specify) _____

4.  Age:      ☐ 18
    ☐ Below 18      ☐ 18–23      ☐ 24–28      ☐ 29–35
    ☐ 36–40      ☐ 41–45      ☐ 46–50      ☐ Above 50

5.  Have you ever moved from one region to another?
    a. To attend primary school?       ☐ Yes (where to?) _____ ☐ No      ☐ 19
    b. To attend secondary school?    ☐ Yes (where to?) _____ ☐ No      ☐ 20
    c. To attend university?              ☐ Yes (where to?) _____ ☐ No      ☐ 21
    d. To take up a job?                  ☐ Yes (where to?) _____ ☐ No      ☐ 22
    e. For another reason? (please specify) _____
                                                 ☐ Yes (where to?) _____ ☐ No      ☐ 23

6.  What was the arrangement of classes when you were studying? *(If you cannot remember the exact number, please give an estimated number.)*

    a.  In primary school
    How many terms were there each year? _____ terms.     □24
    How long was each term? _____ months.     □25
    How many class periods were there each week? _____ periods.     □□26–27
    What was the length of each period? _____ minutes.     □□28–29

    b.  In secondary school
    How many terms were there each year? _____ terms.     □30
    How long was each term? _____ months.     □31
    How many class periods were there each week? _____ periods.     □□32–33
    What was the length of each period? _____ minutes.     □□34–35

    c.  At university
    How many terms were there each year? _____ terms.     □36
    How long was each term? _____ months.     □37
    How many class periods were there each week? _____ periods.     □□38–39
    What was the length of each period? _____ minutes.     □□40–41

FOR
OFFICE USE

# Part II    Putonghua

1.  When did you start learning Putonghua?     □42
    ❑ At home from birth
    ❑ From kindergarten
    ❑ From primary school *(please specify grade)* _____
    ❑ From secondary school *(please specify grade)* _____
    ❑ Only when I went to university *(please specify year)* _____
    ❑ Only when I started working
    ❑ Another time *(please specify)* _____

2.  When did you start learning written Chinese?     □43
    ❑ At home from birth
    ❑ From kindergarten
    ❑ From primary school *(please specify grade)* _____
    ❑ From secondary school *(please specify grade)* _____
    ❑ Only when I went to university *(please specify year)* _____
    ❑ Only when I started working
    ❑ Another time *(please specify)* _____

3.  Please fill in the numbers of the Chinese classes you had:
    *(If you did not attend any Chinese classes, please fill in 0; if you cannot remember the exact number, please give an estimated number.)*
    a.  In primary school, I attended _____ periods of Chinese     □□44–45
    classes each week.

b. In secondary school, I attended _____ periods of Chinese classes each week.

⬚⬚46–47

c. At university, I attended _____ periods of Chinese classes each week.

⬚⬚48–49

4. Did your teacher(s) of Chinese classes teach in Putonghua?
   a. In primary school
   ❑ Yes, all of them    ❑ Yes, some of them    ❑ No, they did not

   ⬚50

   b. In secondary school
   ❑ Yes, all of them    ❑ Yes, some of them    ❑ No, they did not

   ⬚51

   c. At university
   ❑ Yes, all of them    ❑ Yes, some of them    ❑ No, they did not

   ⬚52

5. Did your teacher(s) of other subjects (e.g. mathematics, science) teach in Putonghua?
   a. In primary school
   ❑ Yes, all of them    ❑ Yes, some of them    ❑ No, they did not

   ⬚53

   b. In secondary school
   ❑ Yes, all of them    ❑ Yes, some of them    ❑ No, they did not

   ⬚54

   c. At university
   ❑ Yes, all of them    ❑ Yes, some of them    ❑ No, they did not

   ⬚55

6. Please describe any activity in the classroom or advice from your teacher(s) of Chinese classes that you found **especially useful** in learning Putonghua or written Chinese.

7. Please describe any activity in the classroom or advice from your teacher(s) of Chinese classes that you found **not too useful** in learning Putonghua or written Chinese.

8. Did you use Putonghua when conversing with your classmates outside the classroom?
   a. In primary school
      ❑ Yes, usually      ❑ Yes, sometimes      ❑ Not at all     ❑56

   b. In secondary school
      ❑ Yes, usually      ❑ Yes, sometimes      ❑ Not at all     ❑57

   c. At university
      ❑ Yes, usually      ❑ Yes, sometimes      ❑ Not at all     ❑58

   Note: If you usually used Putonghua when conversing with your classmates outside the classroom from primary school to university, please turn to Question 10 (page 4).

9. If you did not usually use Putonghua when conversing with your classmates outside the classroom, what was the reason? *(you can choose more than one answer)*
   ❑ Their Putonghua was not good enough.     ❑59
   ❑ I could express myself better in my own dialect.     ❑60
   ❑ I was afraid they would laugh at my mistakes.     ❑61
   ❑ I felt uncomfortable when I used Putonghua to communicate with someone who spoke the same Chinese dialect as I.     ❑62
   ❑ I felt it was impolite to use Putonghua when I communicated with someone who spoke the same Chinese dialect as I.     ❑63
   ❑ We felt closer as friends when we used our Chinese dialect.     ❑64
   ❑ It was just my habit not to use Putonghua all the time.     ❑65
   ❑ Another reason *(please specify)* _____ ❑66

10. When you were learning Putonghua, was there anyone at home who would speak Putonghua with you?
    ❑ Yes, very often because everyone at home used Putonghua.
    ❑ Yes, although not everyone at home used Putonghua, at least one of my family members could speak Putonghua.
    ❑ No, all my family members preferred to communicate in another Chinese dialect or minority language.
    ❑ No, none of my family members knew Putonghua.
    ❑ Another answer *(please specify)* _____

11. Did you do anything outside your Chinese classes to help you learn Putonghua or written Chinese better?
    a. Conversing with others
       ❑ Very often      ❑ Sometimes      ❑ Not at all     ❑68

    b. Practise by myself with tapes and materials
       ❑ Very often      ❑ Sometimes      ❑ Not at all     ❑69

    c. Listening to the radio
       ❑ Very often      ❑ Sometimes      ❑ Not at all     ❑70

    d. Watching television
       ❑ Very often      ❑ Sometimes      ❑ Not at all     ❑71

e. Seeing movies or watching video tapes
   ❏ Very often    ❏ Sometimes    ❏ Not at all       ❏72

f. Listening to songs or singing songs
   ❏ Very often    ❏ Sometimes    ❏ Not at all       ❏73

g. Checking the dictionary
   ❏ Very often    ❏ Sometimes    ❏ Not at all       ❏74

h. Reading newspapers or magazines
   ❏ Very often    ❏ Sometimes    ❏ Not at all       ❏75

i. Reading books
   ❏ Very often    ❏ Sometimes    ❏ Not at all       ❏76

j. Writing letters
   ❏ Very often    ❏ Sometimes    ❏ Not at all       ❏77

k. Other activities *(please specify)* _____
   ❏ Very often    ❏ Sometimes    ❏ Not at all       ❏78

12. Of the activities you did outside the classroom to learn Putonghua or written Chinese, which of them were most useful to you? Why?

13. By the time you left secondary school, did you feel your Putonghua was good enough for university education or your working life?
   ❏ Yes      ❏ No                           ❏79

14. After secondary school, did you try to improve your Putonghua further? If so, what did you do?

15. How would you rate your difficulty in learning Putonghua?
   ❏ Very easy         ❏ Easy         ❏ Neutral     ❏80
   ❏ Somewhat difficult    ❏ Very difficult

16. Which aspects of Putonghua did you find easy or difficult to learn?
    a. Pronunciation
       ❏ Easy         ❏ Neutral                                    ☐81
       ❏ Difficult    ❏ Did not use Putonghua in this way

    b. Conversation
       ❏ Easy         ❏ Neutral                                    ☐82
       ❏ Difficult    ❏ Did not use Putonghua in this way

    c. Making a speech
       ❏ Easy         ❏ Neutral                                    ☐83
       ❏ Difficult    ❏ Did not use Putonghua in this way

    d. Listening to news broadcasts
       ❏ Easy         ❏ Neutral                                    ☐84
       ❏ Difficult    ❏ Did not use Putonghua in this way

    e. Listening to academic or technical lectures
       ❏ Easy         ❏ Neutral                                    ☐85
       ❏ Difficult    ❏ Did not use Putonghua in this way

    f. Knowledge of *hanyu pinyin*
       ❏ Easy         ❏ Neutral                                    ☐86
       ❏ Difficult    ❏ Did not use Putonghua in this way

17. How would you rate your difficulty in learning written Chinese?
    ❏ Very easy             ❏ Easy           ❏ Neutral             ☐87
    ❏ Somewhat difficult    ❏ Very difficult

18. Which aspects of written Chinese did you find easy or difficult to learn?
    a. Reading simple instructions
       ❏ Easy         ❏ Neutral                                    ☐88
       ❏ Difficult    ❏ Did not use written Chinese in this way

    b. Reading newspaper articles
       ❏ Easy         ❏ Neutral                                    ☐89
       ❏ Difficult    ❏ Did not use written Chinese in this way Easy

    c. Reading academic or technical materials
       ❏ Easy         ❏ Neutral                                    ☐90
       ❏ Difficult    ❏ Did not use written Chinese in this way

    d. Writing a simple letter
       ❏ Easy         ❏ Neutral                                    ☐91
       ❏ Difficult    ❏ Did not use written Chinese in this way

    e. Writing an academic or technical paper
       ❏ Easy         ❏ Neutral                                    ☐92
       ❏ Difficult    ❏ Did not use written Chinese in this way

    f. Knowledge of simplified characters
       ❏ Easy         ❏ Neutral                                    ☐93
       ❏ Difficult    ❏ Did not use written Chinese in this way

g. Knowledge of complex characters
- ❏ Easy        ❏ Neutral
- ❏ Difficult   ❏ Did not use written Chinese in this way

❏94

h. Writing simplified characters
- ❏ Easy        ❏ Neutral
- ❏ Difficult   ❏ Did not use written Chinese in this way

❏95

i. Writing complex characters
- ❏ Easy        ❏ Neutral
- ❏ Difficult   ❏ Did not use written Chinese in this way

❏96

19. Please explain why you found some aspects in Putonghua or written Chinese easy or difficult to learn.

20. Which of the following sentences **best describes** your feeling about learning Putonghua? *(please choose only one)*

❏97

- ❏ I should learn Putonghua really well because it is our national language.
- ❏ I should learn Putonghua because it is widely used in China.
- ❏ I learnt Putonghua because this was the requirement at school or university.
- ❏ I learnt Putonghua in order to communicate with my family members.
- ❏ I feel more confident if I speak Putonghua well.
- ❏ I like learning Putonghua because I am interested in studying languages.
- ❏ I could not learn Putonghua well because it was not very much used in my region.
- ❏ I could not learn Putonghua well because I was too old to learn.
- ❏ Another answer *(please specify)* _____

21. How would you rate your ability in Putonghua?

a. Pronunciation
- ❏ Not too good  ❏ Okay       ❏ Good
- ❏ Very good     ❏ Excellent  ❏ Did not use Putonghua in this way

❏98

b. Conversation
- ❏ Not too good  ❏ Okay       ❏ Good
- ❏ Very good     ❏ Excellent  ❏ Did not use Putonghua in this way

❏99

c. Making a speech
- ❏ Not too good  ❏ Okay       ❏ Good
- ❏ Very good     ❏ Excellent  ❏ Did not use Putonghua in this way

❏100

d. Listening to news broadcasts
   ❏ Not too good ❏ Okay ❏ Good
   ❏ Very good ❏ Excellent ❏ Did not use Putonghua in this way  ❏101

e. Listening to academic or technical lectures
   ❏ Not too good ❏ Okay ❏ Good
   ❏ Very good ❏ Excellent ❏ Did not use Putonghua in this way  ❏102

f. Knowledge of *hanyu pinyin*
   ❏ Not too good ❏ Okay ❏ Good
   ❏ Very good ❏ Excellent ❏ Did not use Putonghua in this way  ❏103

22. How would you rate your ability in written Chinese?
   a. Reading simple instructions
      ❏ Not too good ❏ Okay ❏ Good
      ❏ Very good ❏ Excellent ❏ Did not use written Chinese in this way  ❏104

   b. Reading newspaper articles
      ❏ Not too good ❏ Okay ❏ Good
      ❏ Very good ❏ Excellent ❏ Did not use written Chinese in this way  ❏105

   c. Reading academic or technical materials
      ❏ Not too good ❏ Okay ❏ Good
      ❏ Very good ❏ Excellent ❏ Did not use written Chinese in this way  ❏106

   d. Writing a simple letter
      ❏ Not too good ❏ Okay ❏ Good
      ❏ Very good ❏ Excellent ❏ Did not use written Chinese in this way  ❏107

   e. Writing an academic or technical paper
      ❏ Not too good ❏ Okay ❏ Good
      ❏ Very good ❏ Excellent ❏ Did not use written Chinese in this way  ❏108

   f. Knowledge of simplified characters
      ❏ Not too good ❏ Okay ❏ Good
      ❏ Very good ❏ Excellent ❏ Did not use written Chinese in this way  ❏109

   g. Knowledge of complex characters
      ❏ Not too good ❏ Okay ❏ Good
      ❏ Very good ❏ Excellent ❏ Did not use written Chinese in this way  ❏110

   h. Writing simplified characters
      ❏ Not too good ❏ Okay ❏ Good
      ❏ Very good ❏ Excellent ❏ Did not use written Chinese in this way  ❏111

   i. Writing complex characters
      ❏ Not too good ❏ Okay ❏ Good
      ❏ Very good ❏ Excellent ❏ Did not use written Chinese in this way  ❏112

23. Do you now use Putonghua?
   a. At home
      ❏ Very often ❏ Sometimes ❏ Not at all  ❏113

b. At work
  ❏ Very often    ❏ Sometimes    ❏ Not at all         □114

c. Conversing with friends
  ❏ Very often    ❏ Sometimes    ❏ Not at all         □115

d. At government offices
  ❏ Very often    ❏ Sometimes    ❏ Not at all         □116

e. When shopping or in restaurants
  ❏ Very often    ❏ Sometimes    ❏ Not at all         □117

f. Another answer *(please specify)* _____
  ❏ Very often    ❏ Sometimes    ❏ Not at all         □118

24. Do you now use written Chinese?
  a. At home
    ❏ Very often    ❏ Sometimes    ❏ Not at all       □119

  b. At work
    ❏ Very often    ❏ Sometimes    ❏ Not at all       □120

  c. Writing letters to friends
    ❏ Very often    ❏ Sometimes    ❏ Not at all       □121

  d. At government offices
    ❏ Very often    ❏ Sometimes    ❏ Not at all       □122

  e. When shopping or in restaurants
    ❏ Very often    ❏ Sometimes    ❏ Not at all       □123

  f. Another answer *(please specify)* _____
    ❏ Very often    ❏ Sometimes    ❏ Not at all       □124

## Part III   Other Chinese dialects

FOR
OFFICE USE

1. Besides Putonghua, do you know any other Chinese dialect? If "Yes", please list them all. If your answer is "No", please turn to Part IV of the survey (page 10).

2. Besides Putonghua, into which of the following types would you classify the Chinese dialect **you know best**? *(please choose only one)*

❏ Beijing Guanhua  (Beijing, Shenyang etc.)
❏ Northern Guanhua  (Jinan in Shandong, Cangzhou etc.)
❏ Jiaoliao Guanhua  (Qingdao, Yantai, Dalian etc.)
❏ Central Guanhua  (South of Huanghe in Henan; western parts of Shandong; southwestern parts of Shanxi and Luoyang, Zhengzhou, Xinyang, Fuyang, Xuzhou, Qufu, Xian, Yuncheng in central parts of Shaanxi)
❏ Lanyin Guanhua  (Lanzhou, Yinchuan etc.)
❏ Southwestern Guanhua  (Chengdu, Zhongqing, Wuhan, Kunming, Guiyang, Guilin etc.)
❏ Jianghuai Guanhua  (Parts of Linjiang between Jiujiang in Jiangxi and Zhenjiang in Jiangsu)
❏ Jiangzhe Hua  (Suzhou Hua or Shanghai Hua) (South of Changjiang and east of Zhenjiang within Jiangsu; Jingjiang, Haimen and Qidong in north of Changjiang; most parts of Zhejiang and Tongling in southern parts of Anhui).
❏ Hunan Hua  (Changsha Hua, Shuangfeng Hua) (Most parts of Hunan; Yiyang, Quanzhou, Ziyuan and Xingan in northern parts of Guangxi; Changsha, Changde and Zhuzhou; around Shuangfeng and Hengyang)
❏ Jiangxi Hua  (Central and northern parts of Jiangxi; southeast corner of Hubei and the marginal area of eastern parts of Hunan)
❏ Kejia Hua  (Eastern and northern parts of Guangdong; western and northern parts of Fujian; southern parts of Jiangxi; southeast corner of Hunan; some stretches in Taiwan, Guangxi and Sichuan)
❏ Guangzhou Hua  (Central and southwestern parts of Guangdong; southeastern parts of Guangxi; Hong Kong and Macau)
❏ Fujian Hua or Minnan Hua  (Fuzhou Hua, Xiamen Hua) (Eastern, southern and central parts of Fujian; around Chaozhou and Shantou in eastern parts of Guangdong; Hainan and some parts of the Leizhou Peninsula; most parts of Taiwan; Pingyang, Yuhuan and Zhoushan Qundao in southern parts of Zhejiang; around Yushan and Yanshan in Jiangxi)

☐125

3. When did you start learning this dialect?
❏ At home from birth
❏ From kindergarten

☐126

❑ From primary school *(please specify grade)* _____
❑ From secondary school *(please specify grade)* _____
❑ Only when I went to university *(please specify year)* _____
❑ Only when I started working
❑ Another time *(please specify)* _____

4. Which of the following sentences **best describes** your feeling about
   learning the Chinese dialect (not Putonghua) you know best? *(please
   choose only one)*
   ❑ I should learn this Chinese dialect because it has been the dialect of
   my parents and ancestors.
   ❑ I should learn this Chinese dialect because it is widely used in my
   region.
   ❑ I learnt this Chinese dialect because it was a requirement at school,
   university or my place of work.
   ❑ I learnt this Chinese dialect in order to communicate with one or more
   of my family members.
   ❑ I feel happy about being able to speak this Chinese dialect.
   ❑ I like learning this Chinese dialect because I am interested in studying
   languages.
   ❑ I could not learn this Chinese dialect well because it was not very much
   used in my region.
   ❑ I could not learn this Chinese dialect well because I was already rather
   old when I tried to learn it.
   ❑ Another answer *(please specify)* _____

   ❑127

5. How would you rate your speaking and listening abilities in this Chinese
   dialect (not Putonghua) you know best?
   a. Pronunciation
      ❑ Not too good  ❑ Okay      ❑ Good
      ❑ Very good     ❑ Excellent  ❑ Did not use the dialect in this way

      ❑128

   b. Conversation
      ❑ Not too good  ❑ Okay      ❑ Good
      ❑ Very good     ❑ Excellent  ❑ Did not use the dialect in this way

      ❑129

   c. Making a speech
      ❑ Not too good  ❑ Okay      ❑ Good
      ❑ Very good     ❑ Excellent  ❑ Did not use the dialect in this way

      ❑130

   d. Listening to news broadcasts
      ❑ Not too good  ❑ Okay      ❑ Good
      ❑ Very good     ❑ Excellent  ❑ Did not use the dialect in this way

      ❑131

   e. Listening to academic or technical lectures
      ❑ Not too good  ❑ Okay      ❑ Good
      ❑ Very good     ❑ Excellent  ❑ Did not use the dialect in this way

      ❑132

6. Do you now use this dialect?
   a. At home
      ❑ Very often ❑ Sometimes ❑ Not at all                □133

   b. At work
      ❑ Very often ❑ Sometimes ❑ Not at all                □134

   c. Conversing with friends
      ❑ Very often ❑ Sometimes ❑ Not at all                □135

   d. At government offices
      ❑ Very often ❑ Sometimes ❑ Not at all                □136

   e. When shopping or in restaurants
      ❑ Very often ❑ Sometimes ❑ Not at all                □137

   f. Another answer *(please specify)* _____
      ❑ Very often ❑ Sometimes ❑ Not at all                □138

## Part IV   Minority languages in China

FOR
OFFICE USE

1. Besides Putonghua and Chinese dialects, do you know any minority
   language? If "Yes", please list them all. If your answer is "No", please
   turn to Part V of the survey.

2. Of the minority languages you list in question 1, which one do you know   □139
   best?

   _____

   _____

3. When did you start learning how to speak this minority language?
   ❑ At home from birth                                    □140
   ❑ From kindergarten
   ❑ From primary school *(please specify grade)* _____
   ❑ From secondary school *(please specify grade)* _____
   ❑ Only when I went to university *(please specify year)* _____
   ❑ Only when I started working _____
   ❑ Another time *(please specify)* _____

4. When did you start learning how to write this minority language?   ☐140a
   - ☐ At home from birth
   - ☐ From kindergarten
   - ☐ From primary school *(please specify grade)* _____
   - ☐ From secondary school *(please specify grade)* _____
   - ☐ Only when I went to university *(please specify year)* _____
   - ☐ Only when I started working
   - ☐ Another time *(please specify)* _____

5. Which of the following sentences **best describes** your feeling about   ☐141
   learning the minority language you know best? *(please choose only one)*
   - ☐ I should learn this minority language because it has been the language of my parents and ancestors.
   - ☐ I should learn this minority language because it is widely used in my region.
   - ☐ I learnt this minority language because it was a requirement at school, university or my place of work.
   - ☐ I learnt this minority language in order to communicate with one or more of my family members.
   - ☐ I feel happy about being able to speak this minority language.
   - ☐ I like learning this minority language because I am interested in studying languages.
   - ☐ I could not learn this minority language well because it was not very much used in my region.
   - ☐ I could not learn this minority language well because I was already rather old when I tried to learn it.
   - ☐ Another answer *(please specify)* _____

6. How would you rate your speaking and listening abilities in this minority language?
   a. Pronunciation   ☐142
      - ☐ Not too good    ☐ Okay    ☐ Good
      - ☐ Very good    ☐ Excellent    ☐ Did not use the minority language in this way

   b. Conversation   ☐143
      - ☐ Not too good    ☐ Okay    ☐ Good
      - ☐ Very good    ☐ Excellent    ☐ Did not use the minority language in this way

   c. Making a speech   ☐144
      - ☐ Not too good    ☐ Okay    ☐ Good
      - ☐ Very good    ☐ Excellent    ☐ Did not use the minority language in this way

   d. Listening to news broadcasts   ☐145
      - ☐ Not too good    ☐ Okay    ☐ Good
      - ☐ Very good    ☐ Excellent    ☐ Did not use the minority language in this way

e. Listening to academic or technical lectures
   ❏ Not too good  ❏ Okay    ❏ Good              ❏146
   ❏ Very good    ❏ Excellent  ❏ Did not use the minority
                                     language in this way

7. How would you rate your reading and writing abilities in this minority language?
   a. Reading simple instructions
      ❏ Not too good  ❏ Okay    ❏ Good              ❏147
      ❏ Very good    ❏ Excellent  ❏ Did not use the minority
                                        language in this way

   b. Reading newspaper articles
      ❏ Not too good  ❏ Okay    ❏ Good              ❏148
      ❏ Very good    ❏ Excellent  ❏ Did not use the minority
                                        language in this way

   c. Reading academic or technical materials
      ❏ Not too good  ❏ Okay    ❏ Good              ❏149
      ❏ Very good    ❏ Excellent  ❏ Did not use the minority
                                        language in this way

   d. Writing a simple letter
      ❏ Not too good  ❏ Okay    ❏ Good              ❏150
      ❏ Very good    ❏ Excellent  ❏ Did not use the minority
                                        language in this way

   e. Writing an academic or technical paper
      ❏ Not too good  ❏ Okay    ❏ Good              ❏151
      ❏ Very good    ❏ Excellent  ❏ Did not use the minority
                                        language in this way

8. Do you now use this minority language?
   a. At home
      ❏ Very often    ❏ Sometimes    ❏ Not at all      ❏152

   b. At work
      ❏ Very often    ❏ Sometimes    ❏ Not at all      ❏153

   c. Conversing with friends
      ❏ Very often    ❏ Sometimes    ❏ Not at all      ❏154

   d. At government offices
      ❏ Very often    ❏ Sometimes    ❏ Not at all      ❏155

   e. When shopping or in restaurants
      ❏ Very often    ❏ Sometimes    ❏ Not at all      ❏156

   f. Another answer *(please specify)* _____
      ❏ Very often    ❏ Sometimes    ❏ Not at all      ❏157

## Part V   First foreign language

1.  Please specify your first foreign language *(the one you know best)*

☐158

2.  When did you start learning how to speak your first foreign language?
    - ☐ At home from birth
    - ☐ From kindergarten
    - ☐ From primary school *(please specify grade)* _____
    - ☐ From secondary school *(please specify grade)* _____
    - ☐ Only when I went to university *(please specify year)* _____
    - ☐ Only when I started working
    - ☐ Another time *(please specify)* _____

☐159

3.  When did you start learning how to write your first foreign language?
    - ☐ At home from birth
    - ☐ From kindergarten
    - ☐ From primary school *(please specify grade)* _____
    - ☐ From secondary school *(please specify grade)* _____
    - ☐ Only when I went to university *(please specify year)* _____
    - ☐ Only when I started working
    - ☐ Another time *(please specify)* _____

☐160

4.  Please fill in the numbers of the first foreign language classes you had:
    *(If you did not attend any first foreign language classes, please fill in 0; if you cannot remember the exact number, please give an estimated number.)*

    a.  In primary school, I attended _____ periods of first foreign language classes each week.

☐☐161–162

    b.  In secondary school, I attended _____ periods of first foreign language classes each week.

☐☐163–164

    c.  At university, I attended _____ periods of first foreign language classes each week.

☐☐165–166

5.  Did teacher(s) of your first foreign language classes teach in the foreign language?

    a.  In primary school
        ☐ Yes, all of them   ☐ Yes, some of them   ☐ No, they did not

☐167

    b.  In secondary school
        ☐ Yes, all of them   ☐ Yes, some of them   ☐ No, they did not

☐168

    c.  At university
        ☐ Yes, all of them   ☐ Yes, some of them   ☐ No, they did not

☐169

6. Did teacher(s) of other subjects (e.g. mathematics, science) teach in your first foreign language?
   a. In primary school
      ❑ Yes, all of them    ❑ Yes, some of them    ❑ No, they did not    ❑170

   b. In secondary school
      ❑ Yes, all of them    ❑ Yes, some of them    ❑ No, they did not    ❑171

   c. At university
      ❑ Yes, all of them    ❑ Yes, some of them    ❑ No, they did not    ❑172

7. Please describe any activity in the classroom or advice from your foreign language teacher(s) that you found e**specially useful** in learning your first foreign language.

8. Please describe any activity in the classroom or advice from your foreign language teacher(s) that you found **not too useful** in learning your first foreign language.

9. Did you use your first foreign language when conversing with your classmates outside the classroom?
   a. In primary school
      ❑ Yes, usually    ❑ Yes, sometimes    ❑ Not at all    ❑173

   b. In secondary school
      ❑ Yes, usually    ❑ Yes, sometimes    ❑ Not at all    ❑174

   c. At university
      ❑ Yes, usually    ❑ Yes, sometimes    ❑ Not at all    ❑175

   Note: If you usually used your first foreign language when conversing with your classmates outside the classroom from primary school to university, please turn to Question 11.

10. If you did not usually use your first foreign language when conversing
    with your classmates outside the classroom, what was the reason? *(you
    can choose more than one answer)*
    ❏ Their foreign language was not good enough.                              ☐176
    ❏ I could express myself better in Putonghua or a Chinese dialect.         ☐177
    ❏ I was afraid they would laugh at my mistakes.                            ☐178
    ❏ I felt uncomfortable if I used a foreign language to communicate with    ☐179
      Chinese-speaking people.
    ❏ I felt it was impolite to use a foreign language to communicate with     ☐180
      Chinese-speaking people.
    ❏ We felt closer as friends when we used our own language.                 ☐181
    ❏ It was just my habit not to use my foreign language so often.            ☐182
    ❏ Another reason *(please specify)* _____            ☐183

11. When you were learning your first foreign language, was there anyone at    ☐184
    home who would speak this language with you?
    ❏ Yes, quite often because this foreign language was also used at home.
    ❏ Yes, although this foreign language was not often spoken at home, at
      least one of my family members could also speak this language.
    ❏ No, my family members preferred to communicate in Putonghua or a
      Chinese dialect or minority language.
    ❏ No, none of my family members knew this foreign language.
    ❏ Another answer *(please specify)* _____

12. Did you do anything outside your first foreign language classes to help
    you learn this language better?
    a. Conversing with others
       ❏ Very often    ❏ Sometimes      ❏ Not at all                          ☐185

    b. Practise by myself with tapes and materials
       ❏ Very often    ❏ Sometimes      ❏ Not at all                          ☐186

    c. Listening to the radio
       ❏ Very often    ❏ Sometimes      ❏ Not at all                          ☐187

    d. Watching television
       ❏ Very often    ❏ Sometimes      ❏ Not at all                          ☐188

    e. Seeing movies or watching video tapes
       ❏ Very often    ❏ Sometimes      ❏ Not at all                          ☐189

    f. Listening to songs or singing songs
       ❏ Very often    ❏ Sometimes      ❏ Not at all                          ☐190

    g. Checking the dictionary
       ❏ Very often    ❏ Sometimes      ❏ Not at all                          ☐191

    h. Reading newspapers or magazines
       ❏ Very often    ❏ Sometimes      ❏ Not at all                          ☐192

    i. Reading books
       ❏ Very often    ❏ Sometimes      ❏ Not at all                          ☐193

j. Writing letters
   ❑ Very often    ❑ Sometimes    ❑ Not at all       ☐194

k. Other activities *(please specify)* _____
   ❑ Very often    ❑ Sometimes    ❑ Not at all       ☐195

13. Of the activities you did outside the classroom to learn your first foreign language, which of them were most useful to you? Why?

14. By the time you left secondary school, did you feel your first foreign language was good enough for university education or your working life?
   ❑ Yes        ❑    No       ☐196

15. After secondary school, did you try to improve your first foreign language further? If so, what did you do?

16. How would you rate your difficulty in learning the oral aspects of your first foreign language?
   ❑ Very easy        ❑ Easy       ❑ Neutral      ☐197
   ❑ Somewhat difficult    ❑ Very difficult

17. Which oral aspects of your first foreign language did you find easy or difficult to learn?
  a. Pronunciation
     ❑ Easy        ❑ Neutral                ☐198
     ❑ Difficult    ❑ Did not use the foreign language in this way

  b. Conversation
     ❑ Easy        ❑ Neutral                ☐199
     ❑ Difficult    ❑ Did not use the foreign language in this way

  c. Making a speech
     ❑ Easy        ❑ Neutral                ☐200
     ❑ Difficult    ❑ Did not use the foreign language in this way

d. Listening to news broadcasts
- ❏ Easy        ❏ Neutral
- ❏ Difficult   ❏ Did not use the foreign language in this way

❏ 201

e. Listening to academic or technical lectures
- ❏ Easy        ❏ Neutral
- ❏ Difficult   ❏ Did not use the foreign language in this way

❏ 202

18. How would you rate your difficulty in learning the written aspects of your first foreign language?
- ❏ Very easy         ❏ Easy          ❏ Neutral
- ❏ Somewhat difficult  ❏ Very difficult

❏ 203

19. Which written aspects of your first foreign language did you find easy or difficult to learn?

a. Reading simple instructions
- ❏ Easy        ❏ Neutral
- ❏ Difficult   ❏ Did not use the foreign language in this way

❏ 204

b. Reading newspaper articles
- ❏ Easy        ❏ Neutral
- ❏ Difficult   ❏ Did not use the foreign language in this way

❏ 205

c. Reading academic or technical materials
- ❏ Easy        ❏ Neutral
- ❏ Difficult   ❏ Did not use the foreign language in this way

❏ 206

d. Writing a simple letter
- ❏ Easy        ❏ Neutral
- ❏ Difficult   ❏ Did not use the foreign language in this way

❏ 207

e. Writing an academic or technical paper
- ❏ Easy        ❏ Neutral
- ❏ Difficult   ❏ Did not use the foreign language in this way

❏ 208

20. Please explain why you found some aspects of your first foreign language easy or difficult to learn.

21. Which of the following sentences **best describes** your feeling about learning the first foreign language? *(please choose only one)*
- ❏ I should learn this foreign language really well because it is an international language.

❏ 209

❏ I should learn this foreign language because it is increasingly used in China.

❏ I learnt this foreign language because it was a requirement at school or university.

❏ I learnt this foreign language in order to communicate with foreigners in my work.

❏ I feel more confident if I can speak this foreign language well.

❏ I like learning this foreign language because I am interested in studying languages.

❏ I could not learn this foreign language well because it was not very much used in my region.

❏ I could not learn this foreign language well because I was too old to learn.

❏ Another answer *(please specify)* _____

□ 209

22. How would you rate your speaking and listening abilities in your first foreign language?

a. Pronunciation
   ❏ Not too good  ❏ Okay  ❏ Good
   ❏ Very good  ❏ Excellent  ❏ Did not use the foreign language in this way

□ 210

b. Conversation
   ❏ Not too good  ❏ Okay  ❏ Good
   ❏ Very good  ❏ Excellent  ❏ Did not use the foreign language in this way

□ 211

c. Making a speech
   ❏ Not too good  ❏ Okay  ❏ Good
   ❏ Very good  ❏ Excellent  ❏ Did not use the foreign language in this way

□ 212

d. Listening to news broadcasts
   ❏ Not too good  ❏ Okay  ❏ Good
   ❏ Very good  ❏ Excellent  ❏ Did not use the foreign language in this way

□ 213

e. Listening to academic or technical lectures
   ❏ Not too good  ❏ Okay  ❏ Good
   ❏ Very good  ❏ Excellent  ❏ Did not use the foreign language in this way

□ 214

23. How would you rate your reading and writing abilities in your first foreign language?

a. Reading simple instructions
   ❏ Not too good  ❏ Okay  ❏ Good
   ❏ Very good  ❏ Excellent  ❏ Did not use the foreign language in this way

□ 215

  b. Reading newspaper articles                                      ☐216
- ❑ Not too good ❑ Okay ❑ Good
- ❑ Very good ❑ Excellent ❑ Did not use the foreign language in this way

  c. Reading academic or technical materials              ☐217
- ❑ Not too good ❑ Okay ❑ Good
- ❑ Very good ❑ Excellent ❑ Did not use the foreign language in this way

  d. Writing a simple letter                                      ☐218
- ❑ Not too good ❑ Okay ❑ Good
- ❑ Very good ❑ Excellent ❑ Did not use the foreign language in this way

  e. Writing an academic or technical paper             ☐219
- ❑ Not too good ❑ Okay ❑ Good
- ❑ Very good ❑ Excellent ❑ Did not use the foreign language in this way

24. Do you now speak or listen in your first foreign language?
  a. At home
- ❑ Very often ❑ Sometimes ❑ Not at all           ☐220

  b. At work
- ❑ Very often ❑ Sometimes ❑ Not at all           ☐221

  c. Conversing with friends
- ❑ Very often ❑ Sometimes ❑ Not at all           ☐222

  d. At government offices
- ❑ Very often ❑ Sometimes ❑ Not at all           ☐223

  e. When shopping or in restaurants
- ❑ Very often ❑ Sometimes ❑ Not at all           ☐224

  f. Another answer *(please specify)* _____
- ❑ Very often ❑ Sometimes ❑ Not at all           ☐225

25. Do you now read or write in your first foreign language?
  a. At home
- ❑ Very often ❑ Sometimes ❑ Not at all           ☐226

  b. At work
- ❑ Very often ❑ Sometimes ❑ Not at all           ☐227

  c. Writing letters to friends
- ❑ Very often ❑ Sometimes ❑ Not at all           ☐228

  d. At government offices
- ❑ Very often ❑ Sometimes ❑ Not at all           ☐229

e. When shopping or in restaurants
   ❑ Very often    ❑ Sometimes    ❑ Not at all    ☐230

f. Another answer *(please specify)* _____
   ❑ Very often    ❑ Sometimes    ❑ Not at all    ☐231

## Part VI   Second foreign language

FOR
OFFICE USE

1. Besides your first foreign language, do you know other foreign languages?
   If "Yes", please list them all. If your answer is "No", please turn to Part
   VII of the survey (page 20).

2. Of the other foreign languages you know (besides your first foreign    ☐232
   language), please specify the one you know best: _____

   We shall refer to this foreign language as your second foreign language
   in this survey from now on.

3. When did you start learning how to speak your second foreign language?
   ❑ At home from birth    ☐233
   ❑ From kindergarten
   ❑ From primary school *(please specify grade)* _____
   ❑ From secondary school *(please specify grade)* _____
   ❑ Only when I went to university *(please specify year)* _____
   ❑ Only when I started working
   ❑ Another time *(please specify)* _____

4. When did you start learning how to write your second foreign language?
   ❑ At home from birth    ☐234
   ❑ From kindergarten
   ❑ From primary school *(please specify grade)* _____
   ❑ From secondary school *(please specify grade)* _____
   ❑ Only when I went to university *(please specify year)* _____
   ❑ Only when I started working
   ❑ Another time *(please specify)* _____

5. Which of the following sentences **best describes** your feeling about learning the second foreign language you know best? *(please choose only one)*
   ❑ I should learn this foreign language because it is an international language.
   ❑ I should learn this foreign language because it is increasingly used in China.
   ❑ I learnt this foreign language because it was a requirement at school or university.
   ❑ I learnt this foreign language in order to communicate with foreigners in my work.
   ❑ I feel more confident if I can speak this foreign language well.
   ❑ I like learning this foreign language because I am interested in studying languages.
   ❑ I could not learn this foreign language well because it was not very much used in my region.
   ❑ I could not learn this foreign language well because I was too old to learn.
   ❑ Another answer *(please specify)* _____

   ☐235

6. How would you rate your speaking and listening abilities in your second foreign language?
   a. Pronunciation
      ❑ Not too good  ❑ Okay      ❑ Good
      ❑ Very good     ❑ Excellent  ❑ Did not use the foreign language in this way

      ☐236

   b. Conversation
      ❑ Not too good  ❑ Okay      ❑ Good
      ❑ Very good     ❑ Excellent  ❑ Did not use the foreign language in this way

      ☐237

   c. Making a speech
      ❑ Not too good  ❑ Okay      ❑ Good
      ❑ Very good     ❑ Excellent  ❑ Did not use the foreign language in this way

      ☐238

   d. Listening to news broadcasts
      ❑ Not too good  ❑ Okay      ❑ Good
      ❑ Very good     ❑ Excellent  ❑ Did not use the foreign language in this way

      ☐239

   e. Listening to academic or technical lectures
      ❑ Not too good  ❑ Okay      ❑ Good
      ❑ Very good     ❑ Excellent  ❑ Did not use the foreign language in this way

      ☐240

7. How would you rate your reading and writing abilities in your second foreign language?
   a. Reading simple instructions
   ❑ Not too good ❑ Okay ❑ Good
   ❑ Very good ❑ Excellent ❑ Did not use the foreign language in this way
   ☐241

   b. Reading newspaper articles
   ❑ Not too good ❑ Okay ❑ Good
   ❑ Very good ❑ Excellent ❑ Did not use the foreign language in this way
   ☐242

   c. Reading academic or technical materials
   ❑ Not too good ❑ Okay ❑ Good
   ❑ Very good ❑ Excellent ❑ Did not use the foreign language in this way
   ☐243

   d. Writing a simple letter
   ❑ Not too good ❑ Okay ❑ Good
   ❑ Very good ❑ Excellent ❑ Did not use the foreign language in this way
   ☐244

   e. Writing an academic or technical paper
   ❑ Not too good ❑ Okay ❑ Good
   ❑ Very good ❑ Excellent ❑ Did not use the foreign language in this way
   ☐245

8. Do you now use your second foreign language?
   a. At home
   ❑ Very often ❑ Sometimes ❑ Not at all
   ☐246

   b. At work
   ❑ Very often ❑ Sometimes ❑ Not at all
   ☐247

   c. Conversing with friends
   ❑ Very often ❑ Sometimes ❑ Not at all
   ☐248

   d. At government offices
   ❑ Very often ❑ Sometimes ❑ Not at all
   ☐249

   e. When shopping or in restaurants
   ❑ Very often ❑ Sometimes ❑ Not at all
   ☐250

   f. Another answer *(please specify)* _____
   ❑ Very often ❑ Sometimes ❑ Not at all
   ☐251

## Part VII  Other comments

Do you have any other comments on your language learning experience?

THANK YOU VERY MUCH FOR YOUR CO-OPERATION.

# Appendix II
# Interview Questions for Han Chinese Learners

An adapted version of these questions was used to interview minority learners.

## Interview for Han Chinese learners (December 2000)

### I. Background

1. Respondent's Project ID No.: _____

2. Respondent's name: _____ Place of birth: _____

3. Age: _____ Sex: _____ Occupation: _____

4. Date: _____ Time: _____ Place of interview: _____

---

### II. Interview probes

1. What languages do you know/speak? Which ones do you know/speak best?

2. How did you learn each of them? At school? From family members? From using it with other people? By yourself?

3. What helped or hindered you in your learning? Any particular incidents you can remember? Was your learning of a new language or dialect affected by:

   a. the language(s) or dialect(s) you already knew? your learning experience?
   b. your personality? how you felt about the language?
   c. how you felt about other learners?
   d. what you thought of your teacher? what he/she did/did not do?
   e. the language circumstances/policies in the community/country? media?

4. Can you remember how much time you spent learning Putonghua/Chinese and learning English? Different at different levels? Can you remember some of the activities in class or the titles of the books you used?

5. What is the best way to learn a language? What are the most important factors? Do you think literature has a place too in the curriculum if we only want to learn how to use a language for specific purposes? Should language skills be taught separately? How much time does a learner need to spend to learn a language well?

6. What would you like your school/university/government to do to help you learn the language(s) you know better?

# Appendix III
# Questionnaire for the Survey of Chinese Panel Heads (Primary Schools)

An adapted version of this questionnaire was used to survey Chinese panel heads in secondary schools and English panel heads in primary and secondary schools.

## Survey of Chinese programme (Primary school), September 1999

Part I     Background information
Part II    Teachers
Part III   Chinese programme
Part IV    Ideas on language learning
Part V     Other comments

Reference number: ☐☐☐-☐☐☐-☐☐☐ 1–9

## Part I    Background information

FOR OFFICE USE

1.  Name of school: _____

2.  Location of school: _____ (*nearest big city*) _____ (*region*)

3.  Type of school
    ❑ Primary school                                            ☐☐☐ 10–12
    ❑ Junior middle school
    ❑ Senior middle school                                      ☐☐☐☐ 13–16

4.  In what year was your school established? _____        ☐ 17

5.  Type of language programme                                       ☐ 18
    ❑ Chinese programme
    ❑ Minority language(s) programme
    ❑ English programme

6.  When did your school start teaching Putonghua?                   ☐ 19
    ❑ Before 1949
    ❑ 1949–1965
    ❑ 1966–1977
    ❑ 1978–1988
    ❑ After 1988

7. Do you have any other information on the history of your Chinese programme? For example, any major changes in its role, the medium of instruction, curricular emphasis or type of students?

8. How many students are there in your school? _____  ☐20

9. Of the total number of students in your school, please estimate the percentages for the following groups.
   a. Students from minority language backgrounds  ☐21
      ☐ 0%
      ☐ 1%–5 %
      ☐ 6%–10%
      ☐ 11%–15%
      ☐ 16%–20%
      ☐ 21%–25%
      ☐ Another percentage (*please specify*) _____

   b. Chinese students from overseas  ☐22
      ☐ 0%
      ☐ 1%–5 %
      ☐ 6%–10%
      ☐ 11%–15%
      ☐ 16%–20%
      ☐ 21%–25%
      ☐ Another percentage (*please specify*) _____

   c. Foreign students from other countries  ☐23
      ☐ 0%
      ☐ 1%–5 %
      ☐ 6%–10%
      ☐ 11%–15%
      ☐ 16%–20%
      ☐ 21% - 25%
      ☐ Another percentage (*please specify*) _____

## Part II  Teachers

1.  List the staff grades and the number of teachers in each grade for teachers teaching Chinese in your school.

2.  What is the highest qualification of the **most junior** teacher teaching Chinese in your school?
    - ❏ Teaching certificate or diploma
    - ❏ Bachelor degree
    - ❏ Master degree
    - ❏ Other (*please specify*) _____

    ❏24

3.  What is the highest qualification of the **most senior** teacher teaching Chinese in your school?
    - ❏ Teaching certificate or diploma
    - ❏ Bachelor degree
    - ❏ Master degree
    - ❏ Other (*please specify*) _____

    ❏25

4.  How many years has your **most junior** teacher been teaching Chinese?
    - ❏ 5 years or less
    - ❏ 6 to 10 years
    - ❏ 11 to 15 years
    - ❏ 16 to 20 years
    - ❏ 21 to 25 years
    - ❏ 26 to 30 years
    - ❏ 31 years or more

    ❏26

5.  How many years has your **most senior** teacher been teaching Chinese?
    - ❏ 5 years or less
    - ❏ 6 to 10 years
    - ❏ 11 to 15 years
    - ❏ 16 to 20 years
    - ❏ 21 to 25 years
    - ❏ 26 to 30 years
    - ❏ 31 years or more

    ❏27

6.  Please provide the following details on the arrangement of classes:
    a.  No. of semesters in a year: _____ semesters
    b.  Length of each semester: _____ weeks
    c.  Average no. of periods taught by each teacher per week: _____ periods
    d.  Average total no. of students taught by each teacher in a semester: _____ students

    ❏28
    ❏❏29–30
    ❏❏31–32
    ❏❏❏33–35

7. Does your school have the following resources to support language teaching? *(You can choose more than one answer.)*
   ❏ Library or reading room      ☐36
   ❏ Cassette recorders and tapes      ☐37
   ❏ Video players and tapes      ☐38
   ❏ Overhead projectors      ☐39
   ❏ CD players and CDs      ☐40
   ❏ Computers      ☐41
   ❏ Computer software for language learning      ☐42
   ❏ Video projectors      ☐43
   ❏ Internet access      ☐44
   ❏ Other resources (*please specify*) _____      ☐45

8. In your school, is there currently a shortage of teachers teaching Chinese?      ☐46
   ❏ Yes, a serious shortage.
   ❏ Yes, but we can still manage.
   ❏ No shortage.
   ❏ No, we have more Chinese teachers than we need.

## Part III    Chinese programme

FOR
OFFICE USE

1. Could you please send us a syllabus for the Chinese curriculum in your school for each grade? If not, please provide a sample syllabus for the **highest grade** in your school and specify what grade it is.

2. Please provide the following information on the arrangement of Chinese classes for each grade:

| | No. of students in each class group | No. of lessons each week | Length of each lesson (minutes) | No. of Chinese lessons each week | Are speaking and listening taught at this grade? | Are reading and writing taught at this grade? | |
|---|---|---|---|---|---|---|---|
| Primary 1 | | | | | | | 47–50 |
| Primary 2 | | | | | | | 51–54 / 55–58 |
| Primary 3 | | | | | | | 59–62 / 63–66 |
| Primary 4 | | | | | | | 67–70 / 71–74 |
| Primary 5 | | | | | | | 75–78 / 79–82 |
| Primary 6 | | | | | | | 83–86 / 87–90 / 91–94 |

3.  Are students required to study literary texts in Chinese?
    - ❏ Yes, for all grades.
    - ❏ Yes, only in some of the grades. (*please specify*) _____ ❏95
    _____
    - ❏ None of the grades requires it. _____

4.  The main teaching materials used in Chinese courses are: ❏96
    - ❏ Published by the Ministry of Education.
    - ❏ Published by the District Education Commission.
    - ❏ Published by commercial publishers.
    - ❏ Published by other educational institutions.
    - ❏ Written by our teachers and only used in our school.
    - ❏ Other (*please specify*) _____

5.  Do students have to pass any Chinese test before they can be admitted to your school? If yes, please give the name of the test(s).

6.  Upon graduation from Primary 6, do students have to pass any national test for Chinese? If yes, please give the name of the test(s).

7.  For students graduating from your school, how would you rate their speaking and listening abilities in Putonghua on the average?
    a.  Pronunciation
        - ❏ Not too good   ❏ Okay        ❏ Good      ❏97
        - ❏ Very good      ❏ Excellent   ❏ Not sure

    b.  Conversation
        - ❏ Not too good   ❏ Okay        ❏ Good      ❏98
        - ❏ Very good      ❏ Excellent   ❏ Not sure

    c.  Making a speech
        - ❏ Not too good   ❏ Okay        ❏ Good      ❏99
        - ❏ Very good      ❏ Excellent   ❏ Not sure

    d.  Listening to news broadcasts
        - ❏ Not too good   ❏ Okay        ❏ Good      ❏100
        - ❏ Very good      ❏ Excellent   ❏ Not sure

e. Listening to academic or technical lectures
  - ❑ Not too good ❑ Okay ❑ Good
  - ❑ Very good ❑ Excellent ❑ Not sure
  
  ❑101

f. Knowledge of *hanyu pinyin*
  - ❑ Not too good ❑ Okay ❑ Good
  - ❑ Very good ❑ Excellent ❑ Not sure
  
  ❑102

8. For students graduating from your school, how would you rate their reading and writing abilities in Chinese on the average?
   a. Reading simple instructions
     - ❑ Not too good ❑ Okay ❑ Good
     - ❑ Very good ❑ Excellent ❑ Not sure
     
     ❑103

   b. Reading newspaper articles
     - ❑ Not too good ❑ Okay ❑ Good
     - ❑ Very good ❑ Excellent ❑ Not sure
     
     ❑104

   c. Reading academic or technical materials
     - ❑ Not too good ❑ Okay ❑ Good
     - ❑ Very good ❑ Excellent ❑ Not sure
     
     ❑105

   d. Writing a simple letter
     - ❑ Not too good ❑ Okay ❑ Good
     - ❑ Very good ❑ Excellent ❑ Not sure
     
     ❑106

   e. Writing an academic or technical paper
     - ❑ Not too good ❑ Okay ❑ Good
     - ❑ Very good ❑ Excellent ❑ Not sure
     
     ❑107

   f. Knowledge of simplified characters
     - ❑ Not too good ❑ Okay ❑ Good
     - ❑ Very good ❑ Excellent ❑ Not sure
     
     ❑108

   g. Knowledge of complex characters
     - ❑ Not too good ❑ Okay ❑ Good
     - ❑ Very good ❑ Excellent ❑ Not sure
     
     ❑109

   h. Writing simplified characters
     - ❑ Not too good ❑ Okay ❑ Good
     - ❑ Very good ❑ Excellent ❑ Not sure
     
     ❑110

   i. Writing complex characters
     - ❑ Not too good ❑ Okay ❑ Good
     - ❑ Very good ❑ Excellent ❑ Not sure
     
     ❑111

## Part IV   Ideas on language learning

There are many different opinions about language learning. What do you think about the opinions listed below?

1.  To learn a language or dialect well, it is best to begin learning as early as possible.
    ❑ Strongly agree      ❑ Agree         ❑ No comment
    ❑ Disagree            ❑ Strongly disagree

    ☐112

2.  After the learner has reached a certain age, for example, puberty, it is easier for the learner to learn a language or dialect perfectly.
    ❑ Strongly agree      ❑ Agree         ❑ No comment
    ❑ Disagree            ❑ Strongly disagree

    ☐113

3.  It is possible to learn a language or dialect well at any age as long as the learner is highly motivated.
    ❑ Strongly agree      ❑ Agree         ❑ No comment
    ❑ Disagree            ❑ Strongly disagree

    ☐114

4.  A learner's own language has no direct influence on how he or she learns a new language or dialect.
    ❑ Strongly agree      ❑ Agree         ❑ No comment
    ❑ Disagree            ❑ Strongly disagree

    ☐115

5.  Learners find it easier to learn a new language or dialect that is similar to their own languages.
    ❑ Strongly agree      ❑ Agree         ❑ No comment
    ❑ Disagree            ❑ Strongly disagree

    ☐116

6.  Some languages or dialects are more difficult to learn than others whatever the learners' own language background.
    ❑ Strongly agree      ❑ Agree         ❑ No comment
    ❑ Disagree            ❑ Strongly disagree

    ☐117

7.  If learners are from the same language background, then their aptitude to learn a new language is the same.
    ❑ Strongly agree      ❑ Agree         ❑ No comment
    ❑ Disagree            ❑ Strongly disagree

    ☐118

8.  Learners with different personalities may have different degrees of success in language learning.
    ❑ Strongly agree      ❑ Agree         ❑ No comment
    ❑ Disagree            ❑ Strongly disagree

    ☐119

9. It is difficult to succeed in learning Putonghua well in countries where it is not widely spoken because there will be little opportunity to use it outside the classroom or at home.
   ❑ Strongly agree  ❑ Agree  ❑ No comment  ❑120
   ❑ Disagree  ❑ Strongly disagree

10. Learners can learn Chinese better if the explanations about Chinese are conducted in their own language.
    ❑ Strongly agree  ❑ Agree  ❑ No comment  ❑121
    ❑ Disagree  ❑ Strongly disagree

11. Teaching other subjects in Putonghua can enable them to learn it better.
    ❑ Strongly agree  ❑ Agree  ❑ No comment  ❑122
    ❑ Disagree  ❑ Strongly disagree

12. There is too much emphasis on reading and writing in the current Chinese programme, so learners are poor in speaking and listening.
    ❑ Strongly agree  ❑ Agree  ❑ No comment  ❑123
    ❑ Disagree  ❑ Strongly disagree

13. The current Chinese programme is too focused on examination preparation.
    ❑ Strongly agree  ❑ Agree  ❑ No comment  ❑124
    ❑ Disagree  ❑ Strongly disagree

14. If the learning of Chinese is for specific purposes such as professional or academic communication, including the study of literature in their programme is wasting their time.
    ❑ Strongly agree  ❑ Agree  ❑ No comment  ❑125
    ❑ Disagree  ❑ Strongly disagree

15. A teacher's proficiency in Chinese is the most important factor in his/her competence to teach the language.
    ❑ Strongly agree  ❑ Agree  ❑ No comment  ❑126
    ❑ Disagree  ❑ Strongly disagree

16. How a teacher teaches in the classroom affects learners' success in language learning the most.
    ❑ Strongly agree  ❑ Agree  ❑ No comment  ❑127
    ❑ Disagree  ❑ Strongly disagree

17. Students must respect and/ or like their teacher before they can learn well.
    ❑ Strongly agree  ❑ Agree  ❑ No comment  ❑128
    ❑ Disagree  ❑ Strongly disagree

18. No matter how well the teacher teaches in the classroom, learners cannot succeed in Chinese learning unless they take responsibility for their own learning.
    ❏ Strongly agree     ❏ Agree     ❏ No comment     ☐129
    ❏ Disagree     ❏ Strongly disagree

19. Besides the textbooks, we do not have enough supplementary learning materials for students.
    ❏ Strongly agree     ❏ Agree     ❏ No comment     ☐130
    ❏ Disagree     ❏ Strongly disagree

20. Please use Numbers 1 to 10 to rank the following factors according to their importance in language learning, with 1 meaning 'Most important'.

    _____ Age of learners     ☐131

    _____ Learners' language background     ☐132

    _____ Learners' motivation, aptitude and/or personality     ☐133

    _____ Opportunity to practise the language outside the classroom     ☐134

    _____ Medium of instruction in the institution     ☐135

    _____ The syllabus of the language programme     ☐136

    _____ The teachers' proficiency in Chinese     ☐137

    _____ The way the teacher teaches     ☐138

    _____ The national language examinations     ☐139

    _____ The availability of resources     ☐140

## Part V  Other comments

Do you have any other comments on your language teaching experience?

THANK YOU VERY MUCH FOR YOUR CO-OPERATION.

# Appendix IV
# Questionnaire for the Survey of Foreign Languages Department Heads (Universities)

An adapted version of this questionnaire was used to survey Chinese department heads in universities.

## Survey of foreign language programmes in higher education institutions, September 1999

Part I     Background information
Part II    Teachers
Part III   English programme
Part IV    Another foreign language programme
Part V     Ideas on language learning
Part VI    Other comments

Reference number: ☐☐☐–☐☐☐–☐☐☐ 1–9

## Part I   Background information

FOR OFFICE USE

1. Name of institution: _____        ☐☐☐ 10–12

2. Location of institution: _____ (*nearest big city*) _____ (*region*)        ☐☐☐☐ 13–16

3. Type of institution        ☐ 17
   ❑ Comprehensive university
   ❑ Science and technology university
   ❑ Teacher education or normal university
   ❑ Other (*please specify*) _____

4. In what year was your institution established? _____

5. Type of language department        ☐ 18
   ❑ Chinese department
   ❑ Minority language(s) department
   ❑ Foreign languages department

6. When was the department established?　　　　　　　　　　□19
   ❑ Before 1949
   ❑ 1949–1965
   ❑ 1966–1977
   ❑ 1978–1988
   ❑ After 1988

7. Do you have any other information on the history of your department? For example, any major changes in its role, the medium of instruction, curricular emphasis or type of students?

8. Are the following foreign languages currently taught in your department? *(You can choose more than one answer.)*

   | | | |
   |---|---|---|
   | ❑ English | ❑ French | □□20–21 |
   | ❑ German | ❑ Japanese | □□22–23 |
   | ❑ Russian | ❑ Another language *(please specify)* _____ | □□24–25 |

9. How many students does your department teach? Are they majors or non-majors in foreign languages? Undergraduates or graduate students?

   | Type of students | Number of students | |
   |---|---|---|
   | Undergraduate majors | | □26 |
   | Undergraduate non-majors | | □27 |
   | Graduate majors | | □28 |
   | Graduate non-majors | | □29 |
   | Non-degree visiting students | | □30 |
   | Total number of students | | □31 |

10. Of the total number of students in your department, please estimate the percentages for the following groups.
    a. Students from minority language backgrounds　　　　　□32
       ❑ 0%
       ❑ 1%–5 %
       ❑ 6%–10%
       ❑ 11%–15%
       ❑ 16%–20%
       ❑ 21%–25%
       ❑ Another percentage *(please specify)* _____

    b. Chinese students from overseas　　　　　　　　　　　□33
       ❑ 0%
       ❑ 1%–5 %
       ❑ 6%–10%

❑ 11%–15%
❑ 16%–20%
❑ 21%–25%
❑ Another percentage (*please specify*) _____

c. Foreign students from other countries
❑ 0%
❑ 1%–5 %
❑ 6%–10%
❑ 11%–15%
❑ 16%–20%
❑ 21%–25%
❑ Another percentage (*please specify*) _____

❑34

# Part II  Teachers

1. Do you have the following teaching staff grades (or their equivalents) in your department?
   ❑ Professors              _____ persons
   ❑ Associate Professors    _____ persons
   ❑ Assistant Professors    _____ persons
   ❑ Tutors/Instructors      _____ persons
   ❑ More junior staff grades _____ persons

☐☐☐ 35–37
☐☐☐ 38–40
☐☐☐ 41–43
☐☐☐ 44–46
☐☐☐ 47–49

2. What is the highest qualification of the **most junior** teacher in your department?
   ❑ Teaching certificate or diploma
   ❑ Bachelor degree
   ❑ Master degree
   ❑ PhD degree
   ❑ Other (*please specify*) _____

❑50

3. What is the highest qualification of the **most senior** teacher in your department?
   ❑ Teaching certificate or diploma
   ❑ Bachelor degree
   ❑ Master degree
   ❑ PhD degree
   ❑ Other (*please specify*) _____

❑51

4. How many years has your **most junior** teacher been teaching?
   ❑ 5 years or less
   ❑ 6 to 10 years
   ❑ 11 to 15 years
   ❑ 16 to 20 years
   ❑ 21 to 25 years
   ❑ 26 to 30 years
   ❑ 31 years or more

❑52

5. How many years has your **most senior** teacher been teaching?        ☐53
   - ❏ 5 years or less
   - ❏ 6 to 10 years
   - ❏ 11 to 15 years
   - ❏ 16 to 20 years
   - ❏ 21 to 25 years
   - ❏ 26 to 30 years
   - ❏ 31 years or more

6. How many (%) of your teachers are foreigners from countries where the   ☐54
   foreign languages are spoken?
   - ❏ 0%
   - ❏ 1%–20%
   - ❏ 21%–40%
   - ❏ 41%– 60%
   - ❏ 61%–80%
   - ❏ 81%–100%

7. How many (%) of your local teachers who teach a foreign language have   ☐55
   lived for at least 3 months in a country where the foreign language is
   widely spoken?
   - ❏ 0%
   - ❏ 1%–20%
   - ❏ 21%–40%
   - ❏ 41%–60%
   - ❏ 61%–80%
   - ❏ 81%–100%

8. Please provide the following details on the arrangement of classes:

| | | |
|---|---|---|
| a. No. of semesters in a year: | _____ semesters | ☐56 |
| b. Length of each semester: | _____ weeks | ☐☐57–58 |
| c. Average no. of periods taught by each teacher per week: | _____ periods | ☐☐59–60 |
| d. Average total no. of students taught by each teacher in a semester: | _____ students | ☐☐☐61–63 |

9. Does your department have the following resources to support language
   teaching? *(You can choose more than one answer.)*
   - ❏ Library or reading room      ☐64
   - ❏ Cassette recorders and tapes      ☐65
   - ❏ Video players and tapes      ☐66
   - ❏ Overhead projectors      ☐67
   - ❏ CD players and CDs      ☐68
   - ❏ Computers      ☐69
   - ❏ Computer software for language learning      ☐70
   - ❏ Video projectors      ☐71
   - ❏ Internet access      ☐72
   - ❏ Other resources *(please specify)* _____   ☐73

10. In your department, is there currently a shortage of teachers?  ☐74
    - ❏ Yes, a serious shortage.
    - ❏ Yes, but we can still manage.
    - ❏ No shortage.
    - ❏ No, we have more teachers than we need.

## Part III   English programme

1.  How many programmes teaching English are there in your department?
    Please name them. *(A programme is defined as a series of courses. For
    example, Beginner's English, Intermediate English, Advanced English
    altogether can be counted as one programme with 3 courses.)*

| Name of programme | This programme is for ... | |
|---|---|---|
| a. | ❏ Undergraduate majors<br>❏ Undergraduate non-majors<br>❏ Non-degree visiting students | ❏ Graduate majors<br>❏ Graduate non-majors |
| b. | ❏ Undergraduate majors<br>❏ Undergraduate non-majors<br>❏ Non-degree visiting students | ❏ Graduate majors<br>❏ Graduate non-majors |
| c. | ❏ Undergraduate majors<br>❏ Undergraduate non-majors<br>❏ Non-degree visiting students | ❏ Graduate majors<br>❏ Graduate non-majors |
| d. | ❏ Undergraduate majors<br>❏ Undergraduate non-majors<br>❏ Non-degree visiting students | ❏ Graduate majors<br>❏ Graduate non-majors |

2. Please provide the following information for the English programme **for undergraduates majoring in English**:

   a. Brief information:

   | Title of programme: | | | |
   |---|---|---|---|
   | Total no. of students: | | students | ☐☐☐☐75–78 |
   | Average no. of students in each class: | | students | ☐☐☐79–81 |
   | Total no. of courses in this programme: | | courses | ☐☐82–83 |
   | Total no. of class periods for each course: | | periods | ☐☐☐84–86 |
   | No. of English courses a student is required to take to fulfil degree requirements: | | courses | ☐☐87–88 |
   | Total no. of class periods in English courses for each student: | | periods | ☐☐☐☐89–92 |
   | Are students in this programme required to take courses in English literature? | ☐ Yes    ☐ No | | ☐93 |

   b. What are the aims of this programme? (*You can choose more than one answer.*)
      ☐ To improve students' general English proficiency.                    ☐94
      ☐ To improve students' Academic English competence.                   ☐95
      ☐ To improve students' Professional English competence.               ☐96
      ☐ To increase students' understanding of literature in English.       ☐97
      ☐ Other (*please specify*)_____            ☐98

   c. How are different aspects of English taught in terms of the organization ☐99
      of lessons?
      ☐ Listening, speaking, reading, writing and literature are taught separately.
      ☐ The above skills and knowledge are taught in an integrated manner.
      ☐ Each course is organized differently, so both arrangements are used.

   d. Could you please send us a course description for this English programme? If not, please provide the names of the courses in this programme.

   e. What are the main teaching materials used in this programme?          ☐100
      ☐ Published by the Ministry of Education.
      ☐ Published by the District Education Commission.
      ☐ Published by commercial publishers.
      ☐ Published by other educational institutions.
      ☐ Written by our teachers and only used in our school.
      ☐ Other (*please specify*) _____

f.  Do students have to pass any language test before they can be admitted to this programme? If yes, please give the name of the test(s).

g.  Upon completion of your programme, do students have to pass any national test for this language? If yes, please give the name of the test.

h.  For students who completed this programme, how would you rate their speaking and listening abilities in English on the average?

    (i).   Pronunciation

       ❏ Not too good   ❏ Okay   ❏ Good       ❑101

       ❏ Very good   ❏ Excellent   ❏ Not sure

    (ii).  Conversation

       ❏ Not too good   ❏ Okay   ❏ Good       ❑102

       ❏ Very good   ❏ Excellent   ❏ Not sure

    (iii). Making a speech

       ❏ Not too good   ❏ Okay   ❏ Good       ❑103

       ❏ Very good   ❏ Excellent   ❏ Not sure

    (iv). Listening to news broadcasts

       ❏ Not too good   ❏ Okay   ❏ Good       ❑104

       ❏ Very good   ❏ Excellent   ❏ Not sure

    (v).  Listening to academic or technical lectures

       ❏ Not too good   ❏ Okay   ❏ Good       ❑105

       ❏ Very good   ❏ Excellent   ❏ Not sure

i.  For students who completed this programme, how would you rate their reading and writing abilities in English on the average?

    (i).   Reading simple instructions

       ❏ Not too good   ❏ Okay   ❏ Good       ❑106

       ❏ Very good   ❏ Excellent   ❏ Not sure

    (ii).  Reading newspaper articles

       ❏ Not too good   ❏ Okay   ❏ Good       ❑107

       ❏ Very good   ❏ Excellent   ❏ Not sure

    (iii). Reading academic or technical materials

       ❏ Not too good   ❏ Okay   ❏ Good       ❑108

       ❏ Very good   ❏ Excellent   ❏ Not sure

    (iv). Writing a simple letter

       ❏ Not too good   ❏ Okay   ❏ Good       ❑109

       ❏ Very good   ❏ Excellent   ❏ Not sure

    (v).  Writing an academic or technical paper

       ❏ Not too good   ❏ Okay   ❏ Good       ❑110

       ❏ Very good   ❏ Excellent   ❏ Not sure

3. Please provide the following information for the English programme for **undergraduates not majoring in English**:

   a. Brief information:

| | | |
|---|---|---|
| Title of programme: | | |
| Total no. of students: | students | ☐☐☐☐111–114 |
| Average no. of students in each class: | students | ☐☐☐115–117 |
| Total no. of courses in this programme: | courses | ☐☐118–119 |
| Total no. of class periods for each course: | periods | ☐☐☐120–122 |
| No. of English courses a student is required to take to fulfil degree requirements: | courses | ☐☐123–124 |
| Total no. of class periods in English courses for each student: | periods | ☐☐☐☐125–128 |
| Are students in this programme required to take courses in English literature? | ☐ Yes    ☐ No | ☐129 |

   b. What are the aims of this programme? (*You can choose more than one answer.*)
      ☐ To improve students' general English proficiency.          ☐130
      ☐ To improve students' Academic English competence.          ☐131
      ☐ To improve students' Professional English competence.      ☐132
      ☐ To increase students' understanding of literature in English.   ☐133
      ☐ Other (*please specify*)_____   ☐134

   c. How are different aspects of English taught in terms of the organization   ☐135
      of lessons?
      ☐ Listening, speaking, reading, writing and literature are taught separately.
      ☐ The above skills and knowledge are taught in an integrated manner.
      ☐ Each course is organized differently, so both arrangements are used.

   d. Could you please send us a course description for this English programme? If not, please provide the names of the courses in this programme.

   e. What are the main teaching materials used in this programme?
      ☐ Published by the Ministry of Education.                     ☐136
      ☐ Published by the District Education Commission.
      ☐ Published by commercial publishers.
      ☐ Published by other educational institutions.
      ☐ Written by our teachers and only used in our school.
      ☐ Other (*please specify*) _____

f. Do students have to pass any language test before they can be admitted to this programme? If yes, please give the name of the test(s).

g. Upon completion of your programme, do students have to pass any national test for this language? If yes, please give the name of the test.

h. For students who completed this programme, how would you rate their speaking and listening abilities in English on the average?

(i). Pronunciation

❑ Not too good  ❑ Okay  ❑ Good  ☐137
❑ Very good  ❑ Excellent  ❑ Not sure

(ii). Conversation

❑ Not too good  ❑ Okay  ❑ Good  ☐138
❑ Very good  ❑ Excellent  ❑ Not sure

(iii). Making a speech

❑ Not too good  ❑ Okay  ❑ Good  ☐139
❑ Very good  ❑ Excellent  ❑ Not sure

(iv). Listening to news broadcasts

❑ Not too good  ❑ Okay  ❑ Good  ☐140
❑ Very good  ❑ Excellent  ❑ Not sure

(v). Listening to academic or technical lectures

❑ Not too good  ❑ Okay  ❑ Good  ☐141
❑ Very good  ❑ Excellent  ❑ Not sure

i. For students who completed this programme, how would you rate their reading and writing abilities in English on the average?

(i). Reading simple instructions

❑ Not too good  ❑ Okay  ❑ Good  ☐142
❑ Very good  ❑ Excellent  ❑ Not sure

(ii). Reading newspaper articles

❑ Not too good  ❑ Okay  ❑ Good  ☐143
❑ Very good  ❑ Excellent  ❑ Not sure

(iii). Reading academic or technical materials

❑ Not too good  ❑ Okay  ❑ Good  ☐144
❑ Very good  ❑ Excellent  ❑ Not sure

(iv). Writing a simple letter

❑ Not too good  ❑ Okay  ❑ Good  ☐145
❑ Very good  ❑ Excellent  ❑ Not sure

(v). Writing an academic or technical paper

❑ Not too good  ❑ Okay  ❑ Good  ☐146
❑ Very good  ❑ Excellent  ❑ Not sure

4. Please provide the following information for the English programme for **graduates majoring in English**:

a. Brief information:

| | | | |
|---|---|---|---|
| Title of programme: | | | |
| Total no. of students: | | students | ☐☐☐☐147–150 |
| Average no. of students in each class: | | students | ☐☐☐151–153 |
| Total no. of courses in this programme: | | courses | ☐☐154–155 |
| Total no. of class periods for each course: | | periods | ☐☐☐156–158 |
| No. of English courses a student is required to take to fulfil degree requirements: | | courses | ☐☐159–160 |
| Total no. of class periods in English courses for each student: | | periods | ☐☐☐☐161–164 |
| Are students in this programme required to take courses in English literature? | ☐ Yes ☐ No | | ☐ 165 |

b. What are the aims of this programme? (*You can choose more than one answer.*)
 ☐ To improve students' general English proficiency.   ☐166
 ☐ To improve students' Academic English competence.   ☐167
 ☐ To improve students' Professional English competence.   ☐168
 ☐ To increase students' understanding of literature in English.   ☐169
 ☐ Other (*please specify*)_____   ☐170

c. How are different aspects of English taught in terms of the organization   ☐171
 of lessons?
 ☐ Listening, speaking, reading, writing and literature are taught separately.
 ☐ The above skills and knowledge are taught in an integrated manner.
 ☐ Each course is organized differently, so both arrangements are used.

d. Could you please send us a course description for this English programme? If not, please provide the names of the courses in this programme.

e. What are the main teaching materials used in this programme?   ☐172
 ☐ Published by the Ministry of Education.
 ☐ Published by the District Education Commission.
 ☐ Published by commercial publishers.
 ☐ Published by other educational institutions.
 ☐ Written by our teachers and only used in our school.
 ☐ Other (*please specify*) _____

f.  Do students have to pass any language test before they can be admitted to this programme? If yes, please give the name of the test(s).

g.  Upon completion of your programme, do students have to pass any national test for this language? If yes, please give the name of the test.

h.  For students who completed this programme, how would you rate their speaking and listening abilities in English on the average?

    (i). Pronunciation

        ❑ Not too good    ❑ Okay    ❑ Good        ☐173

        ❑ Very good    ❑ Excellent    ❑ Not sure

    (ii). Conversation

        ❑ Not too good    ❑ Okay    ❑ Good        ☐174

        ❑ Very good    ❑ Excellent    ❑ Not sure

    (iii). Making a speech

        ❑ Not too good    ❑ Okay    ❑ Good        ☐175

        ❑ Very good    ❑ Excellent    ❑ Not sure

    (iv). Listening to news broadcasts

        ❑ Not too good    ❑ Okay    ❑ Good        ☐176

        ❑ Very good    ❑ Excellent    ❑ Not sure

    (v). Listening to academic or technical lectures

        ❑ Not too good    ❑ Okay    ❑ Good        ☐177

        ❑ Very good    ❑ Excellent    ❑ Not sure

i.  For students who completed this programme, how would you rate their reading and writing abilities in English on the average?

    (i). Reading simple instructions

        ❑ Not too good    ❑ Okay    ❑ Good        ☐178

        ❑ Very good    ❑ Excellent    ❑ Not sure

    (ii). Reading newspaper articles

        ❑ Not too good    ❑ Okay    ❑ Good        ☐179

        ❑ Very good    ❑ Excellent    ❑ Not sure

    (iii). Reading academic or technical materials

        ❑ Not too good    ❑ Okay    ❑ Good        ☐180

        ❑ Very good    ❑ Excellent    ❑ Not sure

    (iv). Writing a simple letter

        ❑ Not too good    ❑ Okay    ❑ Good        ☐181

        ❑ Very good    ❑ Excellent    ❑ Not sure

    (v). Writing an academic or technical paper

        ❑ Not too good    ❑ Okay    ❑ Good        ☐182

        ❑ Very good    ❑ Excellent    ❑ Not sure

5. Please provide the following information for the English programme for **graduates not majoring in English**:

   a. Brief information:

   | | | |
   |---|---|---|
   | Title of programme: | | |
   | Total no. of students: | | students |
   | Average no. of students in each class: | | students |
   | Total no. of courses in this programme: | | courses |
   | Total no. of class periods for each course: | | periods |
   | No. of English courses a student is required to take to fulfil degree requirements: | | courses |
   | Total no. of class periods in English courses for each student: | | periods |
   | Are students in this programme required to take courses in English literature? | ❏ Yes ❏ No | |

   ☐☐☐☐183–186
   ☐☐☐187–189
   ☐☐190–191
   ☐☐☐192–194

   ☐☐195–196

   ☐☐☐☐197–200

   ☐201

   b. What are the aims of this programme? (*You can choose more than one answer.*)
      ❏ To improve students' general English proficiency.
      ❏ To improve students' Academic English competence.
      ❏ To improve students' Professional English competence.
      ❏ To increase students' understanding of literature in English.
      ❏ Other (*please specify*)_____

   ☐202
   ☐203
   ☐204
   ☐205
   ☐206

   c. How are different aspects of English taught in terms of the organization of lessons?

   ☐207

      ❏ Listening, speaking, reading, writing and literature are taught separately.
      ❏ The above skills and knowledge are taught in an integrated manner.
      ❏ Each course is organized differently, so both arrangements are used.

   d. Could you please send us a course description for this English programme? If not, please provide the names of the courses in this programme.

   e. What are the main teaching materials used in this programme?

   ☐208

      ❏ Published by the Ministry of Education.
      ❏ Published by the District Education Commission.
      ❏ Published by commercial publishers.
      ❏ Published by other educational institutions.
      ❏ Written by our teachers and only used in our school.
      ❏ Other (*please specify*) _____

f.  Do students have to pass any language test before they can be admitted to this programme? If yes, please give the name of the test(s).



g.  Upon completion of your programme, do students have to pass any national test for this language? If yes, please give the name of the test.



h.  For students who completed this programme, how would you rate their speaking and listening abilities in English on the average?
    (i). Pronunciation
    - ❏ Not too good    ❏ Okay    ❏ Good
    - ❏ Very good    ❏ Excellent    ❏ Not sure    ☐209

    (ii). Conversation
    - ❏ Not too good    ❏ Okay    ❏ Good
    - ❏ Very good    ❏ Excellent    ❏ Not sure    ☐210

    (iii). Making a speech
    - ❏ Not too good    ❏ Okay    ❏ Good
    - ❏ Very good    ❏ Excellent    ❏ Not sure    ☐211

    (iv). Listening to news broadcasts
    - ❏ Not too good    ❏ Okay    ❏ Good
    - ❏ Very good    ❏ Excellent    ❏ Not sure    ☐212

    (v). Listening to academic or technical lectures
    - ❏ Not too good    ❏ Okay    ❏ Good
    - ❏ Very good    ❏ Excellent    ❏ Not sure    ☐213

i.  For students who completed this programme, how would you rate their reading and writing abilities in English on the average?
    (i). Reading simple instructions
    - ❏ Not too good    ❏ Okay    ❏ Good
    - ❏ Very good    ❏ Excellent    ❏ Not sure    ☐214

    (ii). Reading newspaper articles
    - ❏ Not too good    ❏ Okay    ❏ Good
    - ❏ Very good    ❏ Excellent    ❏ Not sure    ☐215

    (iii). Reading academic or technical materials
    - ❏ Not too good    ❏ Okay    ❏ Good
    - ❏ Very good    ❏ Excellent    ❏ Not sure    ☐216

    (iv). Writing a simple letter
    - ❏ Not too good    ❏ Okay    ❏ Good
    - ❏ Very good    ❏ Excellent    ❏ Not sure    ☐217

    (v). Writing an academic or technical paper
    - ❏ Not too good    ❏ Okay    ❏ Good
    - ❏ Very good    ❏ Excellent    ❏ Not sure    ☐218

## Part IV   Another foreign language

1. Besides English, which other foreign language attracts the greatest number of students in your department? _____

   *Note: We shall refer to this language as the second foreign language from here onwards.*

2. How many programmes teaching this second foreign language are there in your department? Please name them.

| Name of programme | This programme is for ... | |
|---|---|---|
| a. | ❏ Undergraduate majors<br>❏ Undergraduate non-majors<br>❏ Non-degree visiting students | ❏ Graduate majors<br>❏ Graduate non-majors |
| b. | ❏ Undergraduate majors<br>❏ Undergraduate non-majors<br>❏ Non-degree visiting students | ❏ Graduate majors<br>❏ Graduate non-majors |
| c. | ❏ Undergraduate majors<br>❏ Undergraduate non-majors<br>❏ Non-degree visiting students | ❏ Graduate majors<br>❏ Graduate non-majors |
| d. | ❏ Undergraduate majors<br>❏ Undergraduate non-majors<br>❏ Non-degree visiting students | ❏ Graduate majors<br>❏ Graduate non-majors |

3. Please provide the following information for the second foreign language programme for **undergraduates majoring in this second foreign language**:

| | | | |
|---|---|---|---|
| Title of programme: | | | |
| Total no. of students: | | students | ⬚⬚⬚⬚219–222 |
| Average no. of students in each class: | | students | ⬚⬚⬚223–225 |
| Total no. of courses in this programme: | | courses | ⬚⬚226–227 |
| Total no. of class periods for each course: | | periods | ⬚⬚⬚228–230 |
| No. of this foreign language courses a student is required to take to fulfil degree requirements: | | courses | ⬚⬚231–232 |
| Total no. of class periods in this foreign language courses for each student: | | periods | ⬚⬚⬚⬚233–236 |
| Are students in this programme required to take courses in literature in the second foreign language? | ❑ Yes | ❑ No | ⬚237 |

4. Please provide the following information for the second foreign language programme for **undergraduates not majoring in this second foreign language:**

| | | | |
|---|---|---|---|
| Title of programme: | | | |
| Total no. of students: | | students | ⬚⬚⬚⬚238–241 |
| Average no. of students in each class: | | students | ⬚⬚⬚242–244 |
| Total no. of courses in this programme: | | courses | ⬚⬚245–246 |
| Total no. of class periods for each course: | | periods | ⬚⬚⬚247–249 |
| No. of this second foreign language courses a student is required to take to fulfil degree requirements: | | courses | ⬚⬚250–251 |
| Total no. of class periods in this second foreign language courses for each student: | | periods | ⬚⬚⬚⬚252–255 |
| Are students in this programme required to take courses in literature in the second foreign language? | ❑ Yes | ❑ No | ⬚256 |

5. Please provide the following information for the second foreign language programme for **graduates majoring in this second foreign language**:

| Title of programme: | | |
|---|---|---|
| Total no. of students: | students | ☐☐☐☐257–260 |
| Average no. of students in each class: | students | ☐☐☐261–263 |
| Total no. of courses in this programme: | courses | ☐☐264–265 |
| Total no. of class periods for each course: | periods | ☐☐☐266–268 |
| No. of this second foreign language courses a student is required to take to fulfil degree requirements: | courses | ☐☐269–270 |
| Total no. of class periods in this second foreign language courses for each student: | periods | ☐☐☐☐271–274 |
| Are students in this programme required to take courses in literature in the second foreign language? | ☐ Yes ☐ No | ☐275 |

6. Please provide the following information for the second foreign language programme for **graduates not majoring in this second foreign language**:

| Title of programme: | | |
|---|---|---|
| Total no. of students: | students | ☐☐☐☐276–279 |
| Average no. of students in each class: | students | ☐☐☐280–282 |
| Total no. of courses in this programme: | courses | ☐☐283–284 |
| Total no. of class periods for each course: | periods | ☐☐☐285–287 |
| No. of this second foreign language courses a student is required to take to fulfil degree requirements: | courses | ☐☐288–289 |
| Total no. of class periods in this second foreign language courses for each student: | periods | ☐☐☐☐290–293 |
| Are students in this programme required to take courses in literature in the second foreign language? | ☐ Yes ☐ No | ☐294 |

## Part V   Ideas on language learning

There are many different opinions about language learning. What do you think about the opinions listed below?

1. To learn a foreign language well, it is best to begin learning as early as possible.
   - ❏ Strongly agree
   - ❏ Agree
   - ❏ No comment
   - ❏ Disagree
   - ❏ Strongly disagree

   ☐295

2. After the learner has reached a certain age, for example, puberty, it is easier for the learner to learn a language perfectly.
   - ❏ Strongly agree
   - ❏ Agree
   - ❏ No comment
   - ❏ Disagree
   - ❏ Strongly disagree

   ☐296

3. It is possible to learn a language well at any age as long as the learner is highly motivated.
   - ❏ Strongly agree
   - ❏ Agree
   - ❏ No comment
   - ❏ Disagree
   - ❏ Strongly disagree

   ☐297

4. A learner's own language has no direct influence on how he or she learns a new language.
   - ❏ Strongly agree
   - ❏ Agree
   - ❏ No comment
   - ❏ Disagree
   - ❏ Strongly disagree

   ☐298

5. Learners find it easier to learn a new language that is similar to their own languages.
   - ❏ Strongly agree
   - ❏ Agree
   - ❏ No comment
   - ❏ Disagree
   - ❏ Strongly disagree

   ☐299

6. Some languages are more difficult to learn than others whatever the learners' own language background.
   - ❏ Strongly agree
   - ❏ Agree
   - ❏ No comment
   - ❏ Disagree
   - ❏ Strongly disagree

   ☐300

7. If learners are from the same language background, then their aptitude to learn a new language is the same.
   - ❏ Strongly agree
   - ❏ Agree
   - ❏ No comment
   - ❏ Disagree
   - ❏ Strongly disagree

   ☐301

8. Learners with different personalities may have different degrees of success in language learning.
   - ❏ Strongly agree
   - ❏ Agree
   - ❏ No comment
   - ❏ Disagree
   - ❏ Strongly disagree

   ☐302

9. It is difficult to succeed in learning a foreign language well in China because there is little opportunity to use it outside the classroom or at home.
   - ❑ Strongly agree    ❑ Agree    ❑ No comment    ☐303
   - ❑ Disagree    ❑ Strongly disagree

10. Learners can learn a foreign language better if the explanations about the foreign language are conducted in their own language.
    - ❑ Strongly agree    ❑ Agree    ❑ No comment    ☐304
    - ❑ Disagree    ❑ Strongly disagree

11. Teaching other subjects in the foreign language that the learners are trying to learn can enable them to learn the foreign language better.
    - ❑ Strongly agree    ❑ Agree    ❑ No comment    ☐305
    - ❑ Disagree    ❑ Strongly disagree

12. There is too much emphasis on reading and writing in the current foreign language programme, so learners are poor in speaking and listening.
    - ❑ Strongly agree    ❑ Agree    ❑ No comment    ☐306
    - ❑ Disagree    ❑ Strongly disagree

13. The current foreign language programme is too focused on examination preparation.
    - ❑ Strongly agree    ❑ Agree    ❑ No comment    ☐307
    - ❑ Disagree    ❑ Strongly disagree

14. If the learning of the foreign language is for specific purposes such as professional or academic communication, including the study of literature in their programme is wasting their time.
    - ❑ Strongly agree    ❑ Agree    ❑ No comment    ☐308
    - ❑ Disagree    ❑ Strongly disagree

15. A teacher's proficiency in the foreign language is the most important factor in his/her competence to teach the language.
    - ❑ Strongly agree    ❑ Agree    ❑ No comment    ☐309
    - ❑ Disagree    ❑ Strongly disagree

16. How a teacher teaches in the classroom affects learners' success in language learning the most.
    - ❑ Strongly agree    ❑ Agree    ❑ No comment    ☐310
    - ❑ Disagree    ❑ Strongly disagree

17. Students must respect and/or like their teacher before they can learn well.
    - ❑ Strongly agree    ❑ Agree    ❑ No comment    ☐311
    - ❑ Disagree    ❑ Strongly disagree

18. No matter how well the teacher teaches in the classroom, learners cannot succeed in foreign language learning unless they take responsibility for their own learning.
    ❏ Strongly agree     ❏ Agree     ❏ No comment     ☐312
    ❏ Disagree     ❏ Strongly disagree

19. Besides the textbooks, we do not have enough supplementary learning materials for students.
    ❏ Strongly agree     ❏ Agree     ❏ No comment     ☐313
    ❏ Disagree     ❏ Strongly disagree

20. Please use Numbers 1 to 10 to rank the following factors according to their importance in language learning, with 1 meaning 'Most important'.

    _____ Age of learners     ☐314

    _____ Learners' language background     ☐315

    _____ Learners' motivation, aptitude and/or personality     ☐316

    _____ Opportunity to practise the language outside the classroom     ☐317

    _____ Medium of instruction in the institution     ☐318

    _____ The syllabus of the language programme     ☐319

    _____ The teachers' proficiency in Chinese     ☐320

    _____ The way the teacher teaches     ☐321

    _____ The national language examinations     ☐322

    _____ The availability of resources     ☐323

## Part VI   Other comments

FOR OFFICE USE

Do you have any other comments on your language teaching experience?

THANK YOU VERY MUCH FOR YOUR CO-OPERATION.

# Appendix V
# Interview Questions for English Panel Heads (Secondary Schools)

Adapted versions of these questions were used to interview Chinese and English panel heads in primary schools, Chinese panel heads in secondary schools and heads of Chinese departments and foreign languages departments in universities.

## Interview for English Language Head (Secondary) (December 2000)

### I. Background

1.  Respondent's Project ID No.: _____

2.  Respondent's name: _____ Place of birth: _____

3.  Age: _____ Sex: _____ Occupation: _____

4.  Date: _____ Time: _____ Place of interview: _____

### II. Interview probes

1.  What foreign languages are taught in your school? Has it always been so?

2.  Has there been a great increase in the number of students you teach?

3.  What has helped or hindered you in organizing your teaching programme? Any particular incidents you can remember? How has your programme organization been affected by:

    a.  the language(s)/dialect(s) the learners already knew or their experience?
    b.  learners' attitude and motivation? Tuition classes outside the school?
    c.  how learners related to each other? Family support?
    d.  the training your teachers have had? Numbers? Other language educators?
    e.  the language circumstances/policies in the community/country? The media?

4. How much class time is a learner expected to spend learning English in your school? Different for different types of students? Can you give some examples of activities in class or the titles of the books you have used?

5. What is the best way to teach a language? What are the most important factors? Do you think literature has a place too in the curriculum if we only want to learn how to use a language for specific purposes? Should language skills be taught separately? How much time does a learner need to spend to learn a language well?

6. What would you like your school/government to do to support the teaching of foreign languages? Could more be done at other levels of education too?

# References

CHAPTER 1

Adamson, B. (2004). *China's English: A history of English in Chinese education.* Hong Kong: Hong Kong University Press.

Agelasto, M., and Adamson, B. (eds.). (1998). *Higher education in post-Mao China.* Hong Kong: Hong Kong University Press.

Bai, J-H. (1994). Language attitude and the spread of standard Chinese in China. *Language Problems and Language Planning, 18*(2), 128–138.

Belcher, D., and Connor, U. (eds.). (2001). *Reflections on multiliterate lives.* Clevedon: Multilingual Matters.

Benson, P., and Nunan, D. (eds.). (2002). The experience of language learning [Special issue]. *Hong Kong Journal of Applied Linguistics, 7*(2).

Cenoz, J., and Genesee, F. (eds.). (1998). *Beyond bilingualism: Multilingualism and multilingual education.* Clevedon: Multilingual Matters.

Chamberlayne, P., Bornat J., and Wengraf, T. (eds.). (2000). *The turn to biographical methods in social science: Comparative issues and examples.* London: Routledge.

Chen, P. (1999). *Modern Chinese: History and sociolinguistics.* Cambridge: Cambridge University Press.

Cheng, J. Y. S. (1998a). China's foreign policy in the mid-1990s. In J. Y. S. Cheng (ed.), *China in the post-Deng era* (pp. 217–242). Hong Kong: The Chinese University Press.

Cheng, J. Y. S. (ed.). (1998b). *China in the post-Deng era.* Hong Kong: The Chinese University Press.

Cheng, S-W. (2001). *Studies on economic reforms and development in China.* Hong Kong: Oxford University Press (China).

Crystal, D. (1987). *The Cambridge encyclopedia of language.* Cambridge: Cambridge University Press.

Dai, Q-X., Teng, X., Guan X-Q., and Dong, Y. (1997). *Zhongguo shaoshu minzu shuanyu jiaoyu gailun* [Introduction to bilingual education for China's ethnic minorities]. Shenyang: Liaoning Nationalities Publishing House.

Dillon, M. (ed.). (1998). *China: A cultural and historical dictionary.* Richmond: Curzon Press.

Edwards, J. (1994). *Multilingualism.* London: Routledge.

Fairbank, J. K. (1987). *China watch.* Cambridge, MA: Harvard University Press.

Gardner, J., and Hayhoe, R. (1991). The introduction of western higher education. In B. Hook and D. Twitchett (eds.), *The Cambridge encyclopedia of China* (2nd ed., pp. 114–116). Cambridge: Cambridge University Press.

Garnaut, R., and Huang, Y-P. (eds.). (2001). *Growth without miracles: Readings on the Chinese economy in the era of reform.* Oxford: Oxford University Press.

Goodman, D. S. G., and Segal, G. (eds.). (1991). *China in the nineties: Crisis management and beyond.* Oxford: Oxford University Press.

Gray, J. (1991a). Liberation. In B. Hook and D. Twitchett (eds.), *The Cambridge encyclopedia of China* (2nd ed., pp. 253–254). Cambridge: Cambridge University Press.

Gray, J. (1991b). Great leap forward. In B. Hook and D. Twitchett (eds.), *The Cambridge encyclopedia of China* (2nd ed., pp. 265–266). Cambridge: Cambridge University Press.

Gray, J. (1991c). The communes. In B. Hook and D. Twitchett (eds.), *The Cambridge encyclopedia of China* (2nd ed., pp. 266–267). Cambridge: Cambridge University Press.

Gu, M-Y. (2001). *Education in China and abroad: Perspectives from a lifetime in comparative education.* Hong Kong: Comparative Education Research Centre, the University of Hong Kong.

Gu, Y-Q. (1997). *A bibliography on language planning and language policy in China (Materials in English).* Retrieved 26 July 2004, from http://petergu.myplace.nie.edu.sg/bib_lg_plan_cn.htm

Gu, Y-Q., and Hu, G-W. (2002). *EFL in the Chinese context: A bibliography.* Retrieved 26 July 2004, from http://petergu.myplace.nie.edu.sg/china_efl_bib.htm

Hayhoe, R. (1991). The educational achievements of the People's Republic. In B. Hook and D. Twitchett (eds.), *The Cambridge encyclopedia of China* (2nd ed., pp. 117–119). Cambridge: Cambridge University Press.

Herdina, P., and Jessner, U. (2002). *A dynamic model of multilingualism: Perspectives of change in psycholinguistics.* Clevedon: Multilingual Matters.

Howell, J. (1993). *China opens its doors: The politics of economic transition.* Hemel Hempstead: Harvester Wheatsheaf.

Huang, J-H. (1987). *Hanyu fangyanxue* [Chinese dialectology]. Xiamen: Xiamen University Press.

Kissinger, H. (1999). *Years of renewal.* New York, NY: Simon and Schuster.

Lam, A. (2002a). English in education in China: Policy changes and learners' experiences. *World Englishes, 21*(2), 245–256.

Lam, A. (2002b). Language policy and learning experience in China: Six case histories. *Hong Kong Journal of Applied Linguistics, 7*(2), 57–72.

Laurenceson, J., and Chai, J. C. H. (2003). *Financial reform and economic development in China.* Cheltenham: Edward Elgar.

Lee, M. B. (2001). *Ethnicity, education and empowerment: How minority students in Southwest China construct identities.* Aldershot: Ashgate.

Lynch, M. (1998). *The People's Republic of China since 1949.* London: Hodder and Stoughton.

MacFarquhar, R. (1991a). The two lines. In B. Hook and D. Twitchett (eds.), *The Cambridge encyclopedia of China* (2nd ed., p. 270). Cambridge: Cambridge University Press.

MacFarquhar, R. (1991b). Four modernizations. In B. Hook and D. Twitchett (eds.), *The Cambridge encyclopedia of China* (2nd ed., p. 279). Cambridge: Cambridge University Press.

MacFarquhar, R., and Shambaugh, D. (1991). Cultural revolution. In B. Hook and D. Twitchett (eds.), *The Cambridge encyclopedia of China* (2nd ed., pp. 270–273). Cambridge: Cambridge University Press.

Mengin, F., and Rocca, J-L. (eds.). (2002). *Politics in China: Moving frontiers.* New York, NY: Palgrave Macmillan.

Ministry of Education, People's Republic of China. (n.d.). *2002 quanguo jiaoyu shiye fazhan tongji gongbao* [Statistical report on the national educational developments in 2002]. Retrieved 4 June 2003, from http://www.moe.gov.cn

National Bureau of Statistics of the People's Republic of China. (2001). *Communique on major figures of the 2000 population census (No. 1).* Retrieved 11 October 2003, from http://www.stats.gov.cn/english/newrelease/statisticalreports/200204230084.htm

Nunan, D., and Lam, A. (1998). Teacher education for multilingual contexts: Models and issues. In J. Cenoz and F. Genesee (eds.), *Beyond bilingualism: Multilingualism and multilingual education* (pp. 117–140). Clevedon: Multilingual Matters.

Paulston, C. B. (1994). *Linguistic minorities in multilingual settings: Implications for language policies.* Amsterdam: John Benjamins.

Pavlenko, A., and Blackledge, A. (eds.). (2004). *Negotiation of identities in multilingual contexts.* Clevedon: Multilingual Matters.

Peterson, G., Hayhoe, R., and Lu, Y-L. (eds.). (2001). *Education, culture, and identity in twentieth-century China.* Hong Kong: Hong Kong University Press.

Ramsey, S. R. (1987). *The languages of China.* Princeton, NJ: Princeton University Press.

Sichuan Foreign Language Institute. (1993). *Zhongguo waiyu jiaoyu yaoshi lu 1949–1989* [Important events in foreign language teaching in China]. Beijing: Foreign Language Teaching and Research Press.

Singh, S. K. (2001). *Multilingualism.* New Delhi: Bahri Publications.

Spolsky, B. (ed.). (1986). *Language and education in multilingual settings.* Clevedon: Multilingual Matters.

State Language Commission. (1995). *Yuyan wenzi gongzuo bai ti* [100 questions in language orthography work]. Beijing: Yuwen Chubanshe.

State Language Commission. (1996). *Goujia yuyan wenzi zhengce fagui huibian (1949–1995)* [Collection of national language policy papers (1949–1995)]. Beijing: Yuwen Chubanshe.

Turner, Y., and Acker, A. (2002). *Education in the new China: Shaping ideas at work.* Aldershot: Ashgate.

Wang, J., Chen, Z-T., Cao, X-Z., and Chen, N-H. (eds.). (1995). *Dangdai Zhongguo de wenzi gaige* [Contemporary language and script reform in China]. Beijing: Dangdai Zhongguo Chubanshe.

Wang, X-F. (2003). *Education in China since 1976.* Jefferson, NC: McFarland and Co.

Yahuda, M. (1991). The Sino-Soviet conflict. In B. Hook and D. Twitchett (eds.), *The Cambridge encyclopedia of China* (2nd ed., pp. 269–270). Cambridge: Cambridge University Press.

Yang, R. (2002). *The third delight: Internationalization of higher education in China.* New York, NY: Routledge.

Zhou, M-L. (2001). The spread of Putonghua and language attitude changes in Shanghai and Guangzhou, China. *Journal of Asian Pacific Communication 11*(2), 231–253.

Zhou, M-L. (2003). *Multilingualism in China: The politics of writing reforms for minority languages 1949–2002.* Berlin: Mouton de Gruyter.

CHAPTER 2

Barnes, M. D. (1974). *Language planning in Mainland China: A sociolinguistic study of P'u-t'ung-hua and P'in-Yin.* Ann Arbor, MI: University Microfilms.

Chen, P. (1999). *Modern Chinese: History and sociolinguistics.* Cambridge: Cambridge University Press.

Cheng, C-C. (1986). Contradictions in Chinese language reform. *International Journal of the Sociology of Language, 59,* 87–96.

Cheng, X-H. (1991). *Fan jian you zhi* [Complex and simplified choices]. Hong Kong: Joint Publishing (Hongkong) Co. Ltd.

China Education and Research Network. (n.d.). Chinese language education ahead in the world. Retrieved 9 August 2004, from http://www.edu.cn/20040317/3101452.shtml

China Internet Information Center. (2001). More foreigners sit language test. Retrieved 7 August 2004, from http://www.china.org.cn/english/MATERIAL/27574.htm

Consulate General of the People's Republic of China in San Francisco. (n.d.). *Teaching of Chinese as a foreign language.* Retrieved 9 August 2004, from http://www.chinaconsulatesf.org/eng/jy/t46906.htm

Cummins, J. (1984). Bilingualism and cognitive functioning. In S. Shapson and V. D'oyley (eds.), *Bilingual and multilingual education: Canadian perspectives* (pp. 55–67). Clevedon: Multilingual Matters.

Editorial Committee, China Education Yearbook. *China Education Yearbook.* (2001). Beijing: People's Education Press.

Hsia, T-T. (1956). *China's language reforms.* New Haven, CT: Institute of Far Eastern Languages, Yale University.

HSK Center of Beijing Language and Culture University. (n.d.). About HSK. Retrieved 7 August 2004, from http://www.hsk.org.cn/english/Common/shuoming.asp

Jernudd, B. H. (1986). Chinese language planning: Perspectives from China and abroad. *International Journal of the Sociology of Language, 59,* 5–6.

Lam, A. (1998). Orthographic convergence in China. Paper presented at the International Colloquium on Linguistic Convergence, University of Cambridge, Cambridge.

Lam, A. (2001). Bilingualism. In R. Carter and D. Nunan (eds.), *The Cambridge guide to Teaching English to Speakers of Other Languages* (pp. 93–99). Cambridge: Cambridge University Press.

Lam, A. (2002). Chinese language education in China: Policy and experience. Paper presented at the AILA' 2002 World Congress on 'Applied linguistics in the 21st century: Opportunities for innovation and creativity', Singapore, 16–21 December.

Malmqvist, G. (1994). Chinese linguistics. In G. Lepschy (ed.), *History of linguistics: Vol. 1. The eastern traditions of linguistics* (pp. 1–24). London: Longman Group UK Limited.

Ministry of Education and the State Language Commission. (2000). *Guanyu jinyibu jiaqiang xuexiao puji Putonghua he yongzi guifanhua gongzuo de tongzhi* [Notification concerning strengthening the work of promoting Putonghua and the the use of standard characters in schools]. Retrieved 27 July 2004, from http://www.moe.gov.cn/language/tgputonghua/03.htm

Ministry of Education. (2002). Diyipi yixingci zhenglibiao de tongzhi [Notification concerning the standard list of the first batch of variant vocabulary]. *Jiaoyubu Zhengbao 157/158*, 382–384.

National People's Congress. (1999). *Zhongguo Renmin Gongheguo Xianfa* [The Constitution of the People's Republic of China]. Beijing: Falu Chubanshe.

Ni, M-L., Zhao, D-M., and Peng, Z-P. (eds.). (1998). HSK *Zhongguo Hanyu Shuiping Kaoshi yingshi zhinan* [Guide to HSK Chinese Proficiency Test of China]. Beijing: Beijing Language and Culture University Press.

Norman, J. (1988). *Chinese.* Cambridge: Cambridge University Press.

Rohsenow, J. S. (1986). The second Chinese character simplification scheme. *International Journal of the Sociology of Language, 59*, 73–85.

Seybolt, P. J., and Chiang, G. K. (eds.). (1979). *Language reform in China: Documents and commentary.* White Plains, NY: M. E. Sharpe.

State Council, People's Republic of China. (1956). *Guowuyuan guanyu tuiguang Putonghua de zhishi* [Directive from the State Council concerning the propagation of Putonghua]. Retrieved 27 July 2004, from http://www.moe.gov.cn/language/tgputonghua/01.htm

State Language Commission. (1995). *Yuyan wenzi gongzuo bai ti* [100 Questions in the language orthography work]. Beijing: Yuwen Chubanshe.

State Language Commission. (1996). *Goujia yuyan wenzi zhengce fagui huibian (1949–1995)* [Collection of state language policy papers (1949–1995)]. Beijing: Yuwen Chubanshe.

State Language Commission. (1997). *Guanyu banbu 'Putonghua Shuiping Ceshi dengji biaozhun (shixing)' de tongzhi* [Notice concerning the distribution of the Standards for Grades in the Putonghua Proficiency Test (Pilot)]. Retrieved 27 July 2004, from http://www.moe.gov.cn/language/tgputonghua/02.htm

Su, P-C. (1994). *Xiandai hanzixue gangyao* [Principles of Modern Chinese orthographic studies]. Beijing: Peking University Press.

Taylor, I., and Olson, D. R. (eds.). (1995). *Scripts and literacy: Reading and learning to read alphabets, syllabaries and characters.* Dordrecht: Kluwer Academic Publishers.

Wang, J., Chen, Z-T., Cao, X-Z., and Chen, N-H. (eds.). (1995). *Dangdai Zhongguo de wenzi gaige* [Contemporary language and script reform in China]. Beijing: Dangdai Zhongguo Chubanshe.

Zhou, M-L. (2001). The spread of Putonghua and language attitude changes in Shanghai and Guangzhou, China. *Journal of Asian Pacific Communication 11*(2), 231–253.

Zhou, Y-G. (1986). Modernization of the Chinese Language. *International Journal of the Sociology of Language, 59*, 7–23.

## CHAPTER 3

Adamson, B. (2004). *China's English: A history of English in Chinese education.* Hong Kong: Hong Kong University Press.

Beijing Municipality College English Teaching and Research Association. (ed.). (1987). *Daxue yingyu jiaoxue* [The teaching of College English]. Beijing: Beijing Municipality College English Teaching and Research Association.

Bolton, K. (2003). *Chinese Englishes: A sociolinguistic history.* Cambridge: Cambridge University Press.

Chen, Z-L., and Yang, T-F. (eds.). (1997). *Daxue waiyu jiaoxue yu yanjiu* [Research and teaching on foreign languages at college and university level]. Beijing: Tsinghua University Press.

College Foreign Language Teaching and Research Association. (ed.). (1994). *Keji yingyu jiaoxue yanjiu wenji* [Essays on the teaching and research of English for Science and Technology (EST)]. Shanghai: Shanghai Foreign Language Education Press.

Cortazzi, M., and Jin, L-X. (1996). English teaching and learning in China. *Language Teaching, 29*(2), 61–80.

Department of English Quality Review Team. (1992). *Zhongguo yingyu benke xuesheng suzhi diaocha baogao* [Report on quality review of undergraduate English in China]. Beijing: Beijing Foreign Language Institute.

Dillon, M. (ed.). (1998). *China: A cultural and historical dictionary*. Richmond, Surrey: Curzon Press.

Dzau, Y-L. F. (ed.). (1990). *English in China*. Hong Kong: API Press.

Ellis, R. (1994). *The study of second language acquisition*. Oxford: Oxford University Press.

Foreign Language Teaching and Research Association, China. (ed.). (1987). *Gonggong waiyu jiaocai yanjiu wenji* [Foreign language teaching for non-majors: Textbook development]. Shanghai: Shanghai Foreign Language Education Press.

Fu, K. (1986). *Zhongguo waiyu jiaoyu shi* [A history of foreign language teaching in China]. Shanghai: Shanghai Foreign Language Education Press.

Gao, Y-H. (ed.). (2004). *Zhongguo daxuesheng yingyu xuexi shehui xinli: Xuexi dongji yu ziwo rentong yanjiu* [The social psychology of English learning by Chinese college students: Motivation and learners' self-identities]. Beijing: Foreign Language Teaching and Research Press.

Hayhoe, R. (1991). The educational achievements of the People's Republic. In B. Hook and D. Twitchett (eds.), *The Cambridge encyclopedia of China* (pp. 117–119). Cambridge: Cambridge University Press.

Lam, A. (2002). English in education in China: Policy changes and learners' experiences. *World Englishes, 21*(2), 245–256.

Lam, A., and Chow, K. (2001). *English language education in China: An update*. Paper presented at the International Conference on 'Globalization, Culture and English Language Education in China and Hong Kong (SAR)', the Chinese University of Hong Kong, Hong Kong, 1–4 March.

Lehmann, W. P. (ed.). (1975). *Language and linguistics in the People's Republic of China*. Austin: University of Texas Press.

Li, L-Y., Zhang, R-S., and Liu, L. (1988). *Zhongguo yingyu jiaoyu shi* [A history of English language teaching in China]. Shanghai: Shanghai Foreign Language Education Press.

Li, P-Y. (ed.). (1990). *ELT in China: Papers presented at the International Symposium on Teaching English in the Chinese Context*. Beijing: Foreign Language Teaching and Research Press.

Liu, R-Q., and Wu, Y-A. (2000). *Zhongguo yingyu jiaoyu yanjiu* [Studies in English language teaching in China]. Beijing: Foreign Language Teaching and Research Press.

Lynch, M. (1998). *The People's Republic of China since 1949*. London: Hodder and Stoughton Educational.

Ministry of Education. (2002). Jiaoyubu, Zhonghua Cishan Zonghui guanyu kaizhan zhuguang xiangcun yingyu jiaoshi ziyuan peixun zhe peixun (TESOL renzheng) xiangmu de tongzhi [Announcement about the Start of the Candlelight Village English Teacher Voluntary Training Project (Certified by TESOL)]. *Jiaoyubu Zhengbao, 2002 (7/8)*, 374–379.

Pride, J. B., and Liu, R-S. (1988). Some aspects of the spread of English in China since 1949. *International Journal of the Sociology of Language, 74*, 41–70.

Robins, R. H., and Uhlenbeck, E. M. (eds.). (1991). *Endangered languages*. Oxford: Berg Publishers.

Ross, H. A. (1993). *China learns English: Language teaching and social change in the People's Republic*. New Haven: Yale University Press.

Scovel, T. (1995). English teaching in China. Unpublished report for the United States Information Agency.

Shen, L-X., and Gao, Y-H. (2004). *Fengkuang yingyu duiyu xuexizhe de yiyi* [What "Crazy English" means to Chinese students]. In Y-H. Gao (ed.), *Zhongguo daxuesheng yingyu xuexi shehui xinli: Xuexi dongji yu ziwo rentong yanjiu* [The social psychology of English learning by Chinese college students: Motivation and learners' self-identities] (pp. 190–201). Beijing: Foreign Language Teaching and Research Press.

Sichuan Foreign Language Institute. (1993). *Zhongguo waiyu jiaoyu yaoshi lu 1949–1989* [Important events in foreign language teaching in China]. Beijing: Foreign Language Teaching and Research Press.

The British Council and State Education Commission. (1996). English in China: Proceedings from the English 2000 Conference, Beijing, 18–20 January. Unpublished conference proceedings.

Troutner, J. L. (1996). *Language, culture, and politics: English in China, 1840s–1990s*. University of California, San Diego, PhD dissertation. Ann Arbor, MI: UMI.

Wang, L-B. (2001) When English becomes big business. Paper presented at the International Conference on 'Globalization, Culture and English Language Education in China and Hong Kong (SAR)', the Chinese University of Hong Kong, Hong Kong, 1–4 March.

Wardhaugh, R. (1987). *Languages in competition: Dominance, diversity and decline*. Oxford: Basil Blackwell in association with Andre Deutsch.

Xu, G-Z. (1990). China's modernization and its English language needs. In Pengyi Li (ed.), *ELT in China: Papers presented at the International Symposium on Teaching English in the Chinese Context* (pp. 2–10). Beijing: Foreign Language Teaching and Research Press.

Xu G-Z. (ed.). (1996). *ELT in China 1992: Papers from Tianjin Conference*. Beijing: Foreign Language Teaching and Research Press.

Zhou, L-X. (ed.). (1995). *Zhongguo zhongxue yingyu jiaoyu baike quanshu* [An encyclopaedia of English education in middle schools in China]. Shenyang: Northeastern University Press.

## CHAPTER 4

An, J. (1986). *Hezhenyu jianzhi* [A short description of the Hezhen language]. Beijing: Central University of Nationalities Press.

Chinatravel. (2000). *Brief tables of Chinese minor nationalities*. Retrieved 11 October 2003, from http://www.chinatravel.com/china/minorcha.html

Chinese Academy of Social Sciences, Research Institute on Nationalities, and the State Commission on Nationality Affairs. (1992). *Zhongguo shaoshu minzu wenzi* [The orthographies of China's minority languages]. Beijing: Zhongguo Zangxue Chubanshe.

Chinese Academy of Social Sciences. (2002). *The Institute of Linguistics.* Retrieved 28 September 2004, from http://www.cass.cn

Dai, Q-X., and Cui, Z-C. (1985). *Achangyu jianzhi* [A short description of the Achang language]. Beijing: Central University of Nationalities Press.

Dai, Q-X., Teng, X., Guan, X-Q., and Dong, Y. (1997). *Zhongguo shaoshu minzu shuangyu jiaoyu gailun* [Introduction to bilingual education for China's ethnic minorities]. Shenyang: Liaoning Nationalities Publishing House.

Downer, G. B. (1991). The non-Han cultures. In B. Hook and D. Twitchett (eds.), *The Cambridge encyclopedia of China* (2nd ed., pp. 77–83). Cambridge: Cambridge University Press.

Hansen, M. H. (1999). *Lessons in being Chinese: Minority education and ethnic identity in Southwest China.* Seattle, WA: University of Washington Press.

He, J-F. (1998). *Zhongguo shaoshu minzu shuangyu yanjiu: Lishi yu xianshi* [Research on bilingualism among China's ethnic minorities: History and reality]. Beijing: Central University of Nationalities.

He, J-S. (1983). *Gelaoyu jianzhi* [A short description of the Gelao language]. Beijing: Central University of Nationalities Press.

Hu, Z-Y. (1986). *Oroqenyu jianzhi* [A short description of the Oroqen language]. Beijing: Central University of Nationalities Press.

Huang, X. (2000). *Zhongguo shaoshu minzu yuyan huoli yanjiu* [Studies on minority language vitality in China]. Beijing: Central University for Nationalities Press.

Lam, A. (1998). Orthographic convergence in China. Paper presented at the International Colloquium on Linguistic Convergence, University of Cambridge, Cambridge.

Lee, M. B. (2001). *Ethnicity, education and empowerment: How minority students in Southwest China construct identities.* Aldershot: Ashgate.

Liu, Z-X. (1981). *Dongxiangyu jianzhi* [A short description of the Donxiang language]. Beijing: Central University of Nationalities Press.

Lu, S-Z. (1983). *Pumiyu jianzhi* [A short description of the Pumi language]. Beijing: Central University of Nationalities Press.

Mao, Z-W., and Meng, Z-J. (1986). *Sheyu jianzhi* [A short description of the She language]. Beijing: Central University of Nationalities Press.

Ministry of Education, People's Republic of China. (n.d.a). *Zhonghua Renmin Gongheguo falu fagui zhong youguan yuwen wenzi de guiding* [The specifications pertaining to languages and scripts in the law and regulations of the People's Republic of China]. Retrieved 4 June 2003, from http://www.moe.gov.cn

Ministry of Education, People's Republic of China. (n.d.b). *Woguo de shaoshu minzu yuyan wenzi jianjie* [A brief introduction to the languages and scripts among the ethnic minorities in the country]. Retrieved 4 June 2003, from http://www.moe.gov.cn

National Bureau of Statistics of the People's Republic of China. (2001). *Communique on major figures of the 2000 population census (No. 1).* Retrieved 11 October 2003, from http://www.stats.gov.cn/english/newrelease/statisticalreports/200204230084.htm

National People's Congress. (1999). *Zhongguo Renmin Gongheguo Xianfa* [The Constitution of the People's Republic of China]. Beijing: Falu Chubanshe.

National People's Congress. (2001). Quanguo Renmin Daibiao Dahui Changwu Weiyuanhui Guanyu Xiugai 'Zhonghua Renmin Gongheguo Minzu Quyu Zijifa' de jueding [The National People's Congress General Affairs Committee's decision concerning the amendment of 'The Law on Regional Autonomy for Minority Nationalities in the People's Republic of China']. *Quanguo Renmin Daibiao Dahui Changwu Weiyuanhui Gongbao* [National People's Congress General Affairs Committee Notices] *2001 (2)*, 121–148.

Ouyang, J-Y. (1985). *Lhobayu jianzhi* [A short description of the Lhoba language]. Beijing: Central University of Nationalities Press.

Ouyang, J-Y., Cheng, F. and Yu, C-R. (1984). *Ginyu jianzhi* [A short description of the Gin language]. Beijing: Central University of Nationalities Press.

Population Census Office under the State Council and Department of Population, Social, Science and Technology Statistics, National Bureau of Statistics of China. (2002). *Zhongguo 2000 nian ren kou pu cha zi liao* (Vol. 1) [Tabulation on the 2000 Population Census of the People's Republic of China, Vol. 1]. Beijing: Zhongguo Tongji Chubanshe, Xinhua Shudian.

Ramsey, S. R. (1987). *The languages of China.* Princeton, NJ: Princeton University Press.

State Language Commission. (1995). *Yuyan wenzi gongzuo bai ti* [100 questions in language orthography work]. Beijing: Yuwen Chubanshe.

State Language Commission. (1996). *Goujia yuyan wenzi zhengce fagui huibian (1949–1995)* [Collection of national language policy papers (1949–1995)]. Beijing: Yuwen Chubanshe.

Sun, H-K., and Liu, L. (1986). *Nuyu jianzhi* [A short description of the Nu language]. Beijing: Central University of Nationalities Press.

Teng, X. (2001). *Wenhua bianqian yu shuangyu jiaoyu* [Culture change and bilingual education]. Beijing: Jiaoyu Kexue Chubanshe.

Wang, T-Z. (1998). Xin Zhongguo minzu jiaoyu zhengce de xingcheng yu fazhan (Shang) [The formation and development of the educational policy for ethnic groups in New China (Part 1)]. *Minzu Jiaoyu Yanjiu* [Research in Ethnic Education] *35*, 3–9.

Xie, Q-H. (1989). *Zhongguo minzu jiaoyu shigang* [History of minority education in China]. Nanning: Guangxi Education Press.

Zheng, X-R. (2003). A study of ethnic minority teaching materials. *China Education Forum*, *4*(1), 17–18.

Zhou, M-L. (2003). *Multilingualism in China: The politics of writing reforms for minority languages 1949–2002.* Berlin: Mouton de Gruyter.

CHAPTER 5

Beijing Foreign Studies University. (2001). *Beijing Foreign Studies University.* Beijing: Foreign Language Teaching and Research Press.

China Education and Research Network. (2004). *Chinese language education ahead in the world.* Retrieved 9 August 2004, from http://www.edu.cn/20040317/3101452.shtml

China Internet Information Center. (2002). *Nearly 25 million foreigners learning Chinese.* Retrieved 7 August 2004, from http://www.china.org.cn/english/FR/37572.htm

China Internet Information Center. (2003). *Increasing foreigners show desire to learn Chinese.* Retrieved 7 August 2004, from http://www.china.org.cn/english/international/55150.htm

Consulate General of the People's Republic of China in San Francisco. (n.d.). Teaching Chinese as a foreign language. Retrieved 9 August 2004, from http://www.chinaconsulatesf.org/eng/jy/t46906.htm

English Team, Steering Committee for Foreign Language Teaching in Higher Education. (2000). *Gaodeng xuexiao yingyu zhuanye yingyu jiaoxue dagang* [Syllabus for English majors in higher education]. Shanghai: Shanghai Foreign Language Education Press and Foreign Language Teaching and Research Press.

Gao, Y-H. (ed.). (2004). *Zhongguo daxuesheng yingyu xuexi shehui xinli: Xuexi dongji yu ziwo rentong yanjiu* [The social psychology of English learning by Chinese college students: Motivation and learners' self-identities]. Beijing: Foreign Language Teaching and Research Press.

Grosjean, F. (1992). Another view of bilingualism. In R. J. Harris (ed.), *Cognitive processing in bilinguals* (pp. 51–62). Amsterdam: North-Holland.

Jen-Siu, M. (2002). Worrying signs for Beijing's language campaign. *South China Morning Post*, 2 December, p. 1.

Jiang, Z-Q. (2004). 'Green card' available to foreigners. *China Daily*, 21 August, p. 1.

Kramsch, C. (2001). Intercultural communication. In R. Carter and D. Nunan (eds.), *The Cambridge guide to teaching English to speakers of other languages* (pp. 201–206). Cambridge: Cambridge University Press.

Lam, A. (2002). Biscriptal reading in Chinese. In H. S. R. Kao, C. K. Leong and D. G. Gao (eds.), *Cognitive and neuroscience studies of the Chinese language* (pp. 247–261). Hong Kong: Hong Kong University Press.

Leech, G. N. (2001). *A linguistic guide to English poetry* (with teaching notes by X-B. Qin). Beijing: Foreign Language Teaching and Research Press. (First published by Longmans in 1969.)

Liu, Y. (ed.). *Primary English for China: Teachers' Book 4*. Beijing: People's Education Press and Pan Pacific Publishing Ltd.

Ministry of Education, People's Republic of China. (2001). *Yingyu kecheng biaozhun: Shiyan gao* [Standards for the English curriculum: Pilot version]. Beijing: Beijing Normal University Press.

Ministry of Education, People's Republic of China. (2002). *Yingyu kecheng biaozhun: Shiyan gao: Jiedu* [Standards for the English curriculum: Pilot version: Explanation]. Beijing: Beijing Normal University Press.

Ministry of Education, People's Republic of China. (n.d.). *Zhongguo Renmin Gongheguo Guojia tongyong yuyan wenzi fa* [The law on the commonly used language and script in the People's Republic of China]. Retrieved 4 June 2003, from http://www.moe.gov.cn

Nunan, D., and Lam, A. (1998). Teacher education for multilingual contexts: Models and issues. In J. Cenoz and F. Genesee (eds.), *Beyond bilingualism: Multilingualism and multilingual education* (pp. 117–140). Clevedon: Multilingual Matters.

Nunan, D. (1999–2000). *Go for it* (Books 1 to 4). Boston, MA: Heinle and Heinle/International Thomson Publishing.

Revision Team for College English Syllabus. (1999). *Daxue Yingyu Jiaoxue Dagang: Xiudiingben* [College English syllabus: Revised version]. Shanghai: Higher Education Press and Shanghai Foreign Language Education Press.

State Council. (2002). *Guowuyuan guanyu shenhua gaige jiakuai fazhan minzu jiaoyu de jueding* [The State Council's decision about intensifying changes to accelerate the development of minority education]. Retrieved 4 June 2003, from http://www.moe.gov.cn

Yian, X-Z. (2004). Scholars talk at 1st forum on Chinese studies in Shanghai. *China Daily*, 21 August, p. 3.

Zhou, M-L. (2003). *Multilingualism in China: The politics of writing reforms for minority languages 1949–2002*. Berlin: Mouton de Gruyter.

# Index